HUME

The Arguments of the Philosophers

EDITED BY TED HONDERICH
Grote Professor of the Philosophy of Mind and Logic
University College, London

The purpose of this series is to provide a contemporary
assessment and history of the entire course of philosophical thought.
Each book constitutes a detailed, critical introduction to the work
of a philosopher of major influence and significance.

* *Available in Paperback*

HUME

Barry Stroud

London and New York

First published in 1977
by Routledge & Kegan Paul plc
Printed in Great Britain by
St Edmundsbury Press Ltd, Bury St Edmunds, Suffolk

Reprinted and first published as a paperback in 1981
Reprinted in 1984, 1985, 1988, 1990, 1991, 1994
by Routledge
11 New Fetter Lane, London EC4P 4EE
29 West 35th Street, New York, NY 10001

British Library Cataloguing in Publication Data

Stroud, Barry
Hume.—(The arguments of the philosophers; 5).
1. Hume, David—Criticism and interpretation
I. Series
192   *B1498*   *77-72347*
ISBN 0–415–03687–9 Pbk

FOR SARAH,
BOOKLOVER

Contents

Preface

In this book I try to provide a comprehensive interpretation of Hume's philosophy and to expound and discuss his central problems against the background of that general interpretation. But there are several ways in which the task had to be limited. Hume had important things to say on almost every question of human concern.

I say nothing, for example, about religion, and that is a serious omission since the topic was of life-long importance to Hume, both philosophically and, in another way, personally. Nor do I consider any of his philosophical writings about economics. Of Hume's politics I discuss only the most general features of the theory of society and government. His detailed treatment of particular passions or emotions is ignored, but I do discuss at some length the role of what he calls 'passions' in the production of human action, and therefore in morality. I also say nothing about his historical writings, although on the general interpretation I offer they can be seen as much more of a piece with his philosophical work than has usually been supposed. But these limitations of subject-matter were necessary in order to deal more fully with what must be regarded as the most fundamental parts of Hume's philosophy.

In discussing those central parts I do not try to give an exhaustive treatment of Hume's views or of the philosophical issues in question. My aim throughout is to illustrate and support the general interpretation by particular instances of its application, and thereby to show how Hume's views on those fundamental questions are best to be understood and evaluated. If I am even partly successful I hope it will be apparent how much of what has come to be the conventional wisdom about Hume and the defects of his views is mistaken or misguided. I do not suggest that those views are ultimately defensible, or even fully coherent, but if they are not we must come to understand

ix

the real source of their failure and not be content with superficial or merely fashionable diagnoses. I have found that many widespread objections to Hume miss the mark in not going deeply enough, usually because they attack only small, isolated bits of what he says without taking into account the more general theoretical framework that gives those particular bits their sense. But I have not encumbered the text with extensive references to commentators and critics, nor have I tried systematically to document what I would regard as the shortcomings of other interpretations. I concentrate on presenting and supporting my own understanding of Hume.

I do think that in what follows I have managed to clear away some of the accumulated fog from several different windows into Hume's philosophy, but I remain fully conscious in most cases of not having gone far towards illuminating what lies in the darker recesses within. My hope is only that now it will be easier and more fruitful to continue scholarly and philosophical investigations along some of the lines I have sketched but not fully explored.

I have also tried to indicate some connections between Hume's treatment of particular topics and more recent discussions of those same, or related, topics, and there too I have not aspired to, or achieved, completeness. Hume's especially prominent position in Western philosophy makes that impossible. An exhaustive guide to discussions of Hume's problems and their descendants as they appear in twentieth-century philosophy would be an almost exhaustive guide to twentieth-century philosophy. In a speculative and wide-ranging last chapter I try to indicate in general terms those aspects of Hume's philosophy that are, or ought to be seen as, most alive for philosophers today.

I have tried throughout to make what I say intelligible to beginners, or virtual beginners, in philosophy, while also providing something of interest to Hume scholars and to philosophers dealing with the problems he discussed. I think I know how difficult it is to satisfy those different demands simultaneously, but members of the relevant groups will be able to judge for themselves how far I succeed in satisfying any one of them.

Like any student of philosophy, I have been reading and thinking about Hume or his problems in one way or another for a long time, and it is difficult to pin-point specific influences on my present understanding of him. My greatest debt is undoubtedly to the writings of Norman Kemp Smith. Every student of Hume is, or ought to be, in his debt. It is additional evidence, if more were needed, of the close connection between philosophy and the study of the history of philosophy that Kemp Smith's revolutionary historical work on Hume never received the widespread acceptance it deserved in the philosophical world, largely because philosophy itself was not ready for it. The rigid analytic empiricism of the first half of this century could not appreciate the philosophical importance, and therefore tended to deny the existence, of what Kemp Smith was right in identifying as Hume's philosophical naturalism. It will be obvious that my own interpretation owes a great deal to Kemp Smith, but I think that, partly on the basis of his work, I have been able to present a more systematic and more consistent naturalistic interpretation, and in many cases to discuss important questions of interpretation and assessment with attention to more detail and more recent philosophical criticism than was available to Kemp Smith. The infrequent references to him in what follows are therefore no measure of my real debt to him.

E. C. Mossner's marvellous biography of Hume has also been important for my understanding. It is invaluable for the study of the writings of someone whose person is so immediately present in his philosophical work, even though I make no direct reference to those agreeable human characteristics in what I say in this book about Hume's philosophy. I include a bibliography listing many other works I have found especially interesting and helpful, but that is insufficient indication of my indebtedness to other writers on Hume, and I am glad to be able to acknowledge it here, if only in a sweeping and impersonal way.

I have lectured and given seminars on Hume for a number of years in Berkeley, and in 1974 in Oslo, and I am grateful to those patient audiences for their sympathetic responses and their helpful criticisms and suggestions. I also would like to thank the sub-faculty of philosophy in Oxford for their hospitality when I was beginning to write the book. During that year in Oxford I also was fortunate to be able to discuss Hume's *Treatise* in classes given by John Passmore, and to present some thoughts on Hume's scepticism to the Jowett Society.

In my treatment of Hume's moral philosophy, which I found very difficult, I have had the benefit of correspondence and discussion with Gilbert Harman and extensive discussion over the years with Philippa Foot and Derek Parfit. Their writings too have taught me much about moral philosophy.

Dagfinn Føllesdal and Bernt Vestre have read parts of some version of the text and have made comments and suggestions that have led to its improvement. I have gained more from the shrewdness and persistence of Jean Austin than the apparent inconclusiveness of our many discussions of Hume might have suggested to her, and from both the conversation and the writings of David Pears I have learned more about Hume and about philosophy than I am afraid will be evident in what follows.

In Berkeley, a paper by Paul Grice and John Haugeland and discussions with them on Hume's views on personal identity were especially useful to me. I have talked about most parts of Hume's philosophy and about my reading of it with Barbara Winters and have always learned things from her judicious response. Discussions on Hume (and almost everything else) over the years with Thompson Clarke, Michael Frede, John Searle, and Hans Sluga have had deeper effects than I am sure any of us now can identify, and I am grateful to each of them for that, and for their encouragement. I value especially the insight and sensitivity of Thompson Clarke who, while not advancing interpretations of specific parts of Hume's philosophy, has contributed more to my philosophical understanding than this book, or any better one, could possibly have revealed.

Barry Stroud

I

The Study of Human Nature

Account for moral as for nat'ral things:

David Hume is generally considered to be a purely negative philosopher—the arch sceptic whose primary aim and achievement was to reduce the theories of his empiricist predecessors to the absurdity that was implicitly contained in them all along. This view, part of which started in Hume's own day, was strongly encouraged by nineteenth-century historians of philosophy who saw all intellectual changes as necessary stages in a predetermined process of the unfolding of something called History or the Absolute. In that scheme of things Hume's assigned role was to carry the empiricist philosophy of Locke and Berkeley to its logical and incredible conclusion, thus setting the stage for Kant and eventually for the final Hegelian liberation. Even today many philosophers not noticeably sympathetic to that intellectual tradition regard Hume as little more than the third and final step in the downfall of classical British empiricism. No doubt some passages in Hume, taken alone, might support this line of inter-pretation, but it is an extreme and unfortunate distortion of what he actually wrote. Not only is it mistaken; it would make Hume much less interesting and important for us as a philosopher than he actually is.

Hume is a philosopher of human nature. He puts forth a new theory or vision of man, and one that he thinks differs significantly from those of his predecessors. It is a bold and simple theory, and is much more an expression of the unbounded optimism of the enlightenment than of the clever negativism of a man at the end of his intellectual rope. Although most of its details have been rejected, the spirit and the general outlines of that theory are very much with us today. They still represent, for most people, the very paradigm of what it is to have an explanation of something, and therefore in particular of what it is to understand human behaviour.

1

Hume's first and most comprehensive philosophical work, *A Treatise of Human Nature*,[1] was written while he was in his middle twenties, and published in 1739 and 1740. His *Enquiry Concerning Human Understanding* (1748) and *Enquiry Concerning the Principles of Morals* (1751)[2] are closely related to it, and in fact attempt to achieve more smoothly and more palatably the same general philosophical aims. The *Treatise* carries the subtitle 'An Attempt to Introduce the Experimental Method of Reasoning into Moral Subjects'. That gives an excellent indication of what is to be found in the book, and in Hume's work generally. It alone should make one suspicious of the traditional 'sceptical' interpretation.

'Moral' philosophy, in Hume's sense, is to be contrasted with 'natural' philosophy, which deals with objects and phenomena in the world of nature. Natural philosophy is roughly the same as what is now called physics, chemistry and biology. Of course, men are objects of nature too, and are therefore part of the subject-matter of natural philosophy. A man falling off a bridge accelerates at the same rate and hits the water at the same time as a stone that falls off with him. Moral philosophy differs from natural philosophy only in the *way* it deals with human beings—it considers only those respects in which they differ from other 'objects of nature'. Men think, act, feel, perceive and speak, so 'moral subjects' deal with human thought, action, feelings, perception, passions and language. Hume is concerned with what it is like to be human, with what is special or different about being human—with human nature. The non-human parts of animate nature come under his scrutiny only briefly, but the question of how humans differ from animals is in fact extremely important for Hume. He sees men as much more like the animals than most earlier theories had done.

So although the word 'moral' in Hume's subtitle does not mean only 'having to do with questions of good and bad, right and wrong, duty and obligation, and so on', it does mean at least that. Humans are special in that considerations of good and bad, right and wrong, do play a role in their behaviour. Precisely what role they play, and how, is one of the topics that interests Hume most, but by 'moral' he means more. His subject is everything that is distinctively human.[3]

The concern with human nature is probably as old as human nature itself. Certainly it did not begin with Hume. But there are different ways of examining and portraying humanity, and Hume pursues only one of them. He thinks the ancients, and the poets and dramatists of his own time, paint man's virtues 'in the most amiable colours', usually for the purpose of moral or spiritual exhortation. But in doing so they show:

2

more of a delicacy of sentiment, a just sense of morals, or a greatness of soul, than a depth of reasoning and reflection. They content themselves with representing the common sense of mankind in the strongest lights, and with the best turn of thought and expression, without following out steadily a chain of propositions, or forming the several truths into a regular science. (Hume (2), pp. 5–6)

To the complaint of his friend and mentor, Francis Hutcheson, that the third book of the *Treatise* 'lacks a certain warmth in the cause of virtue' Hume replies:

There are different ways of examining the Mind as well as the Body. One may consider it either as an Anatomist or as a Painter; either to discover its most secret Springs & Principles or to describe the Grace & Beauty of its actions. I imagine it impossible to conjoin these two Views. (Hume (7), vol. 1, p. 32)

There is no attempt to disparage the portrayal of the 'grace and beauty' of human nature; Hume means only to distinguish it from his own more 'scientific' investigation.

He thinks that studying human nature 'as an anatomist' is a relatively new enterprise which can be as accurate and reliable as natural philosophy has proven itself to be. The science of man, like natural philosophy, should seek to explain, and thus help us to understand, the diverse phenomena of human life in all their complexity by appeal to general principles. His attempt to 'anatomize human nature in a regular manner' (Hume (2), p. 6) is a search for just such 'principles of human nature'. He wants to do for the human realm what he thinks natural philosophy, especially in the person of Newton, had done for the rest of nature.

Newtonian theory provides a completely general explanation of why things in the world of nature happen as they do. It explains various and complicated physical happenings in terms of relatively few extremely general, perhaps universal, principles. Similarly, Hume wants a completely general theory of human nature to explain why human beings act, think, perceive and feel in all the ways they do. Of course, he does not think he can actually explain all aspects of human nature, but he thinks he has a general framework within which the job eventually could be done. He is really content simply to emphasize the fact that human nature can be the subject of scientific study, and to suggest some of the general principles involved, without providing all the details required on a fully successful theory. In his *Dissertation of the Passions*, a brief rewriting of Book II of the *Treatise*, he concedes:

3

I pretend not to have here exhausted this subject. It is sufficient for my purpose, if I have made it appear, that, in the production and conduct of the passions, there is a certain regular mechanism, which is susceptible of as accurate a disquisition, as the laws of motion, optics, hydrostatics, or any part of natural philosophy. (Hume (5), p. 166)

So the key to understanding Hume's philosophy is to see him as putting forward a general theory of human nature in just the way that, say, Freud or Marx did. They all seek a general kind of explanation of the various ways in which men think, act, feel and live. The theories of Freud and Marx are of course much more specific and detailed than Hume's. And the details themselves—the kinds of explanations offered—are also very different in each case. And all three are interested in different things. But although it would be ludicrous to press the comparison in many ways, there are two very general and important similarities. The aim of all three is completely general—they try to provide a basis for explaining *everything* in human affairs. And the theories they advance are all, roughly, deterministic. In that respect they differ from the views of man found in Christianity or in so-called 'existentialist' writers where there is an emphasis on will and free choice, and on man's 'making himself into something', thus to some extent creating his own nature independently of the world in which he finds himself. The views of Hume, Freud and Marx differ even more radically from that libertarian conception than they differ among themselves. That is perhaps because they all claim to be scientific.

But Hume's science of man requires more than general, even universal, principles. They must be arrived at by what he calls 'the experimental method of reasoning'. By that he means nothing more specific than drawing only those conclusions that are somehow authorized or supported by experience.

For to me it seems evident, that the essence of the mind being equally unknown to us with that of external bodies, it must be equally impossible to form any notion of its powers and qualities otherwise than from careful and exact experiments, and the observation of those particular effects, which result from its different circumstances and situations. (p. xxi)

It might seem hardly worth remarking that the way to discover how and why human beings behave, think and feel as they do is to observe them in various circumstances and be prepared to check your conclusions against further observable facts. But Hume thinks it needs to be

4

emphasized since most views of human nature apparently were not arrived at by following such a simple precept.

The talk of 'the nature of man' or 'man's essence' with which literature abounds had not depended very closely on an examination of actual men as they exist in the world.

> I found that the moral Philosophy transmitted to us by Antiquity, labor'd under the same Inconvenience that has been found in their natural Philosophy, of being entirely Hypothetical, & depending more upon Invention than Experience. Every one consulted his Fancy in erecting Schemes of Virtue & of Happiness, without regarding human Nature, upon which every moral Conclusion must depend. (Hume (7), vol. 1, p. 16)

Since great progress had been made in natural philosophy by rejecting this merely *a priori* theorizing, Hume thinks 'the experimental method of reasoning' will lead to parallel improvements in the science of man, or 'moral subjects'.

He does not regard himself as the first practitioner of this new science, but he does consider his theory more complete and more systematic than what had gone before—if successful, it would produce a complete revolution in philosophy. Some measure of his youthful conception of the importance of his work can perhaps be gleaned from the remark:

> 'Tis no astonishing reflection to consider, that the application of experimental philosophy to moral subjects should come after that to natural at the distance of above a whole century; since we find in fact, that there was about the same interval betwixt the origins of these sciences; and that reckoning from Thales to Socrates, the space of time is nearly equal to that betwixt my Lord Bacon and some late philosophers in *England*, who have begun to put the science of man on a new footing, and have engaged the attention, and excited the curiosity of the public. (pp. xx—xxi)

He sees those 'late philosophers in *England*'—Locke, Shaftesbury, Mandeville, Hutcheson, Butler, etc.—as playing a role in the development of the science of man analogous to that of Bacon, whom he regards as 'the father of experimental physics' (Hume (2), p. 7). Newton represents the capstone, the final realization, of what Bacon started. Carrying out the analogy, that would make Hume into the Newton of the science of man.[4]

And he takes that analogy seriously. Like Newton, he advocates the end of merely 'hypothetical' science. This does not mean that we are to adopt no hypotheses in trying to find out the truth about man, but that we must not simply impose our conjectures and fancies on the world and then accept them as certain or well-established truths. Rather we must carry the search for simple and general principles as far as we can on the basis of experience, and then, when it is impossible to discover anything further by that means, stop. Hume too can say in the Newtonian spirit *'Hypotheses non fingo'*.

Moral philosophy must labour under the disadvantage of not being able to design and carry out experiments as freely as in natural philosophy, but although this is an inconvenience it does not represent a fundamental distinction between the two kinds of investigations. We can find the effect of one physical body on another by artificially placing them together and observing the result, but Hume thinks this will not usually work with human actions. His reasons are obscure. He seems to think the only way to observe human behaviour is to observe one's own. And that is unreliable, since:

> by placing myself in the same case with that which I consider,
> 'tis evident this reflection and premeditation would so disturb the
> operation of my natural principles, as must render it impossible
> to form any just conclusion from the phenomenon. (p. xxiii)

However accurate this might be about self-observation, it does not apply to experiments in which an observer watches the behaviour of one or more 'subjects', not himself. Even there, perhaps, if the subjects know they are being observed the results will be unreliable grounds for conclusions about people outside artificially contrived experimental situations. But Hume does not deny that we have some reliable access to the natural behaviour of human beings without interference. In fact it provides the only source of data for his science of human nature.

> We must . . . glean up our experiments in this science from a
> cautious observation of human life, and take them as they
> appear in the common course of the world, by men's behaviour
> in company, in affairs, and in their pleasures. (p. xxiii)

Astronomers are no better off; the objects of their study are likewise beyond human manipulation.

Hume's remarks about following the experimental method are to be taken seriously, and should be kept in mind when examining the procedures he himself follows in his examination of human nature. Many will object that that is irrelevant to our judgment of him as a philosopher, since philosophy is not an empirical science. If Hume really is interested in giving a general empirical theory of human nature, it will be argued, then he is simply doing what we now think of as psychology, or perhaps sociology. They are empirical sciences whose results are, or ought to be, experimentally testable, but if that is all he is doing, then he is not really making contributions to philosophy at all.

This objection, in one form or another, has been the foundation of many recent interpretations of Hume. The view behind it is that since philosophy is not an empirical discipline, but is rather the *a priori* study of meanings or the logical relations among concepts, then in so far as Hume is a philosopher that is what he is doing too. His properly philosophical work is therefore really a contribution to something called logical or conceptual analysis, despite the apparently psychological form in which he usually expresses it. Of course, it is conceded that he is interested in empirical psychological questions as well, but what he says about them is thought to be crude and amateurish, and in any case of no philosophical interest.

I think this roughly positivistic conception of what Hume the philosopher is, or must be, doing is responsible for much serious misunderstanding of his intentions, and therefore of his work as a whole. No real test of its adequacy is possible without looking closely at the structure and the details of what he actually says and does. That is the task of later chapters. But it is worth pointing out here that the objection rests on the questionable assumption of a clear and recognizable distinction between *a priori* and empirical investigations, and on the further contention that philosophy falls on the *a priori* side of the line. Only the positivists' confidence in that distinction allowed them to make such sweeping claims about the history of philosophy. It is true that Hume himself distinguishes between knowledge based on 'relations among ideas' and knowledge of 'matters of fact', and that was taken as a precursor of the positivists' distinction between analytic and synthetic judgments. But Hume would certainly deny that philosophy, or what he is writing in the *Treatise* and the *Enquiries*, is *a priori*, or is based on 'relations among ideas' alone. A purely *a priori* mode of philosophizing is precisely what he is trying to supplant in recommending the experimental method of reasoning for investigating the nature of man.

The positivists believed there could be no *philosophical* investigation of the nature of man or of the nature of anything else in the world. They agreed with Hume that we must rely on experience in studying man, but they would conclude that, for that very reason, the results could not be contributions to philosophy. But then the dispute should be seen as one about the nature of philosophy, and not about what Hume is actually doing—and my concern is only with the latter. Hume seeks extremely general and illuminating truths about important aspects of all of human life and thought, and he considers himself a philosopher. In the eighteenth century philosophy was not thought of as a separate technical subject marked off by clear boundaries from every other area of intellectual concern. Our mainly administrative or institutional distinctions between subjects did not exist in Hume's day—and perhaps they exist today primarily in merely administrative minds. In fact it seems to me that the confidence that philosophy in particular is only *a priori* analysis of concepts is based on an epistemological and semantical theory that is now largely discredited. In any case, only those who are both obsessed with compartmentalization and equipped with an adequate definition of philosophy will want to press at the outset the question whether Hume is really doing philosophy or something else.

Hume is Newtonian in much more than method. The very terms and models of his theory are inspired in part by the atomic theory of matter and Newton's theory of universal gravitation. For Hume the basic contents of human experience are particular entities called 'simple perceptions' which combine in different ways to form 'complex perceptions'. To explain how and why these elements and their combinations come and go in the mind in just the patterns and arrangements that they do would be to explain human thought, feeling and behaviour. Just as Newton's law of universal gravitation accounts for the movement and subsequent position of all physical particles in the universe, so Hume's official view is that what he calls 'the principle of the association of ideas' will account for every mental or psychological phenomenon by explaining how and why various perceptions come to be 'present to the mind'.

> Here is a kind of ATTRACTION, which in the mental world will
> be found to have as extraordinary effects as in the natural,
> and to shew itself in as many and various forms. (pp. 12–13)

In fact, to discover the various forms or 'principles' of association would seem to be the key to the science of man, since:

> so far as regards the mind these are the only links that bind the
> parts of the universe together or connect us with any person or
> object exterior to ourselves. For as it is by means of thought
> only that anything operates upon our passions, and as these are
> the only ties of our thoughts, they are really *to us* the cement
> of the universe, and all the operations of the mind must, in a
> great measure, depend on them. (Hume (2), p. 32)

Hume even claims that the use he makes of the principle of the association of ideas is his most original contribution to philosophy (Hume (2), p. 31).

8

There is no doubt that he tends to think of the mind in these mechanistic Newtonian terms, and that his model of mental dynamics has a profound influence on many of his philosophical conclusions. And this fact lends support to the interpretation of Hume as the arch sceptic. Since his conclusions seem much more negative than those of Locke, Berkeley and others, and his adherence to, and application of, the 'Newtonian' theory of ideas seems more rigorous and consistent than theirs, it was supposed that Hume's originality consists simply in having pushed that theory to its logical conclusion, and that he stops there and throws up his hands in despair. This was the view his contemporary, Thomas Reid, took of Hume's achievement. He claimed that the theory of ideas had seemed obviously true to him also until Hume demonstrated so convincingly that it leads to a dead end.[5] For Reid the obvious way out was simply to give up the theory of ideas.

But Hume's originality does not consist in his commitment to the theory of ideas, even if that theory is understood as a kind of Newtonian 'atomistic' picture of the human mind. That commitment alone would hardly distinguish him from any other philosopher from Descartes to Berkeley. Nor is he simply straightening out some of the difficulties and pushing farther some of the implications of a widely shared theory of the mind. Of the *Treatise* he writes:

> My principles are also so remote from all the vulgar sentiments
> on the subject, that were they to take place, they would
> produce almost a total alteration in philosophy: and you know,
> revolutions of this kind are not easily brought about. (Hume
> (7), vol. 1, p. 26)

This judgment of the revolutionary character of his philosophy could scarcely be based on nothing more than a demonstration of certain limitations, however fundamental, in the theory of ideas. It is clear to any reader of Locke and Berkeley that that theory, taken strictly, is too limited to account for all the phenomena it is supposed to explain. If Hume were simply pointing that out—even explicitly and in detail—he would be at most an interesting minor philosopher of the eighteenth century. But he is considerably more than that.

His 'revolution' in philosophy takes for granted the theory of ideas, and concentrates on what must be added to it, what else must be true of human beings, in order to explain why they think, feel and act in the ways they do. There had traditionally been a largely inherited or *a priori* framework of thinking about human nature—in particular about man's rationality—that Hume seeks both to discredit and to supplant. And he tries to do so by an experimental investigation of human thought, feeling and behaviour rather than by what he regards as traditional *a priori* theorizing about 'human nature' or the 'essence

9

of man'. His originality and greatness as a philosopher lie in the power and brilliance with which he carries out those tasks, and not in any alleged contributions to, or criticisms of, the theory of ideas as such. He never questions that theory, nor is he particularly interested in defending it. He is unquestioningly confident that, as far as it goes, it provides the best model for understanding the human mind.

The seeds of Hume's 'revolution' in philosophy are to be found in a 'new scene of thought' that opened up to him in his eighteenth year.[6] It is, in effect, a systematic generalization of Francis Hutcheson's views on aesthetics and morals.[7] According to Hutcheson, just as we are naturally constituted to receive sensations of certain colours, sounds and smells when objects affect our sense organs in certain ways, so we naturally feel certain sentiments of moral or aesthetic approval or disapproval on contemplating certain actions or objects. We do not make a rational inference from something we discover objectively in the object to the verdict that it is red, nor do we carry with us some abstract definition of beauty or of moral goodness and try rationally to discover which objects in our experience in fact fulfil that definition. Our moral and aesthetic judgments are based on feelings or sentiments, and if we never had such feelings we would never make any moral or aesthetic judgments at all. But it is a fundamental fact about us that we do get such feelings. We are naturally endowed with characteristics responsible for our feeling what we do, and therefore for our approving and disapproving what we do, completely independently of reasoning and reflection. We do not *decide* what to approve; we simply 'find' ourselves with a certain feeling and thus approve of certain things, just as we 'find' ourselves with a sensation of red on certain occasions and thus believe there is something red before us. Of course, there might be some features possessed by all and only the things we call red, or the things we call good or beautiful, but in no case do we make an inference from the presence of such features to the judgment in question. In fact, most of us do not even know what such features, if any, are. For a moral or aesthetic judgment an actual feeling must intervene, and feelings are not arrived at by reasoning or inference. So for Hutcheson morality and aesthetics are primarily matters of feeling, not of reason. That is the point Hume seizes on.

He agrees with the essentials of Hutcheson's theory of morality and aesthetics—in fact his work on morals contains many passages only loosely paraphrased from Hutcheson's own writings.[8] But in Hume's hands the denigration of the role of reason and the corresponding elevation of feeling and sentiment is generalized into a total theory of man.[9] Even in the apparently most intellectual or cognitive spheres of human life, even in our empirical judgments about the world and in the process of pure ratiocination itself, feeling is shown to be the dominant force. Even 'belief is more properly an act of the sensitive, than of the cogitative part of our natures' (p. 183). Like sensations of red, it arises in us simply as a result of the interaction between certain features of the world and various 'principles of human nature' of which we are not masters. We simply 'find' ourselves on certain occasions with thoughts, beliefs and propensities to act, just as we 'find' ourselves on certain occasions with sensations of red. And the task of the science of man is to discover empirically why those thoughts, beliefs, feelings and actions arise as they do.

So part of Hume's special contribution is to supplement the theory of ideas with a general empirical theory about why and how items come and go in the mind, and in doing so to appeal to nothing more than certain characteristics, propensities and dispositions with which human beings are naturally endowed. The existence of such characteristics or propensities provides the best explanation of what we observe to be true of human behaviour, and that is the way Hume usually argues for them. He asks, in effect, what properties the human mind must have in order for us to think, feel and act as we do. So his interests, if not his way of satisfying them or the status he accords to his results, are in this respect similar to Kant's. But for Hume there is no transcendental investigation, and there are no absolutely necessary conclusions about man. There is only empirical study of the way men contingently, however unchangeably, are.

At some point it will be impossible, given present knowledge, to explain more fully why human beings are the ways they are, but that is characteristic of scientific investigation generally. Not everything can be explained. That is no reason to deny that man can be studied scientifically. And when he is studied scientifically, according to Hume, it will be seen that feeling, not reason, is responsible for his thinking and acting as he does. It is true quite generally that 'Reason is . . . the slave of the passions, and can never pretend to any other office than to serve and obey them' (p. 415).

This 'revolutionary' view completely reverses the traditional conception of the nature of man. According to the ancient definition, man is a rational animal. He therefore fully realizes his true nature, or fully expresses his essence, only in so far as he controls his life and thought by reason. To the extent that he falls short of that ideal he ceases to be distinctively human, and exists only as part of the merely animate world. Descartes, for example, believed that non-human animals have no souls—they are physical automata all of whose behaviour can be given a purely naturalistic, even mechanistic, explanation.[10] A human being, on the other hand, is partly a 'spiritual substance', and therefore has a free and completely unlimited will. With respect to the scope of his will, man is indeed made in the image

11

of God, who is infinite (Descartes (1), vol. 1, p. 175).

On Descartes' view, it is only because man is free and thus responsible for his own actions and beliefs that the existence of evil and error in the world can be accounted for without attributing them to the author of nature himself. Although God makes the world of nature what it is—He is responsible for all the regularities in our experience and hence for everything that happens within the natural causal order—He is not responsible for the existence of human evil and error, since all actions and beliefs result from the exercise of some human being's free will. Man increases his chances of avoiding evil and error only by trying to be as rational as possible in his actions and beliefs, and not deciding to do something or to believe something until he has weighed all the available considerations on both sides and determined which alternative has the preponderance of good reasons in its favour. He is guaranteed to avoid evil and error completely if he accepts and acts on only those precepts that are intuitively or demonstrably true, or can be clearly and distinctly perceived to be true 'by the pure light of reason alone'. The fact that it is not always possible for men to avoid adopting or acting on beliefs that fail to reach this highest degree of rational certainty is simply a consequence of their worldly, animal nature.

For example, Descartes in his *Meditations* resolves to avoid error by accepting only those propositions for which he can find conclusive reasons, or those for which he can find no possible grounds for doubting. In the fourth *Meditation*, in considering whether the thing that thinks, whose existence has already been established, is physical or not, he says:

I here suppose that I do not yet know any reason to persuade me to adopt the one belief rather than the other. From this *it follows* that I am entirely indifferent as to which of the two I affirm or deny, or even whether I abstain from forming any judgment in the matter. (Descartes (1), vol. 1, p. 176, my italics)

Without any convincing argument *pro* or *con* he thinks a rational man simply cannot believe one side or the other.

This is a result of Descartes' conception of rational belief, according to which there are:

two general modes [of thinking], the one of which consists in perception, or in the operation of the understanding, and the other in volition, or the operation of the will. Thus sense-perception, imagining, and conceiving things that are purely intelligible, are just different methods of perceiving; but desiring, holding in aversion, affirming, denying, doubting, all these are the different

12

modes of willing. (Descartes (1), vol. 1, p. 232)

The exercise of one's free will is absolutely essential for the acquisition of any belief, although of course it is not enough.

> I admit that we can judge of nothing unless our understanding is made use of, because there is no reason to suppose we can judge of what we in no wise apprehend; but the will is absolutely essential for our giving our assent to what we have in some manner perceived. (Descartes (1), vol. 1, p. 233)

On this theory, whenever we believe something we do so as a result of a free choice or decision, and the fully rational believer is one who decides to believe only what has the strongest reasons in its favour.

This view was thought to have the consequence that human thought and behaviour, at least in so far as it issues from what is uniquely human in man, cannot be explained as part of the natural causal order. That is precisely what made it attractive to those who regarded mechanical, causal explanation of human thought and behaviour as incompatible with man's freedom and responsibility. The possibility of such explanation was thought to deny the distinction between men and the rest of the animals. Any 'explanation' of the beliefs or actions of a distinctively rational agent could therefore do no more than show that, on the evidence then available to him, those beliefs or actions were the most reasonable ones for that agent to adopt. That of course does not alone imply that he did adopt them. His actually believing or acting in the ways he does results only from a free act of his will, and that act itself cannot be explained as the inevitable result of some sequence of events in the natural causal order. Thus distinctively human thought and behaviour is forever beyond the scope of empirical science—or at any rate beyond the scope of the science of man as Hume envisages it.

Hume's theory sees every aspect of human life as naturalistically explicable. It places man squarely within the scientifically intelligible world of nature, and thus conflicts with the traditional conception of a detached rational subject. That conception was added to something like the theory of ideas in philosophers as diverse as Descartes, Berkeley, Leibniz and Locke. But Hume is not content simply to put forward a theory that conflicts with it, although he does think his own theory is borne out by the facts. Some of his most original contributions to philosophy are made in his attempt actually to discredit the traditional 'rationalistic' conception on its own terms. He does not just advance a positive theory that plays down the role of reason; he tries to show independently that reason does not, and in fact cannot, have the kind of role in human life that had traditionally been supposed. It is this part of his programme that has led to the interpretation of Hume as a mere sceptic.

He argues that none of our beliefs or actions can ever be shown to be rational or reasonable in the way the traditional theory requires. No beliefs or actions can be justified by reason or reasoning alone, even if that reasoning proceeds from the indubitable deliverances of experience. In fact, Hume claims that, for any particular thing any human being believes about what he has not yet experienced, the person has no more reason to believe it than he has to believe its contradictory. That is what brings down on him the charge of negativism and mere paradox-mongering. But Hume's philosophy does not stop with what is usually called his scepticism. The powerful negative arguments have an important positive point. They show that reason, as traditionally understood, has no role in human life. If man, the rational animal, had to have good reasons to believe something before he could believe it, then Hume's arguments would show that no rational man would ever believe anything. But of course we all do believe all kinds of things all the time. In fact, we cannot help it. 'Nature, by an absolute and uncontroulable necessity has determin'd us to judge as well as to breathe and feel' (p. 183).

If no beliefs can be reasonably or rationally acquired, but we do get countless beliefs anyway, then the traditional 'rationalistic' idea of man as a detached rational agent must be rejected. Human beings as we find them in the world do have beliefs. It follows that either human beings are not such detached rational agents at all or, if they are, they never in fact manage to be rational in any of their beliefs or actions, and hence never perform in a way that is distinctively human. In either case, it follows that nothing on this earth lives up to the traditional conception of man. That is not to say that Hume denies that man is a rational animal, or that he finds no important differences between human beings and the rest of the animals. But he wants to look at human beings and see what they are actually like, and thereby see what humanity—or rational animality—really is. When he denies that men's actions and beliefs 'arise from reason' or 'have a foundation in reason' he is denying that actual human beings are rational in the way they would have to be if the traditional conception were correct. That conception embodies a notion of rationality that is simply imposed *a priori* on worldly human beings who are then observed to see how closely they measure up—to what extent they realize what is already 'known' to be their essence. Hume thinks we can find out what rationality and true humanity really are only by examining the creatures that actually exemplify them. Everything about man must be subject to naturalistic, scientific investigation.

14

It is very important to keep clearly in mind the presence of two distinct aspects or phases of Hume's overall task. For instance, he begins a discussion of religious belief by insisting that:

> there are two questions in particular, which challenge our attention, to wit, that concerning its foundation in reason, and that concerning its origin in human nature. (Hume (4), p. 21)

In *The Natural History of Religion* he deals only with the latter question, and in fact offers an interesting, if oversimplified, anthropological account of the origins of polytheism and of its natural development towards monotheism as man's knowledge and sophistication increase. What reasons can be found in the world to support our traditional monotheistic religious belief is a quite different question, and in fact is dealt with in a completely separate book, *Dialogues Concerning Natural Religion*, published only posthumously. It is undoubtedly one of the greatest books ever written on the subject.

Although in the rest of his philosophy Hume does not separate his discussions of the two different questions into different books, he remains quite clear about the distinction between them. Both the *Treatise* and the *Enquiries*, in their positive phases, deal with the 'origin in human nature' of our most fundamental ideas, beliefs, attitudes and reactions. Those psychological phenomena are explained naturalistically by appeal to the nature of our experience and to certain fundamental properties and dispositions of the human mind. But an essential part of that positive programme is the deflation of the pretensions of reason. That clears the stage so that feeling and sentiment can more easily be seen to play their true role. So the *Treatise* and *Enquiries* also deal with the alleged 'foundation in reason' of many of our most fundamental beliefs and attitudes. That can be called the 'negative' phase, since they are shown to have no rational support at all.

Hume usually looks first for the 'foundation in reason' of the beliefs and attitudes he examines, and only after demonstrating that they have none does he then proceed to his positive causal explanation of their origin. He has a much firmer grasp of the distinction between the two different investigations than many of his expositors and critics, and many later theorists of human nature, have sometimes exhibited. Virtually nowhere does he argue that a particular belief or attitude is unjustifiable, unreasonable, or without rational foundation *because* it is simply caused in such-and-such a way by discoverable features of our minds and the world.[11] The positive psychological or naturalistic explanation is introduced only after the negative sceptical argument has been deemed independently successful. So there is in effect a two-pronged attack on the traditional conception of reason. Hume shows negatively that, on its own terms, it implies the extinction of all human beliefs and actions; and he has a positive theory to explain all human beliefs and actions without it.

The 'atomistic' theory of ideas is clearly present in both phases, but always in the background, not as something open to dispute or investigation. Although it plays a role in Hume's negative arguments against the pretensions of reason—and so, strictly speaking, he reduces to absurdity only the conjunction of the traditional conception of reason together with a certain 'atomistic' picture of the mind—he is never led explicitly to doubt the adequacy of that Newtonian picture. And although it provides the framework for his positive theory of man, he does not appear to consider that model any better confirmed after he has made his scientific discoveries than it was before. It is, literally, not open to question either way. Hume nowhere acknowledges the possibility that in this respect he too might be guilty of inherited *a priori* theorizing about man.

II

The Theory of Ideas

Remembrance and Reflection how ally'd;
What thin partitions Sense from Thought divide:

Part I of Book I of the *Treatise* is taken up with the theory of ideas. Hume gives a quick, not very careful or thorough, exposition of the theory of the mind that he adopts without criticism from his predecessors. In the *Enquiry* he spends less than eight pages on it altogether. It is perhaps inaccurate to describe it as a 'theory' at all for Hume. It represents what for him was the unquestionable truth about the human mind. He never asks himself whether the theory of ideas is correct, and he never gives any arguments in support of it; he is interested in expounding only those details that he thinks will be useful to him later.

Students of philosophy are very familiar with this theory. It is an attractive conception, and seems to come naturally to mind when we think about perception, knowledge, thought and language in certain plausible ways. But despite its appeal and its long and illustrious career, it is extremely difficult even to state the theory precisely and intelligibly. That was no obstacle to its having the enormous historical influence it has had.

Its most detailed formulation is perhaps to be found in Locke's *Essay Concerning Human Understanding*. Locke used the term 'idea' to stand for 'whatsoever is the *object* of the understanding when a man thinks' (Locke (1), vol. 1, p. 32), and thinking here includes perceiving, imagining and willing, as well as thinking in the stricter sense of cogitation. For any of these activities to be occurring is for an idea to be before the mind. Having thoughts and having ideas were the same for Locke. In fact, he conceived of ideas as the *materials* of thinking, as the things that the mind, so to speak, 'operates' with in thinking, or the items that come and go and alter as the course of our thinking changes. They are things with which a mind must be furnished if it is to think at all, and one of Locke's main questions was

17

where all our ideas come from. That was, in effect, to ask what makes thought and therefore knowledge possible.

His answer was simple. All our ideas are derived from experience. Within the class of ideas he distinguished between ideas of sensation, which are before the mind when we perceive, sense or feel, especially as a result of the operation of external bodies on our sense organs, and ideas of reflection, which are representations of what goes on within the mind. These we do not get through the sense organs.

> Let us then suppose the mind to be, as we say, white paper, void of all characters, without any ideas:—How comes it to be furnished? Whence comes it by that vast store which the busy and boundless fancy of man has painted on it with an almost endless variety? Whence has it all the *materials* of reason and knowledge? To this I answer in one word, from EXPERIENCE. In that all our knowledge is founded; and from that it ultimately derives itself. Our observation employed either, about external sensible objects, or about the internal operations of our minds perceived and reflected on by ourselves, is that which supplies our understandings with all the *materials* of thinking. These two are the fountains of knowledge, from whence all the ideas we have, or can naturally have, do spring. (Locke (1), vol. 1. pp. 121–2)

After making a number of necessary distinctions, Locke set out to explain, perhaps more thoroughly than anyone else either before or since, precisely how some of our more important ideas could have arisen in the mind from these two sources.

Hume calls all the 'objects of the mind' not ideas, as Locke had done, but 'perceptions', and he divides them into two classes—'impressions' and 'ideas'. Although it is very difficult to say with any precision just what those classes are, and what the principle of distinction between them is, it is fairly clear what Hume wants to do with the distinction and why he tries to draw it in the way he does.

He agrees with Locke that the mind is originally 'white paper', in the sense that it contains no ideas, and that all its 'materials' come from experience. But he insists on a distinction between the entities involved when we are feeling or experiencing, on the one hand, and those involved when we are thinking or reasoning, on the other. Since there must be some 'materials' already in the mind in order for thinking or cogitation to occur, the source of everything in the mind is ultimately something other than thinking or reasoning. Hume calls it perceiving, sensing or feeling. He agrees that there must be a perception before the mind if any mental phenomenon is occurring, but since he thinks Locke has no easy way to make the distinction between sensation and thought, he uses different words to refer to the different kinds of perceptions he thinks are before the mind in each case. So Locke and Hume do not mean the same by 'idea'. What Locke calls ideas Hume calls perceptions, and for Hume every perception is either an impression or an idea. Hume thinks this restores the term 'idea' to its original sense, from which he says Locke had perverted it.

Hume first draws the distinction between impressions and ideas as follows:

> The difference betwixt these consists in the degrees of force
> and liveliness with which they strike upon the mind, and make
> their way into our thought or consciousness. Those perceptions,
> which enter with most force and violence, we may name
> *impressions*; and under this name I comprehend all our
> sensations, passions and emotions, as they make their first
> appearance in the soul. By *ideas* I mean the faint images of
> these in thinking and reasoning; such as, for instance, are all the
> perceptions excited by the present discourse, excepting
> only, those which arise from the sight and touch, and excepting
> the immediate pleasure or uneasiness it may occasion. (p. 1)

He thinks the distinction does not need much explanation, since, as he says, 'every one of himself will readily perceive the difference betwixt feeling and thinking' (pp. 1–2). We know there is a difference between actually perceiving something and just thinking about that thing in its absence, and that, Hume says, is the difference between having an impression of something and having an idea of it. And the distinction between impressions and ideas is simply a distinction between the degrees of force and liveliness with which perceptions strike upon the mind. I shall return in a moment to the question whether perceiving something does really differ from merely thinking about it only in this way, but first I want to look briefly at the rest of what Hume says about the basic furniture of the mind.

A moment's thought about the contents of our minds shows that, as Hume puts it, 'all the perceptions of the mind are double, and appear both as impressions and ideas' (pp. 2–3). That is to say, when we examine what is in our minds we seem to find that all the contents come in pairs, the only difference between the members of each pair being a difference in the degrees of force and liveliness with which they strike upon the mind.

> When I shut my eyes and think of my chamber, the ideas I form
> are exact representations of the impressions I felt; nor is
> there any circumstance of the one, which is not to be found

in the other. In running over my other perceptions, I find still the same resemblance and representation. Ideas and impressions appear always to correspond to each other. (p. 3)

So not only is every perception of the mind either an impression or an idea, it also looks as if there is an exactly resembling idea for every impression, and vice versa. But this, on closer inspection, turns out to be a mistake.

There is an exact resemblance between some of our ideas and some of our impressions, but obviously there are also many perceptions of which that is not true. For example, I can now imagine the New Jerusalem, whose pavement is gold and walls are rubies, but I have never had an impression which exactly resembles the idea I have just formed. Also, I have had a breathtaking impression of Paris from the steps of Sacré Coeur, but I cannot now form an idea which exactly resembles that impression. So there are ideas without exactly resembling impressions, and impressions without exactly resembling ideas.

The hypothesis of a one—one correlation between ideas and impressions does hold, however, in a more restricted domain. This can be seen by invoking the distinction Locke had relied on between *simple* and *complex* perceptions.

Simple perceptions or impressions and ideas are such as admit of no distinction nor separation. The complex are the contrary to these, and may be distinguished into parts. Tho' a particular colour, taste, and smell are qualities all united together in this apple, 'tis easy to perceive they are not the same, but are at least distinguishable from each other. (p. 2)

Both an impression and an idea of an apple are therefore complex, since they consist of parts which are distinguishable.

From this example it is natural to conclude that our impressions or ideas of the colour, taste and smell of this particular apple are simple perceptions, and in fact Hume does speak this way. But he, like Locke, was not sufficiently concerned with what simplicity consists in. Locke at least discussed the question, without much success, but Hume appears to find no difficulty at all. He does not actually say in this passage that the ideas of the colour, taste and smell of this particular apple *are* simple ideas; he says only that, since those constituents can be distinguished, the idea of the apple must be complex. But elsewhere he does speak of ideas of colours as simple ideas.[1] Using the vague criterion of simplicity suggested by what Hume says, it would seem that the idea of this particular red is itself complex, since it has a particular hue and a specific intensity, both of which can be distinguished from each other. Similarly, a particular note sounded on a piano would seem to give us a complex impression, since its pitch is something different from its timbre. And perhaps those features in turn could be broken down into 'parts' or dimensions that are distinguishable even further. Hume gives us no general guidance about how to tell that we have got down to a simple perception, so we will have to be satisfied with the examples he gives—perceptions of a particular shade of a colour, or of a particular sound.

A straightforward inspection of the mind is said to reveal a one—one correlation between our simple ideas and our simple impressions. For every simple idea in the mind there is an exactly resembling simple impression, and vice versa. The apparent counter-examples noted earlier were complex perceptions, and so they can safely be ignored. Of course, to say that this general proposition is discovered by an inspection of the mind is not to say that it is established by an exhaustive enumeration of each one of the perceptions of the mind. Nevertheless, Hume is bold enough to 'venture to affirm' it, and in partial support he offers a typical Humean challenge.

> Every one may satisfy himself in this point by running over as many as he pleases. But if any one should deny this universal resemblance, I know no way of convincing him, but by desiring him to shew a simple impression, that has not a correspondent idea, or a simple idea, that has not a correspondent impression. If he does not answer this challenge, as 'tis certain he cannot, we may from his silence and our own observation establish our conclusion. (pp. 3–4)

No real proof of this correspondence is possible because the only way to see what the objects of the mind are like is for each of us to examine his own mind.

We have now discovered what Hume later calls a 'constant conjunction' between two kinds of things—for every simple idea there is a corresponding simple impression.[2] This conjunction or correlation holds so universally that it cannot be due simply to chance; there must be some connection between things of the two sorts. Either impressions cause their corresponding ideas to appear in the mind, or the causal connection operates in the opposite direction.

Whenever we find a correlation like this we can determine the direction of the causal link by finding out which of the two kinds of things always occurs first in time. For example, if there is found to be a correlation between cigarette smoking and lung cancer, and we come to think that smoking is a contributing cause of cancer, we will do so because we believe that smoking occurs before contracting the disease. Someone who had never smoked a cigarette in his life, who then developed lung cancer, and then began to smoke, would not support the hypothesis that smoking is part of the cause of lung cancer. Similarly, Hume is saying that since for every simple impression there is a corresponding simple idea, and for every simple idea there is a corresponding simple impression, we can find out which causes which if we can find that there is a certain member of the pair that always comes first in time.

Hume then appeals to experience to show that simple impressions always precede their corresponding simple ideas in the mind, and so he concludes that simple impressions cause their corresponding simple ideas. But all complex perceptions are made up of simple perceptions alone, and so without simple perceptions there would be no complex perceptions at all. Therefore, if everything in the mind is either an impression or an idea, and is either simple or complex, then everything in the mind is either a simple impression, or is made up of simple impressions, or comes to be there as the result of the appearance in the mind of simple impressions, because all simple ideas are caused by their corresponding impressions. All simple impressions are either impressions of sensation or impressions of reflection. But impressions of reflection occur only as a result of something's appearing before the mind. And since impressions and ideas are the only things that appear there, it could not be the case that the only impressions that ever occur in a mind are impressions of reflection. So there would be no impressions of reflection unless there were some impressions of sensation. Taken all together, this implies that everything that comes into the mind comes there as a result of our having impressions of sensation. Such impressions are causally required for the appearance before the mind of any other perceptions.

Some of the steps of this theory of the mind might be set out as follows:

(1) There is no thought or mental activity unless there is a perception before the mind.
(2) Every perception is either an impression or an idea.
(3) Every perception is either simple or complex.
(4) Every complex perception consists completely of simple perceptions.
(5) For every simple idea there is a corresponding simple impression.
(6) Every simple idea arises in the mind as the effect of its corresponding simple impression.
(7) There are no impressions of reflection without some impression of sensation.

Therefore,

(8) There is no thought or mental activity unless there are impressions of sensation.

22

This argument provides the background for most of the methodological pronouncements and for some of the actual procedures to be found in Hume's philosophy. He thinks that, in order to understand the human mind, and therefore to understand why we think in the ways we do, we must try to discover the *origins* of those ways of thinking. Modes of thought are to be given, as much as possible, genetic or developmental explanations. This is to account for human behaviour and human mental activity in much the same way as we try to understand diseases. We understand the state the organism is now in by seeing how it got from its original state to its present condition. But according to the theory of ideas, thinking and mental activity generally consists in the presence before the mind of perceptions. Therefore the proper study of the human mind is the study of how those perceptions got into the mind in the first place, and why they are making their appearance there now. From the outline of Hume's theory sketched in (1) through (8) we know that the perceptions got there at least partly as a result of our having certain impressions of sensation, and so Hume's examination of the human mind proceeds by attempting to discover in sense-experience the origins of the ideas we find in our minds. ' 'Tis impossible perfectly to understand any idea, without tracing it up to its origin, and examining that primary impression, from which it arises' (pp. 74–5).

Of course, the impression is only part of the total causal story, but an indispensable part. Another important part, and one that Hume comes to emphasize more and more, is that set of complicated, but primitive operations or dispositions of the mind which lead us to acquire, manipulate, shuffle and even confuse the multitude of perceptions that come to us. In fact, most of the interest of Hume's own positive theory centers on these operations of the mind and their effects, although he usually speaks officially as if only the 'atoms' that come and go in the mind were important.

Hume also thinks that his theory of the mind sketched in (1) through (8) incidentally settles quite conclusively in the negative the question of the existence of innate ideas, in so far as that issue is intelligible or interesting at all:

the present question concerning the precedency of our impressions or ideas, is the same with what has made so much noise in other terms, when it has been disputed whether there be any *innate ideas*, or whether all ideas be derived from sensation and reflection. (p. 7)

In this he follows Locke, and in fact he supposes Locke's denial of innate ideas to have been nothing more than the thesis that all ideas are copies of impressions, even though, as we have seen, Locke lacked the terminology to put it that way.

If Hume's theory is to have the consequence that there are no innate ideas it must be understood as stronger than the contention that we would never have any ideas, thoughts or beliefs unless we had at least some impressions of sensation. That weak claim is quite compatible with our having a host of innate ideas lying dormant in the mind, as it were, waiting for the occurrence of a few random sensations to activate them, after which we can think all those thoughts that were 'innately' in us all along without having encountered anything in experience to which they or their constituents correspond. Hume's stronger conclusion is really that each simple idea that is ever in the mind 'first makes its appearance in a correspondent impression' (p. 33), and without the impression there would be no corresponding idea in the mind at all. The first general principle he takes himself to have established in the science of man is:

> *That all our simple ideas in their first appearance are deriv'd from simple impressions, which are correspondent to them, and which they exactly represent.* (p. 4)

And that does seem incompatible with any interesting theory of innate ideas.

Obviously the most important part of Hume's theory is the claim that every simple idea enters the mind as an effect of its corresponding simple impression. That gives the rationale for Hume's methodology, and is decisive on the innateness issue as he understands it. He thinks step (6) has the same kind of support as any other causal hypothesis. Given the fact that:

(5) For every simple idea there is a corresponding simple impression.

and the further discovery that:

(5a) Every simple idea is preceded into the mind by its corresponding simple impression.

he concludes (not, of course, deductively):

(6) Every simple idea arises in the mind as the effect of its corresponding simple impression.

This is an inference from a constant conjunction between things of two kinds, A and B, and the temporal priority of things of kind A to corresponding things of kind B, to the conclusion that things of kind A are the causes of things of kind B.

24

If this argument is to establish its conclusion there must be some support for its premises. Hume says that (5) is seen to be true by an inspection of our minds, and he thinks the temporal claim (5a) will be accepted if we look to experience and 'consider the order of first appearance' in the mind of the two kinds of perceptions. He finds:

> by constant experience, that the simple impressions always take the precedent of their correspondent ideas, but never appear in the contrary order. (p. 5)

He appeals to various familiar facts to confirm this.

We are all said to be aware of the following 'plain and convincing' phenomena.

> To give a child an idea of scarlet or orange, of sweet or bitter, I present the objects, or in other words, convey to him these impressions; but proceed not so absurdly, as to endeavour to produce the impressions by exciting the ideas. (p. 5)
> . . . where-ever by any accident the faculties, which give rise to any impressions, are obstructed in their operations, as when one is born blind or deaf; not only the impressions are lost, but also their correspondent ideas; so that there never appear in the mind the least traces of either of them. Nor is this only true, where the organs of sensation are entirely destroy'd but likewise where they have never been put in action to produce a particular impression. We cannot form to ourselves a just idea of the taste of a pine-apple, without having actually tasted it. (p. 5)

These represent to Hume obvious and uncontroversial truths about human beings—things we know by observing human life. Perhaps it does seem obvious that to give a child an idea of orange I most typically will present him with an orange object, or that we cannot form a correct idea of the taste of pineapple without actually tasting one. But the question that must be asked is whether these mundane facts support Hume's temporal hypothesis (5a), and if so, how.

The above 'phenomena' support (5a) only if at least two further assumptions are true, or are to some extent justified. That Hume was making at least one of those assumptions is obvious from the very way he describes the familiar facts. The other, as we will see, leads to fundamental difficulties in the theory of ideas.

Taken literally, the 'plain and convincing' facts that we present a child with an orange object in order to give him an idea of orange, or that we cannot form a correct idea of the taste of pineapple without actually tasting one, show at most that those simple ideas are preceded into the mind by our actually seeing, tasting, hearing, smelling, etc., something. But this is not to say that:

> (5a) Every simple idea is preceded into the mind by its corresponding simple impression.

If the 'phenomena' are to confirm (5a), then, something like the following assumptions will have to be made in order to narrow the gap between it and the evidence.

> (P) Whenever anyone actually sees, tastes, hears, smells, etc., something there is a perception before the mind.
>
> (I) The perceptions that are before the mind when anyone sees, tastes, hears, smells, etc., something are *impressions*.

With these two assumptions the argument from the 'phenomena' to (5a), and therefore ultimately to Hume's causal conclusion, is much more plausible.

Of course, it is not an objection to Hume to point out that what he says is justified only on the assumption of something like (P) and (I). He thinks they are both true. But it is important to see that some such assumptions are required, since that will expose to view more of the theory of ideas, and will locate the source of a number of difficulties Hume gets into as a result of accepting that theory.

Assumption (P) is perhaps the most important part of the theory of ideas. It is in fact simply a special case of the basic general principle (1) that for any mental event or phenomenon to be occurring is for a perception to be before the mind. In the particular case of seeing, tasting, hearing, etc., this is a precursor of what has come to be called the 'sense-datum theory' of perceiving, and it has been held in one form or another by most philosophers since Descartes. Hume gives little or no explicit argument for it, and none at all at the very beginning of the *Treatise* or the *Enquiry*, where it would seem to be most needed. The legacy of Descartes, Locke and others made that part of the theory of ideas completely uncontroversial to Hume—so much so that he speaks of having objects presented to one's senses as if it were simply the same thing as having certain impressions (p. 5). Hume is not alone in this. There is very little argument for the basic principle of the theory of ideas in Locke, either, but Berkeley's *Dialogues* provide an almost complete catalogue of the familiar considerations in support of some such view.[3]

Later in the *Treatise* Hume does mention some facts about the 'variability' of perception, or the dependence of what is perceived on the state of the perceiver and the medium through which it is perceived (pp. 210–11, 226–7), but they appear more as reminders of well-known facts and their implications than as attempts to support the foundations of the theory of ideas. Hume's own attitude towards that theory is perhaps best summed up in his remark:

26

> We may observe, that 'tis universally allowed by philosophers, and is besides pretty obvious of itself, that nothing is ever really present with the mind but its perceptions or impressions and ideas, and that external objects become known to us only by those perceptions they occasion. (p. 67)

Of course, the fact that Hume is not concerned to give arguments in support of the basic principle of the theory of ideas, and the fact that he thinks it is 'pretty obvious of itself', should not suggest that he thinks he knows it in some way other than by observation or experience. For him, it is known by the same kind of 'cautious observation of human life' that informs him of most of the rest of his philosophical system. There are many facts about us and the world we live in that are obvious to any intelligent man who looks in the right place, so Hume's not giving any very systematic evidence to support his basic assumption does not imply that he thinks there is none. But at this point I will not venture further into a discussion of the idea that to see, hear, taste, etc., something is to have a perception before the mind.[4] I want to look more closely at the other assumption Hume is relying on.

Before we can assess, or even look for support for, the claim that the perceptions that are before the mind when anyone sees, hears, tastes, etc., something are impressions and not ideas, we must have some understanding of the distinction between impressions and ideas. Hume gets into great difficulties on this question. Since an idea can differ from an impression in very many ways that are irrelevant to the point of the distinction, we need to ask, not simply how ideas differ from impressions, but how an idea differs from its 'corresponding' impression. Hume thinks that all simple perceptions, and many complex perceptions, have partners or correlates which they resemble and hence 'correspond' to. One member of each pair is an impression, the other is an idea. What is it to belong to one class rather than the other? To this question Hume gives different, and not always compatible, answers.

The official answer, and one that there is good theoretical reason for Hume to give, is that impressions differ from their corresponding ideas only in the degree of 'force and liveliness with which they strike upon the mind, and make their way into our thought and consciousness' (p. 1). Assuming that we can determine by inspection or observation the relative force or liveliness with which perceptions strike upon the mind, this criterion would enable us to look into our minds and sort our perceptions into the impressions and the ideas. If we find that the member of the pair which strikes with greater force and liveliness is present, then we are having an impression, and if we find that the member which strikes with less force and liveliness is present, then we are having an idea. And, as Hume intends, this would also enable us to tell by inspection of the mind that for every simple idea there is a corresponding simple impression, and vice versa.[5] That is just step (5) of Hume's argument, which he says is known by inspecting the mind.

But Hume's general aim in making the distinction is to distinguish perceiving or feeling from thinking. Only then will he be able to make the point that there can be no thoughts or ideas unless there are first some sensations or feelings. Since, according to the theory of ideas, for us to perceive or think about something is for there to be a perception before the mind, Hume thinks that the difference between perceiving and thinking is just a difference between the kinds of perceptions that are before the mind in each case. And so he suggests that his distinction between two kinds of perceptions in terms of the degrees of force and liveliness with which they strike upon the mind is just the same as the distinction between perceiving or feeling something, on the one hand, and thinking about it, on the other. At least, that is the account he usually gives, and it fits in best with the demands of his theory.

Are the two distinctions really the same? Is the difference between perceiving and thinking simply a difference between the degrees of force and liveliness with which certain 'objects' strike upon the mind? Obviously we need some understanding of what 'degrees of force and liveliness' are, and how they are to be recognized. Hume is not helpful in this regard. He sees that he has not drawn the distinction clearly, but he suggests that he need not bother, since 'every one of himself will readily perceive the difference betwixt feeling and thinking' (pp. 1–2).

Certainly everyone will acknowledge that there is a difference between feeling or perceiving something and merely thinking about it in its absence, and not many words are needed to convince people of that distinction. But Hume is putting forward a view about what that difference is. He says it is merely a difference in the degree of 'force and liveliness' with which certain perceptions strike upon the mind. And that does need explanation and defence. The obviousness of the fact that there is a distinction between perceiving and thinking does not make Hume's account of that difference obvious. In fact, it is not even clear what his account comes to. If it is taken fairly literally it does not seem to be very plausible.

A detective examining the scene of a murder might look closely at the room in which the body was found and take careful mental note of it. He might find nothing unusual, nothing that gives any clue; it strikes him as just the way the room would have been if it had been occupied only by the victim. But he might later try to run over in his mind exactly what he has seen, and, with a good memory and strong eidetic powers, he might reproduce it quite accurately. According to Hume he would then have an idea which exactly resembles his earlier impression of the room. Suppose he is now aware of a room in which the poker is leaning against the left side of the fireplace, and he remembers, as he knew earlier, that the victim was right-handed. That part of his present idea that includes the fireplace and the poker now strikes upon his mind or consciousness with much greater force and liveliness than the corresponding part of the exactly similar scene had done earlier. Given the theory of ideas, it would seem that the detective had a perception before the mind when he was just thinking about the fireplace and the poker in their absence that struck his mind or consciousness with a greater degree of force and liveliness than did the perception he had before the mind when he originally perceived them. And such things seem to happen often.

If that is so, then Hume's main assumption to the effect that the perceptions that are before the mind when anyone sees, hears, tastes, etc., something are impressions and not ideas, is not true. If impressions are defined as those perceptions that strike the mind with greater force and liveliness than their partners or correlates, then the detective was having an impression when he was merely thinking about the room, and an idea when he was actually perceiving it. In that case an impression would have been preceded into the mind by its corresponding idea, contrary to the principle Hume is trying to establish. There is no doubt that Hume would reject this implication of the example of the detective, but he never explains the grounds on which he could do so.[6] Either he must explain in more detail what 'force and liveliness' of perceptions are, and how they are recognized, or else he must explain the distinction between perceiving and thinking in some other way.[7]

One possible way of making the distinction would be to say that impressions are those perceptions that are before the mind when and only when we are actually perceiving or being stimulated by some external physical object. That would certainly render Hume's main assumption uncontroversial, since it would then say no more than that the perceptions that are before the mind when anyone actually perceives something are impressions, i.e. perceptions that are before the mind when anyone actually perceives something. But that cannot help explain how perceiving differs from thinking.

In any case Hume explicitly denies that impressions are to be defined or identified in terms of the way in which, or the source from which, they actually come to appear in the mind (pp. 2n, 84; *E*, p. 28). He wants to distinguish impressions from ideas on the basis of some features the two kinds of perceptions can be found to possess by a straightforward inspection of the contents of the mind. That is how he claims to know that there is a one—one correlation between simple perceptions of the two different kinds. He restricts the range of evidence to the contents of the mind alone. That is perhaps what makes it so difficult for him to explain the distinction between perceiving and thinking.

Some philosophers, notably Descartes and Berkeley, have emphasized the fact that some of our perceptions come to us independently of our wills. Whatever we might want to see, however hard we try to have before our minds an idea of, say, a mermaid, if we open our eyes in good light and look at the stones on the beach before us, we will see the stones on the beach before us, whether we want to or not. Both Descartes and Berkeley took this as a fact about perceptions that inclines us to believe that they come to us from without, or are produced by something other than ourselves.

This distinction between two kinds of perceptions, even if it could be noticed by introspection of the contents of the mind alone, is not the one Hume draws between impressions and ideas. It is fundamental for Hume's theory of human nature that many of our ideas, as well as our impressions, come to us independently of our wills—they also 'force' themselves upon us whether we want them to or not. In many cases we are powerless to resist. One of the main aims of the science of human nature is to explain just how and why certain ideas inevitably come to us when they do. It is true that ideas are subject to the will in a way impressions are not—we can deliberately and directly 'call up' or construct a particular idea whenever we want to, as long as the mind has been furnished with the necessary ingredients, and we cannot do that with impressions. But such deliberate production is not necessary in order for an idea to appear before the mind, so no distinction between impressions and ideas along these lines will be useful to Hume.

It can sometimes look as if Hume actually identifies impressions, and distinguishes them from ideas, precisely in terms of their appearing in the mind first, earlier than their corresponding ideas. He says, for example:

> under this name [impression] I comprehend all our sensations, passions and emotions, *as they make their first appearance in the soul.* (p. 1, my italics)

> Original impressions or impressions of sensation are such as *without any antecedent perception* arise in the soul. . . .
> (p. 275, my italics)

But if impressions differ from ideas only in preceding their corresponding perceptions into the mind, then no 'experiments' of the sort mentioned earlier are required to establish that simple ideas are always preceded into the mind by their corresponding simple impressions. Whichever member of a pair of corresponding perceptions comes into the mind earlier is *ipso facto* the impression, and so the important premiss of the temporal priority of impressions over ideas need not be confirmed by experience at all. Granted, that would make the premiss true and uncontroversial, but it would no longer serve Hume's purposes, since the connection between having an impression and perceiving or feeling something would have been severed.

The principle that every simple idea is the effect of its corresponding simple impression is supposed to supply the justification for the procedures Hume follows in examining the mind, and to settle the question of innate ideas. It could do neither if an impression were simply that member of a pair of corresponding perceptions that appears in the mind earlier than its correlate. Hume is concerned with the origins of our ideas—his way of understanding the mind is to ask how and why it comes to be furnished with the materials it has—and he tries to trace all our ideas back to impressions. That task is perhaps still feasible if an impression is just a perception that occurs earlier than its corresponding perception, but it would not provide the kind of understanding Hume seeks, and it would leave the innateness issue untouched.

As Hume understands it, the question whether we have any innate ideas is the question whether all our thoughts and beliefs employ only materials that have been derived from perceiving or sensing something. Are any ideas 'native' to the mind whatever experience might be like, or can every mental object be traced back to some 'data' provided by perceiving, sensing or feeling? He thinks he has shown the latter to be true by showing that every simple idea is derived from its corresponding impression, and hence we can trace ideas back to their origins in perceiving or feeling. But if impressions are just those perceptions that occur earlier than their corresponding ideas, Hume would have shown only that every idea in the mind is the effect of some earlier perception in the mind. No defender of innate ideas need deny that. That I can now think of, say, God only because there was an earlier perception of God in my mind is just what he wants to say. The mere fact that there was an earlier corresponding perception does not connect the present idea with any particular source or origin—and in particular, not with perceiving or sensing—and so it is quite possible that that earlier perception was innate, or was put there by God. But that is not true of impressions as Hume understands them.

It is true that Hume makes no claims about the source of our impressions. He says:

> As to those *impressions*, which arise from the *senses*, their
> ultimate cause is, in my opinion, perfectly inexplicable by
> human reason, and 'twill always be impossible to decide with
> certainty, whether they arise immediately from the object, or
> are produc'd by the creative power of the mind, or are
> deriv'd from the author of our being. (p. 84)

And this seems to leave open the possibility that God provides us with all our impressions. That is true, but the possibility Hume envisages here is that God provides us with all impressions 'which arise from the senses', i.e. that God makes us sense or perceive what we do. Even if that were so, as Berkeley believed, there would still be a point to the denial of innate ideas, since to say that some ideas are innate is to say that sensing or perceiving is not required in order for those ideas to get into the mind. So Hume can afford to be non-committal about God's role in producing our impressions, but he must show that, even if God does produce them, He does so by making us perceive and feel, and not just by endowing our minds with certain primitive perceptions that are in the mind earlier than certain other perceptions that correspond to them.

In short, both Hume's denial of innateness and his own positive method rest on the contention that there is nothing in the mind unless we perceive or sense something, and that all the materials in the mind can ultimately be traced back to something that first entered the mind during such a perceiving or sensing. That is precisely why Hume must find some way to distinguish perceiving, sensing or feeling from thinking. It is not enough just to make some distinction or other between two classes of perceptions.

Of course, he says that the distinction between feeling and thinking just *is* a distinction between more and less forceful and lively perceptions, and I have tried to suggest that the only indications he offers for understanding those troublesome terms do not really support that view. But he is looking in the right place, given his theoretical aims and his commitment to the theory of ideas. He wants to find an identifiable feature of all and only all impressions that will distinguish them by inspection from the ideas that correspond to them. Then he can establish by experience that simple ideas are always preceded into the mind by their corresponding simple impressions. Given the one—one correlation between simple impressions and simple ideas— also discovered by direct observation—he then can assert the causal principle that every simple idea is caused by its corresponding simple impression. That is the heart of Hume's theory of the mind.

It is therefore clear why he feels constrained to appeal to something like the degrees of force and liveliness with which certain perceptions strike upon the mind. With such an introspectible criterion he can observe the required correlation between greater force and earlier appearance in the mind that he needs to support the causal theory. Differences in degrees of force and liveliness of perceptior.s—or some other directly recognizable distinction between the perceptions involved—must therefore match the differences between perceiving and thinking. If not, Hume will not have shown that there is no thinking unless something corresponding at least to the ingredients of the thought in question has been perceived, sensed or felt. It is safe to say that Hume does not really succeed in showing that. He does not, and probably cannot, find the right kind of distinction between perceiving and thinking within the only terms he allows himself to use.[8]

Hume is fully aware of the importance of the principle that every simple idea arises in the mind as the effect of its corresponding simple impression. In fact, his only point in sketching the theory of ideas is to establish that principle. But, having established it to his own satisfaction, he immediately raises an objection to it. It is significant that the objection appears in both the *Treatise* and the *Enquiry*. Hume tended to leave out of the *Enquiry* anything he saw as a real difficulty in writing the *Treatise*.

Suppose someone is presented with a spectrum of all the different shades of blue except one—a shade he has never actually seen before in his life. He would certainly perceive a blank where that shade is missing, and would see that there is a greater distance between the contiguous colours there than at any other place in the spectrum. Is it possible for him to get the idea of the missing shade of blue 'from his own imagination, . . . tho' it had never been conveyed to him by his senses' (p. 6)? Hume allows, realistically, that it is possible. But then the man would have a simple idea of a particular shade of blue without ever having had any corresponding simple impression, and so Hume's first principle of the science of human nature would seem to have been refuted.

Hume's response is puzzling:

this may serve as a proof, that the simple ideas are not
always derived from the correspondent impressions; tho' the
instance is so particular and singular, that 'tis scarce worth
our observing, and does not merit that for it alone we should
alter our general maxim. (p. 6)

If exceptions have been found, why should the 'maxim' not be altered or abandoned?

For one thing, all the example really shows, as Hume is sometimes aware, is that it is *not impossible* for someone to get a simple idea in that way. The example is a hypothetical one, and there is no suggestion that anyone actually ever has been, or ever will be, in that position. But Hume also does concede that 'the simple ideas *are not* always derived from the correspondent impressions', and that is perhaps because he easily imagines some circumstances in which, as a matter of causal fact, a simple idea *would* be acquired without an intervening impression. To understand Hume's acceptance of the example one must remember that he puts forward his 'general maxim' that simple ideas are derived from simple impressions as a straightforward causal hypothesis. It is to be taken as contingent, as something that might well have been, or might even be found to be, false. But if there are exceptions it might well be possible to explain how they could occur without having to invoke any general principles that are not part of, or in line with, Hume's theory of the mind. And if the possible exceptions were perforce rare and very special, one might be fully justified in ignoring them and basing one's scientific investigations on the general principle. It is a good general maxim that water boils at 100°C, although that is not true on the tops of high mountains. But anyone living on a flat desert at sea-level could scarcely be faulted for acting as if it were the whole truth.

Still, Hume's rather cavalier attitude towards the exception is unsettling. It is difficult to see how far he would allow it to be generalized. Could ideas of a whole range of shades—in fact, all the shades of a certain colour—spring into the mind as a result of impressions of the other colours? Later in the *Treatise* Hume discovers a basic principle of the mind that he might have used to account for the example of the missing shade of blue, but he draws no limits to the range of its application:

> the imagination, when set into any train of thinking, is apt to
> continue, even when its object fails it, and like a galley put
> in motion by the oars, carries on its course without any new
> impulse. (p. 198)

Can the imagination be set into a certain chain of thinking by only one, or a few, impressions? And how long can those trains continue without needing new 'data'?

Whatever answers Hume were to give to these questions they would have to be understood in such a way that the case of the missing shade of blue and similar possibilities gives no comfort to defenders of innate ideas. Even if the mind is naturally disposed to continue getting new ideas in a certain dimension after it has stopped receiving similar impressions, the ideas in question are to be thought of as derived from

34

those impressions and that disposition of the mind; they are not ideas that do, or could, come to us independently of our perceiving or sensing something. Hume agrees with Locke that the mind's having certain natural or primitive dispositions to acquire ideas under certain circumstances is not the same as its being naturally endowed with certain innate ideas. Although he nowhere succeeds in making that distinction clear enough, his confidence in it no doubt partly explains his willing acceptance of the exception to his 'first principle in the science of human nature'. But it must be confessed that most of the puzzle remains.[9]

The theory of ideas does not deal only with the origins of our ideas. It also gives an account of what happens after the ideas get into the mind—how thinking takes place. We can come to have a particular idea before the mind in a variety of ways. For example, we might remember an earlier impression. Having visited New College chapel in the past, I might now 'call up' the idea which exactly resembles the impression I had earlier. If this really is a case of memory there will be a resemblance between the present idea and the original impression, both in terms of the elements included in it, and the 'order and position' or structure of those elements. The distinction between remembering something, on the one hand, and merely imagining it or having an idea of it that is not a memory-idea, on the other, gives Hume a lot of difficulty. He thinks there ought to be a way of telling, from inspecting the idea alone, whether or not it is a real or veridical memory-idea, but, not surprisingly, he finds no such recognizable criterion.[10]

There are other ways we come to have particular ideas before the mind. We might perform on one of our complex ideas an operation of analysis or separation, and thus bring more clearly before the mind one or another of the simple ideas out of which our original complex idea was composed. Or we might deliberately synthesize or combine various simple ideas into previously unknown combinations. In this way, for example, we can form an idea of a creature with the head and shoulders of a goat and the body of a zebra. No such animal has ever been seen, or perhaps even imagined before, but we have no difficulty in forming an idea of one as long as we have the necessary components at hand.

We can perform various 'actions' of combining or juxtaposing our ideas, and thus get new ideas in the mind. In fact, Hume says that nothing is more free than the imagination (p. 10). It is constantly in 'motion', and nothing is faster than the swiftness of thought. But it does not follow from its freedom or its constant motion that events in the mind occur randomly, in utter chaos. There is an order and coherence in the happenings in the mind, just as there is in the most chaotic-seeming occurrences in the physical world.

> It is evident that there is a principle of connexion between
> the different thoughts or ideas of the mind, and that,
> in their appearance to the memory or imagination, they introduce
> each other with a certain degree of method and regularity. In
> our more serious thinking or discourse this is so observable
> that any particular thought, which breaks in upon the regular
> tract or chain of ideas, is immediately remarked and rejected.
> And even in our wildest and most wandering reveries, nay,
> in our very dreams, we shall find, if we reflect, that the
> imagination ran not altogether at adventures, but that there
> was still a connexion upheld among the different ideas,
> which succeeded each other. Were the loosest and freest
> conversation to be transcribed, there would immediately be
> observed something which connected it in all its transitions.
> (E, p. 23)

Behind the apparently random and fluctuating course of ideas there is a 'gentle force' operating. It leads the mind from one idea to another; it is a 'kind of attraction' by which an idea, 'upon its appearance, naturally introduces its correlative' (p. 289). It is this bond or association between ideas that causes ideas to come into our minds as a result of other ideas that are already there. To discover the principles of this association we must find relations that hold between two ideas when the presence of one of them naturally introduces the other into the mind. That will explain what makes us think in the ways we do; it will show what is really responsible for our thinking in those terms. The analogy with the theory of gravitation is obvious here, and in his discussion of the association of ideas Hume makes it look as if his theory will be much more systematic and much more like the theory of gravitation than it actually turns out to be. He says that there are only three principles of association of ideas, and he strongly suggests that all the various and complicated operations of the mind can be completely accounted for in terms of those three principles alone.

The three 'principles', or relations between ideas such that the presence in the mind of one of them naturally gives rise to the other, are *resemblance, contiguity in time or place* and *cause and effect*. For example:

> A picture naturally leads our thoughts to the original: the
> mention of one apartment in a building naturally introduces an
> enquiry or discourse concerning the others: and if we think
> of a wound, we can scarcely forbear reflecting on the pain
> which follows it. (E, p. 24)

It is difficult to believe that all the operations of the human mind take place only in accord with the principles that are so crudely exemplified here. This is not to deny that resemblance and cause and effect are extremely important relations among our ideas; without them we probably could not think at all. But there are many other 'principles' operating, and Hume appeals to them, as he does to the principles of association, as 'natural', 'primitive', or basic dispositions or operations of the mind. They are basic at least in the sense that the reasons why such principles operate are not known to us. Therefore, they can be taken, at least for now and perhaps for ever, as '*original* qualities of human nature, which I pretend not to explain' (p. 13).

Despite the suggestions in the more programmatic parts of Hume's writings that the association of ideas, on the analogy of the principle of universal gravitation, can account for everything that goes on in the mind, when he actually gets down to the detailed business of explaining the origins of some of our most pervasive forms of thinking, feeling and acting, he does not force everything into a rigid associationist mould. What he says about the origin of our belief in an external world, or of our conception of the self, for example, is incompatible with the general remarks about the universal efficacy and explanatory power of the simple principles of association. This is to Hume's credit. His perceptiveness and philosophical acumen lead him to discoveries that are, as he thinks, dictated by the facts, despite their not being straightforward applications of the general theory he says he is defending. That is one reason why the attempt to understand him as merely the shrewd defender of a simple theory, or as the 'reducer to absurdity' of the theories of his predecessors, leads to a distortion and impoverishment of his actual views.

Even in the brief Part I of the *Treatise*, where he sketches the general outlines of the theory of ideas, Hume strays from the rigid associationist picture, and from the strict analogy with the theory of gravitation, as soon as he tries to explain something important that his theory should be able to account for. How is it possible for us to have general ideas, i.e. ideas which represent or stand for a number of different particulars? We have an idea of man, under which all particular men fall, so it seems that we somehow think of *all* men by means of only one idea. The problem arises for Hume, as it did for Locke and Berkeley, partly because to have an idea is to have a distinct, particular item before the mind, and the question is how that one item can represent all the many things it is said to be an idea of. There are a great many men, and they are of different sizes, shapes, colours, and so on. It would seem that we could represent, or think about, all such creatures at once by means of our idea of man only if either that idea represents all the sizes and all the qualities it is possible for men to have, or it represents no particular size or quality at all. According to Hume, most philosophers have thought that the first alternative implies that the mind has an infinite capacity, since there are an infinite number of sizes and other qualities men could have, and since that is absurd they have concluded that all our general ideas represent no particular degree either of quantity or of quality. But then how could there be an idea of man that is not an idea of a man of any particular size or any particular qualities at all? Hume, acknowledging his debt to Berkeley,[11] thinks there could not be.

He argues that, although the mind does not have infinite capacity, and although it 'cannot form any notion of quantity or quality without forming a precise notion of degrees of each', still we can represent all possible degrees of quantity and quality 'in such a manner at least, as, however imperfect, may serve all the purposes of reflexion and conversation' (p. 18). We can think and speak intelligibly of men, dogs, triangles, and so on, and thereby represent to ourselves and to others all possible varieties of things of those kinds, and although thinking and speaking intelligibly of such things involves having an idea before the mind, there is no need to suppose that our idea is anything but a particular image with determinate degrees of quantity and quality.

We come to be able to think and speak in general terms in the following way. When we find a resemblance among a number of objects we have encountered, we come to apply the same name to them. Thus, a kind of connection is established in the mind between that name and things of that sort. When we hear the name, a particular idea of one of those things immediately comes into the mind. For example, when, after having applied the word 'man' to particular resembling items I have encountered—Tom, Dick, Harry and others—I hear the word again, then the idea of, say, Harry comes into my mind. Of course, Harry differs in many ways from Tom, Dick and the others, and my idea of Harry is therefore an idea of a man with just the characteristics which he, but not the others, has. My idea is an idea of a short, bald, white man, and Tom is tall, hirsute and black. But hearing the word on this occasion did not produce the idea of Tom in my mind; it produced only the idea of Harry. Still, the idea I do have in my mind can be said to represent all men—or at any rate, all men I have encountered—since a connection has been established between the *word* 'man' and all those men. My custom is to apply that word to all of them. The ideas of Tom, Dick and the other individuals are not actually present in my mind, but they are potentially there, so to speak.

38

[We] keep ourselves in a readiness to survey any of them, as we may be prompted by a present design or necessity. The word raises up an individual idea, along with a certain custom; and that custom produces any other individual one, for which we may have occasion. (pp. 20–1)

To say that the idea of Tom, the idea of Dick and the ideas of each of the others, are only 'potentially' in the mind, is to say that some of them would in fact automatically appear there under certain conditions. The custom of applying the same name to each of those men puts us in a state of readiness to receive any of the particular ideas that would constitute counter-examples to claims we make about all things to which the term applies.

Thus shou'd we mention the word, triangle, and form the idea of a particular equilateral one to correspond to it, and shou'd we afterwards assert, *that the three angles of a triangle are equal to each other*, the other individuals of a scalenum and isosceles, which we overlook'd at first, immediately crowd in upon us, and make us perceive the falshood of this proposition, tho' it be true with relation to that idea, which we had form'd. (p. 21)

This fortunate state of affairs would seem to make error virtually impossible, since a recalcitrant idea associated with the general word readily springs to mind 'if by chance we form any reasoning, that agrees not with it' (p. 21). In fact, Hume gives no satisfactory explanation of how we could ever be wrong in our generalizations, although he agrees we sometimes are.

In any case, he clearly believes that our thinking in general terms results just as much from the customary application of a word to a number of resembling things as from the presence before the mind of a certain particular item. In fact, the custom is more important, since the very same mental item may be involved in our thinking of figures, rectilineal figures, regular figures, triangles and equilateral triangles. Different 'customs' are involved in each case—those words are customarily applied to things of different classes—even though an image of an equilateral triangle of an inch perpendicular would serve as the idea present to the mind in each case. But even if we had ideas of several different figures, rather than just one, the essentials of Hume's explanation would remain unchanged.

'tis certain *that* we form the idea of individuals, whenever we use any general term; *that* we seldom or never can exhaust these individuals; and *that* those, which remain, are only represented by means of that habit, by which we recall them,

whenever any present occasion requires it. . . . A particular idea
becomes general by being annex'd to a general term; that is,
to a term, which from a customary conjunction has a relation
to many other particular ideas, and readily recalls them in
the imagination. (p. 22)

It is simply a fundamental fact about the human mind that the
customary association between a word and a number of resembling
things has this effect—it cannot be explained further.

This explanation of general thoughts is much more complicated
than the simple associationist model of the theory of ideas would lead
us to expect. When I hear the word 'man' why does the idea of Harry
come into my mind? Why does that particular item appear, rather than
one of the others? The immediate stimulus was hearing the word
'man', and I follow the custom of applying that word to each of a
number of things. Since it can hardly be said that the word, or the
sound or look of it, resembles any of those things, or is causally related
to them, it cannot be by means of those principles of association that
the idea of Harry appears in my mind. Perhaps some vague notion of
'contiguity' can be evoked here—the word 'man' is somehow (but not
literally) 'attached' to Harry, and to others like him. But the theory is
obviously being considerably stretched. There is a sense in which the
word 'man' is 'associated with' Tom, Dick, Harry and others, but that
is not enough to support Hume, since he thinks that all 'associations'
are instances of either resemblance, contiguity or cause and effect.
Without some specific modes of association in mind, his appeal to
association to explain why certain ideas follow others into the mind
would have no interest.

The official theory is strained even more when it comes to explain
how the 'custom' works on me to prevent false generalizations. I hear
the word 'man' and the idea of Harry comes into my mind. If, on the
basis of that idea, I then come to believe or assert that men are
fair-skinned, the idea of Tom 'immediately crowds in upon' me, and
makes me see the falsity of what I have just said. The idea of Tom does
not appear in the mind solely as a result of the appearance there of the
idea of Harry, but only as a result of a certain 'custom', and of my
having asserted a false generalization. But the only relevant item
before the mind when I assert that generalization is my idea of
Harry—so to speak, standing in as my exemplar for men. And
although Tom resembles Harry in certain respects, it is not solely in
virtue of that resemblance that the idea of him appears in the mind.
Something else makes it come there and not simply the truth of the
principle of association alone. Something like a desire to believe and
speak the truth, and an ability to remember or produce

counter-examples to our claims, would seem to be needed in addition to those principles in order to explain why that idea arises when it does. The behaviour of mental 'atoms' must be governed by much more than an associationist principle of 'gravitation', and Hume in effect acknowledges as much in almost every explanation he gives of important psychological phenomena.

III

Causality and the Inference from the Observed to the Unobserved: The Negative Phase

Together let us beat this ample field,
Try what the open, what the covert yield,

Seeing, hearing, smelling—in short, perceiving—something is for Hume 'a mere passive admission of the impression thro' the organs of sensation' (p. 73). But not everything that goes on in the mind, or that is important for human life, is a case of perceiving in this sense. People think about and have beliefs about matters of fact that they are not perceiving at the moment. And it is very important for human life that this is so. If we had no such beliefs, Hume says:

> We should never know how to adjust means to ends, or to employ our natural powers in the production of any effect. There would be an end at once of all action, as well as of the chief part of speculation. (*E*, p. 45)

Acting often involves deliberation, and that in turn requires beliefs about various means to the ends we seek and the probable results of those possible courses of action. Since the actions have yet to occur, their consequences have not occurred either, and so any beliefs we have about them must be beliefs about something 'absent', something that is not present to our minds at the moment. In fact, a little reflection is enough to show that almost all our beliefs are at least partly about what is not currently being observed by us. How do we get them?

> If you were to ask a man, why he believes any matter of fact, which is absent; for instance, that his friend is in the country, or in France; he would give you a reason; and this reason would be some other fact; as a letter received from him, or the knowledge of his former resolutions and promises. . . . All our reasonings concerning fact are of the same nature. And here it is constantly supposed that there is a connexion between the present fact and that which is inferred from it. Were there

42

nothing to bind them together, the inference would be
entirely precarious. (*E*, pp. 26–7)

We think there is some kind of connection between what we observe
and what we believe to be the case about what is not currently
observed, and we follow up that connection and *infer* from one to the
other. So we get beliefs about the unobserved by some kind of
inference. We make a transition from observing something to a belief
in something that is not observed.

Hume believes that all such transitions are causal inferences, or
'reasonings . . . founded on the relation of *Cause and Effect*' (*E*, p.
26). Therefore he thinks that to understand what it is that assures us of
any matter of fact that is not currently observed, we must understand
the relation of causality.

> 'Tis impossible to reason justly, without understanding perfectly
> the idea concerning which we reason; and 'tis impossible
> perfectly to understand any idea, without tracing it up to
> its origin, and examining that primary impression, from
> which it arises. (pp. 74–5)

The previous chapter sketched the justification Hume gives for this
general methodological principle. It will soon be clear, however, that
there are several other important tasks he is engaged in.

To find the origin in experience of the idea of causality Hume first
looks at an example of two things we would regard as being related as
cause and effect and asks what impressions we get when we perceive
them.

> I find in the first place, that whatever objects are consider'd as
> causes or effects, are *contiguous*; and that nothing can
> operate in a time or place, which is ever so little remov'd
> from those of its existence. Tho' distant objects may sometimes
> seem productive of each other, they are commonly found
> upon examination to be link'd by a chain of causes, which are
> contiguous among themselves, and to the distant objects; and when
> in any particular instance we cannot discover this connexion,
> we still presume it to exist. (p. 75)

He concludes that contiguity is 'essential' to causality (p. 75).

It is widely believed that for Hume contiguity is a necessary
condition for two things' being related as cause and effect, but he can
hardly be said to have established that. He actually claims to be looking
for the impressions from which the idea of causality is derived, and he

admits that we do not get an impression of contiguity *every* time we observe a pair of objects which we take to be related as cause and effect. We see the sun and melted butter, and we believe that the one is the cause of the other, but we do not get an impression of the contiguity between them or of a chain of intermediate, contiguous objects. It might well be, as Hume suggests, that in such cases 'we presume' that there is contiguity nevertheless, but that is irrelevant to the search for the *impressions* we always get in every case of causality. It might be that, once we have the idea of causality, and hence know that contiguity is 'essential' to it, we presume that there is a chain of intermediate objects, and that the cause and the effect are therefore contiguous, but we certainly do not get an impression of contiguity in every case of what we take to be a causal connection. How then do we know, if at all, that contiguity is 'essential' to causality?

Do we even presume contiguity to hold in every case? Where one thought or idea causes another do we believe that there is literally some contact between cause and effect? Hume is especially interested in this form of what might be called mental causality, but the requirement that cause and effect be contiguous makes it difficult to see what he thinks contiguity is. In any case, nothing he says even begins to show that 'X caused Y' implies 'X and Y are contiguous'. In the *Enquiry* he never mentions contiguity as part of the notion of causality.[1]

Another relation said to be 'essential' to causality is the priority in time of the cause to the effect. Hume does not even suggest that we always get an impression of this priority, although he claims to be searching for what is 'essential' to causality by trying to discover the impressions from which the idea is derived. Here too it would seem that we do not always, or perhaps ever, get an impression of the priority in time. We do not actually see the contact of two billiard balls to be slightly earlier than the beginning of the motion of the second ball. Hume thinks there must be such priority, and he thinks he has a general argument to prove it.[2] But even if the argument is successful, and priority is shown to be 'absolutely necessary' for causality, that will not necessarily help Hume in his search for the impressions from which the idea of causality is derived. To show that something Y is an essential ingredient of the idea of X is not to show that every time we observe an X we have an impression of Y. The crudest interpretation of Hume's 'first principle of the science of human nature' might suggest that it is, but Hume himself seems to recognize the difference.

The important point Hume goes on to make is that, even if in every case of causality we did get impressions of contiguity and priority, that would not be enough to explain the origin of the idea of causality. Two objects might be related by contiguity and priority in time 'merely coincidentally'. If, at the very moment that I look at the traffic light it turns green, I do not regard my looking as the cause of the light's turning. So there must be some other ingredient in the idea of causality, or in the origin of it, that has yet to be accounted for.

What is the difference between what we call a 'coincidence' and a genuine case of causality? Obviously, in the case of causality one thing *produces* another, but to say that is to say no more than that they are causally connected. We believe that when two events are related causally the second one happens *because* of the first, but that is really no better. We might believe that the second thing *would not* have happened unless the first one had; or that, given the first, the second *had to* happen. These are not equivalent, and they do not really explain anything, but they represent different rough and ready ways of expressing what we believe when we think that two contiguous events, one of which is temporally prior to the other, are related causally and not just coincidentally. Hume says that we think there is a 'necessary connection' between cause and effect.

When we consider any particular instance of causality which we observe, we can find no impression which is an impression of the necessary connection between cause and effect. We might observe that A happened before B and was contiguous with it, but we cannot have an impression of B's happening *because* A happened, or an impression of the fact that B *would not have happened* unless A had. Of course, we often say things like 'I saw the white ball knock the red ball into the pocket', or 'I saw the stone break the window', and 'knock . . . into' and 'break . . .' are causal verbs. But for Hume such sentences are not the reports of single impressions. They could not be reports of the only impression a person ever had. Some reasons for this will become clearer later.

If we never get an impression of the necessary connection between cause and effect in any particular instance of causality, it would seem that Hume's main methodological principle must be abandoned. The idea of causality appears to be a counter-example to the principle that all ideas arise in the mind as the result of their corresponding earlier impressions. Hume is aware of the threat this poses, and admits, albeit somewhat disingenuously, that the principle will have to be given up if the impressions from which the idea of causality is derived cannot be found (p. 77). This gives some further evidence that he regards the principle as contingent.

Hume makes some of his greatest contributions to philosophy when he gives up the direct search in perceptual experience for the impression of necessary connection and tries to save his fundamental principle by a more roundabout technique. He focuses on the inference or transition we make from cause to effect, or from the observed to the unobserved, and asks what determines us to make it at all, and in the particular ways that we do. He is to be understood as asking straightforward empirical questions whose answers will contribute to the science of man. The main part of his discussion of causality is clearly 'an attempt to introduce the experimental method of reasoning into moral subjects'.

Seen simply in terms of the theory of ideas, the investigation of what we *do* and what leads us to do it—i.e. why we make the inference from the observed 'to the unobserved that we do—might look like a considerable detour. The questions Hume spends most time answering are not really about the impressions from which the idea of causality is derived at all, but rather about how and why we get beliefs about what is not currently being observed. He is concerned with certain natural human ways of thinking, certain more or less mental phenomena that occur in certain circumstances.

On particular occasions, when presented with a certain object or event, all of us uniformly expect some other particular object to exist, or some other event to happen. Or, more generally, we get a belief about something that is not currently being observed by us. It is this bit of human life he wants to understand. We have already seen how important it is that it goes on.

It might seem plausible to say that no one could even understand what it is for something to happen, or for something to begin to exist, without also believing that it had a cause. On this view, knowing or believing that something began to exist would necessarily involve believing that something else existed and was its cause. That would be to accept the traditional causal maxim that whatever begins to exist must have a cause of its existence. Now Hume believes that all inferences from the observed to the unobserved are 'founded on the relation of cause and effect', and there is a sense in which he agrees that every event must have a cause, but he thinks that the traditional way of understanding the causal maxim is completely wrong.

It had been thought that it was 'intuitively' or 'demonstratively' certain that every event has a cause—merely understanding that principle was enough to guarantee its acceptance. Hume argues that that is not so, and that the maxim is incapable of conclusive deductive proof. Whatever certainty we have that every event has a cause, it is not derived solely from our understanding the idea of an event, or of something's beginning to exist. But intuitive or demonstrative certainty can come only from 'the comparison of ideas', so the maxim is not intuitively or demonstratively certain.

Hume allows that it is demonstratively certain that every *effect* has a cause, 'effect being a relative term, of which cause is the correlative' (p. 82). So a thing could not possibly be an effect unless it had a cause. But that does not establish the causal maxim that every *event*, or everything that begins to exist, must have a cause. Although every husband must have a wife, it does not follow that every man must be married. The causal maxim needs more proof than that.

Hume argues quite generally that the maxim could never be demonstrated to be true by any argument. If it were 'demonstratively true' that everything that begins to exist must have a cause of its existence, then it would be absolutely impossible for something to begin to exist without a cause. But he says it is not absolutely impossible for something to begin to exist without a cause, for the following complicated reason. All distinct ideas are separable from each other. The idea of A's beginning to exist is 'evidently distinct' from the idea of a cause of A's beginning to exist. Therefore we can separate the one idea from the other in the mind; we can conceive of an object's coming into existence without having to conjoin to it the idea of a cause of its coming into existence. Whatever we can conceive is possible in the sense of not implying any contradiction. But nothing that is possible in that sense can be refuted 'by any reasoning from mere ideas' (p. 80). And since it is impossible to demonstrate the necessity of anything except by reasoning from mere ideas, the necessity of a cause for everything that begins to exist can never be demonstrated. So the traditional causal maxim is not demonstratively certain.

This is a very important argument for Hume, but it is difficult to know what to make of it. To begin with, he thinks the idea of A's beginning to exist is 'evidently distinct' from the idea of a cause of A's beginning to exist. But what is it for two ideas to be 'distinct'? How can we tell whether the idea of X is distinct from the idea of Y or not? One suggestion is that we have two distinct ideas only when they can be separated without contradiction. It is contradictory to say of something that it is a husband and does not have a wife, but apparently not contradictory to say of something that it began to exist but had no cause.

There are at least two difficulties in this. First, if this is what Hume had in mind, then he can scarcely be said to have *argued* to the conclusion that it is not impossible (in the sense that it implies no contradiction) for something to begin to exist without a cause. It first looked as if he were arguing to that end from the distinctness of two ideas, but if separability without contradiction is the test for distinctness then he is simply *stating* that the negation of the causal maxim is not contradictory. There is no independent argument.

Second, even if Hume were relying directly on the absence of contradiction as the test of possibility, there would still be the question how that test is known to be fulfilled. What is a contradiction? If it is simply a proposition which could not possibly be true, Hume's 'argument' again would shrink to a mere assertion of the possibility of something's beginning to exist without a cause. But what grounds are there for that assertion? To say that 'A began to exist without a cause' is not contradictory on the grounds that it is possible for something to exist without a cause is to put the putative argument backwards. Hume is trying to establish that it is possible.

It will not help to say simply that a contradiction is a proposition which is 'logically' incapable of being true—that it violates or is the negation of a principle of logic. Even if the principles of logic could be independently identified, this would not be enough. It is supposed to be demonstratively certain that every husband has a wife, and therefore contradictory to say of someone that he is a husband but lacks a wife, but what is the principle of logic of which that is the negation? The statement appears to be of the form '$(\exists x)\ (Fx. \sim Gx)$', and that is a satisfiable schema, and so does not contradict any theorem of logic.

Of course, it is natural to reply that 'There is a husband who lacks a wife' is really not of that form. Involved in the very idea of being a husband, it will be argued, is the idea of having a wife. Having a wife is just what it is to be a husband—they are one and the same idea, or the former is included in the latter. Therefore, 'There is a husband who lacks a wife' is really of the form '$(\exists x)\ (Gx.Hx. \sim Gx)$', and that is not a satisfiable schema. So 'There is a husband who lacks a wife' is the negation of a truth of logic after all, and is thus contradictory.

Obviously this line of argument, however plausible, makes essential use of the notion of the 'same' or 'distinct' ideas. It says in effect that a statement is contradictory if it is the negation of a principle of logic either directly or when any terms in the statement are replaced by other terms which stand for the same idea. But then the notion of sameness or distinctness of ideas is being used in the test for contradictoriness, whereas contradictoriness was originally invoked to explain the sameness or distinctness of ideas. Hume really has no non-circular argument on this point at all. He thinks he can start from the 'evident' distinctness of two ideas, but he never says how he can recognize that distinctness.[3]

It might be thought that he can recognize it by a kind of thought-experiment. Take the ideas in question and see whether you can in fact hold one in your mind without the other, or whether you can apply one of the ideas to a certain thing while not applying the other to it. Presumably one cannot do this with the idea of being a husband and the idea of having a wife. Since the thought-experiment fails, the ideas are not distinct. If Hume were to take this line as a way of proving that something can begin to exist without a cause it would not be all smooth sailing.

First, the test is not really a test of the identity or non-distinctness of ideas. According to Hume 'the mind cannot form any notion of quantity or quality without forming a precise notion of degrees of each' (p. 18), so it is impossible for us to form an idea of a straight line without forming an idea of a line of a certain specific length. But if on a particular occasion we form an idea of a straight line one inch in length, that does not show that the idea of being a straight line and the idea of being one inch in length are the same idea, or that the second is included in, or is part of, the first. There is a sense in which it is not true that 'all ideas, which are different, are separable' (p. 24), although this does not prevent us from making what was traditionally called a 'distinction of reason' between them.

When considering a globe of white marble, for example, we do not have separable ideas of the colour and the shape. But if we think of the globe of white marble first in relation to a globe of black marble and then in relation to a cube of white marble, 'we find two separate resemblances, in what formerly seem'd, and really is, perfectly inseparable' (p. 25). So we distinguish between the colour and the shape of the white globe, not directly, by actually separating them, but only by viewing it 'in different aspects'.

> When we wou'd consider only the figure of the globe of white marble, we form in reality an idea both of the figure and colour, but tacitly carry our eye to its resemblance with the globe of black marble: And in the same manner, when we wou'd consider its colour only, we turn our view to its resemblance with the cube of white marble. By this means we accompany our ideas with a kind of reflexion, of which custom renders us, in a great measure, insensible. A person, who desires us to consider the figure of a globe of white marble without thinking on its colour, desires an impossibility; but his meaning is, that we shou'd consider the colour and figure together, but still keep in our eye the resemblance to the globe of black marble, or that to any other globe of whatever colour or substance. (p. 25)

So the test is not a matter of straightforward introspection. How it turns out will depend on what particular 'reflexion' we engage in—what features we take as relevant, and what 'resemblances' we keep in mind.

But since in the present argument Hume is interested in the distinctness, rather than the identity, of two ideas, it might be thought that this does not really matter. If we *can* conceive of a thing's beginning to exist without conceiving of it as having a cause, doesn't that prove everything Hume needs?

The answer to that question, I think, is 'No'. If the test of whether or not a certain thing is conceivable involves only a conscientious attempt to perform a certain mental act and a sincere judgment of the degree of one's success, then the conceivability of something's beginning to exist without a cause does not establish the possibility of something's beginning to exist without a cause. It does not show that there is no contradiction involved in that alleged possibility. And that is what Hume has to show.

The point has been made by William Kneale (Kneale (1), pp. 79–80). Goldbach's Conjecture to the effect that every even number is the sum of two primes has never been proved or disproved. A great many even numbers have been tested and each has been found to be the sum of two primes, but no general proof one way or the other has ever been found. It seems easy to conceive of Goldbach's Conjecture's being proved one day, although that is not to say that it is easy to believe that it will be proved. But I can also conceive of its being disproved, of someone's proving its negation, perhaps by finding a very large even number that is not the sum of two primes. I can conceive of a computer's coming up with one tomorrow.

If I conscientiously try, then, I sincerely find that I can conceive of Goldbach's Conjecture's being proved, and of its being disproved. But it is either true or false, and if true, necessarily true, and if false, necessarily false. If it is true, then in conceiving of its being disproved I have conceived of something that is necessarily false, and therefore impossible; and if it is false, then in conceiving of its being proved I have conceived of something that is necessarily false, and therefore impossible. In one case or the other I must have conceived of something that is actually impossible. So conceivability is not an adequate test of possibility. Of course, if 'conceivable' is taken to mean simply 'non-contradictory', then it could be said to imply possibility, and so not everything I have said I can conceive of would really be conceivable after all. But that would lead back to the first criticism of Hume's argument—that no non-circular test for contradictoriness, conceivability or possibility has been given. We would be back on the treadmill.

Despite its importance, Hume's treatment of this whole subject is perfunctory at best. He nowhere gives even the beginnings of a satisfactory account of 'reasoning from mere ideas'. That is probably because his real interests lie elsewhere.

He argues against the intuitive or demonstrative certainty of the causal maxim in order to show that the 'opinion' that every event[4] must have a cause can arise only from experience. As a student of the human mind, he wants to know *how* that 'opinion' arises. What is it about human nature and human experience that leads people to believe that every event must have a cause? In rejecting the intuitive or demonstrative certainty of the causal maxim he thinks he has exposed one wrong answer to that question, but he is mainly interested in offering his own positive account. He does not just seek the origin of the 'opinion' that every event must have some cause or other; he asks what leads us to believe that this particular event was caused by that particular event and will itself have such-and-such particular effects. He wants to know why and how we make the particular inferences that we do from one event or state of affairs to another. That is the question about causality that Hume spends most of his time trying to answer.[5]

We can look out the window and see rain, and, although we cannot see the street, still infer, and hence come to believe, that the street is wet. Why, having the first belief, do we get the particular belief about the street that we do? Why don't we come to believe that it is paved with gold? Hume tries to answer this question by asking under what conditions we actually make such inferences.

First, all inferences must start from something, and the inferences we are interested in all start from something present to the mind and proceed to a belief in something that is not present to the mind at the time. Hume says that all such inferences start from an *impression*, either from the senses or from the memory. Without an impression as starting-point or foundation, reasoning from causes to effects would be merely hypothetical; we could reason that if A exists then B exists and if B exists then C exists, and so on, but at no point could we detach an unconditional belief unless there were some impression present to the mind to serve as the foundation of that inference. But although an impression is required in order for us to infer from the observed to the unobserved, it is by no means enough. Merely having an impression of A is never enough in itself to give rise to any belief about something not then present to the mind.

It might be thought that having an impression of A would be enough to give rise to such a belief if we could prove, by demonstrative reasoning alone, that if A exists, then something else B also exists. If B is something not then present to the mind, we would then have made an inference from what is present to the mind to what is not, and on the basis of the impression alone. Again, as he did in the case of the traditional causal maxim, Hume argues that this is impossible. Just as he earlier tried to show that from the fact that an object exists we cannot deduce that it has some cause or other, he now claims on the same grounds that we cannot deduce from the fact that a certain object exists that it has this or that particular cause or effect (pp. 86–7). If the earlier argument were successful, this conclusion would follow directly.

The present argument, like the earlier one, obviously turns on the uncritical use of such notions as 'distinct ideas', 'separability', 'conceivability', 'contradiction', and so on, and even less effort is made here to explain or justify them. But the point of the argument is clear enough. He thinks that if our mere understanding of something A, which is now present to the mind, is not enough in itself to lead us to believe anything about the unobserved—if the inference from the observed to the unobserved is never a demonstrative one—then we can be led to make it only by experience. And he is mainly interested in what our experience must be like, what it must contain in addition to the impression of A, to lead us to have a particular belief about some particular thing that is not present to our minds at that moment.

In what situations do we actually make inferences from the observed to the unobserved? Under what circumstances do we come to believe that two things are related causally, or to believe that something B will occur because something A is observed to be occurring now? 'After the discovery of the constant conjunction of any objects', Hume says, 'we always draw an inference from one object to another' (p. 88). Whenever men observe a particular object or event which belongs to a class of things that have been constantly conjoined in their experience with things of another class, then they come to believe that an object or event of the second class exists or will occur. We observe constant conjunctions between things of two kinds, and then upon observing something of the first kind we come to believe that a thing of the second kind exists. This, Hume believes, is a true universal generalization about human behaviour.

How can the truth of this generalization be explained? Hume claims to have discovered the circumstances under which inferences from the observed to unobserved take place, but he wants to understand the mechanism, as it were, by means of which those inferences occur in those circumstances. *How* does an experienced constant conjunction work on us to give us a belief about the unobserved? What is it about experiencing a constant conjunction of As and Bs that 'determines' us, when we observe a particular A, to get an idea of a B, and then to believe that a B will follow? Hume asks:

> Whether experience produces the idea by means of the
> understanding or of the imagination; whether we are determin'd
> by reason to make the transition, or by a certain association
> and relation of perceptions. (pp. 88–9)

In giving his answer to this question he rejects 'reason' or 'the understanding' as the source of such inferences on the grounds that none of them are ever reasonable or rationally justifiable. This is his most famous sceptical result. And there is no doubt that it was meant to be sceptical. But his contribution to philosophy does not stop with that negative result; it was put forward for a definite, positive purpose, and understanding that purpose is the best way to see the kind of theory of human nature he is advancing.

According to the traditional theory of belief, men come to believe something, in so far as they are rational, by weighing the considerations on both sides and deciding to believe that for which they have the best evidence or the most adequate justification. By showing that no inference from a past constant conjunction of As and Bs and a currently observed A to a belief that a B will occur is ever reasonable or justified, Hume rejects this account. Past and present experiences of that sort give us no reason at all to believe anything about the unobserved. But he thinks there is no doubt that we do get beliefs about the unobserved in just such circumstances. Therefore, either the traditional theory of belief is wrong about how we in fact get the beliefs we do, or else we are not rational beings with respect to any of those beliefs that are most important and most fundamental for human life.

If, as Hume believes, we are not 'determin'd by reason' to infer from the observed to the unobserved, then some other explanation of how and why we do it must be found. He looks for that explanation in what he calls 'the imagination'. He tries to find those principles 'of association and relation of perceptions', those natural and primitive dispositions of the mind, that are responsible for our making the inferences we do. The search for such principles is just the experimental, naturalistic study of human nature that Hume advocates, and the need for such a study is exposed more clearly after the traditional theory of reason and belief has been exploded. That destructive or negative task is the point of Hume's sceptical argument.

He condemns as unjustifiable a whole mode of inference or pattern of reasoning. He says that past experience of a constant conjunction between As and Bs, and a present impression of an A, gives us 'no reason at all' to believe that a B will occur.[6] So the mode of inference he is interested in might be represented in completely general terms as follows:

(PE) All observed As have been followed by Bs.

(PI) An A is observed now.

Therefore, (FE) A B will occur.[7]

According to Hume, whenever statements of the form of PE and PI are true about a particular person's experience, then that person will always in fact infer, and hence come to believe, a statement of the form of FE. But, he argues, the person is not 'determin'd by reason' to do so. Of course, there will be a reason *why* the man believes what he does. That is just what Hume, as a student of the science of man, is trying to find out; he seeks causal explanations of human behaviour. But in order to show that the operation of the man's 'reason' is not what leads him to that belief Hume claims that the man has no reason *to* believe what he does. His belief has no rational support or justification. He does not, and cannot, have a reasonable belief that a B will occur. To put it most strongly, even if PE and PI are true about someone, it is no more reasonable for that person to believe that a B will occur than for him to believe that a B will not occur. As far as the competition for degrees of reasonableness is concerned, all possible beliefs about the unobserved are tied for last place. But of course the man will in fact believe that a B will occur. That is not in question.

The first and most important step of the argument to this startling conclusion is:

> If reason determin'd us, it wou'd proceed upon that principle, *that instances, of which we have had no experience, must resemble those, of which we have had experience, and that the course of nature continues always uniformly the same.*
> (p. 89)

I call the italicized proposition the uniformity principle. Hume here claims that all inferences from the observed to the unobserved 'proceed upon the supposition' that it is true. The rest of his argument is designed to establish that no one could ever reasonably believe the uniformity principle, and therefore that no one could ever reasonably believe anything about the unobserved on the basis of what has been observed.

One way to support one's belief in a particular proposition is to discover a demonstrative or deductive proof of it. According to Hume, that would be to show that the proposition in question could not possibly be false. But no demonstrative arguments of this sort could be used to establish the uniformity principle, since:

> We can at least conceive a change in the course of nature;
> which sufficiently proves, that such a change is not absolutely
> impossible. To form a clear idea of any thing, is an
> undeniable argument for its possibility, and is alone a
> refutation of any pretended demonstration against it.
> (p. 89)

But either one supports one's belief by demonstrative reasoning, which proceeds from ideas alone, or one must rely on the findings of sense-experience. For Hume those are the only two ways in which beliefs can be supported or justified.

The uniformity principle cannot be established by observation alone, since it makes a claim about some things that are not, and have not been, observed. It says that *un*observed instances resemble observed ones in certain respects. Therefore, any experiential justification for the uniformity principle must consist of a justified inference from what *has* been observed to the truth of the principle. But according to the first step of the argument *every* inference from the observed to the unobserved is 'founded on the supposition' that the uniformity principle is true, so by instantiation it follows that any inference from the observed to the truth of the uniformity principle is itself 'founded on the supposition' that that principle is true. Therefore, no experiential justification can be given for the uniformity principle without already assuming that it is true, and that would be 'evidently going in a circle, and taking that for granted, which is the very point in question' (*E*, p. 36). So no one could ever be justified in any way in believing the uniformity principle. And since all inferences from the observed to the unobserved are 'founded' on that principle, no one could ever reasonably believe anything about the unobserved. We are not 'determin'd by reason' to believe what we do about the unobserved.

There are many different points at which this sceptical argument might be attacked, but I want to concentrate on one line of criticism which seems to be fundamental. Not surprisingly, it focuses on the first step of the argument. What does Hume mean by saying that every inference from the observed to the unobserved 'proceeds upon' or is 'founded on the supposition' that the uniformity principle is true? Only when we understand what that means can we see the real source of his scepticism.

One thing that makes the claim obscure is the uniformity principle itself. Can a principle even be formulated which can serve as the 'foundation' of all such inferences without being so obviously false that no sane man would even be inclined to accept it?[8] I do not want to minimize the importance of this problem, but I prefer to concentrate on the *role* that the uniformity principle is said to play in all inferences from the observed to the unobserved. We need some understanding of what that role is supposed to be if we are to formulate something that might fulfil it. The question is what Hume means by saying that all inferences from the observed to the unobserved are 'founded on the supposition' that that principle is true.

One thing he means is fairly clear. Having said that all inferences from the observed to the unobserved depend upon the uniformity principle, he immediately begins to look for 'all the arguments upon which such a proposition may be suppos'd to be founded' (p. 89). So he means at least that one whose experience is correctly described by statements of the form of PE and PI will not have reason to believe a statement of the form of FE unless he has reason to believe the uniformity principle. That is why he then goes on to ask what reasons there are to believe the uniformity principle. To say that an inference is 'founded' on a particular supposition is to say at least that no one will be justified in inferring the conclusion from the premisses unless he is also justified in believing the supposition on which the inference is 'founded'.[9]

If that is part of what Hume means, why does he think that inferences from the observed to the unobserved are 'founded' on the uniformity principle in that sense? One plausible suggestion leaps to mind. It is an obvious feature of all such inferences that they are logically invalid as they stand.[10] It is quite possible for a statement of the form of FE to be false even though statements of the form of PE and PI are true. Hume himself in effect points this out when he shows that a change in the course of nature is always at least possible, in the sense of not implying a contradiction. Many have supposed that that is Hume's *only* support for saying that no one is justified in believing the conclusion of an inference from the observed to the unobserved unless he is justified in believing the uniformity principle.

If that is Hume's only support, he must think that the conjunction of the uniformity principle with PE and PI logically implies FE. If something else is needed only because the original argument is not deductively valid, then what is needed must be such that, when it is found, the augmented argument *is* deductively valid. But then if he thinks that someone of whom only PE and PI are true does not have reason to believe FE, and that he would have reason to believe FE if he had reason to believe the uniformity principle as well, Hume must be assuming that no one has reason to believe anything unless he has reason to believe something that logically implies it. He must believe that all reasoning is deductive, or that an inference is a 'good' or 'reasonable' one only if it is deductively valid. It is widely believed that Hume's negative argument relies on precisely that view of reasons.[11]

On this interpretation Hume's conclusion, in the sense in which he is said to mean it, would be perfectly correct. He demonstrates that no set of statements about what has been observed ever logically implies anything about what has not been observed, and on the assumption that no one is justified in believing a proposition unless he is justified in believing something that logically implies it it follows immediately that no one is ever justified in believing anything about the unobserved on the basis of what has been observed. But most defenders of this interpretation go on to point out that this conclusion, although correct, does not really have any general sceptical force. The most that Hume can be said to have established, on this interpretation, is a conditional statement to the effect that *if* no one is ever justified in believing a proposition unless he is justified in believing something that logically implies it, *then* no one is ever justified in believing anything about the unobserved. That conditional statement is true: it is equivalent to the admitted truth that no set of statements about what has been observed logically implies anything about what has not been observed. But, the criticism continues, Hume is wrong simply to assume that the antecedent of that conditional is true—in fact it is not true—and so Hume's general sceptical conclusion has not been established.[12]

Hume's assumption is said to be false because an argument or inference does not need to be deductively valid in order to be a 'good' one, or to justify belief in its conclusion on the basis of its premises. Not all justification or reasons need be deductively sufficient. A man is reasonable or justified in believing something about the unobserved as long as his past and present experience entitles him to believe it, or makes it reasonable for him to believe it, or makes it more reasonable for him to believe it than to believe its negation. And he could be reasonable in believing it even though it turned out to be false.

According to the present interpretation, Hume simply does not take account of that possibility. From the admitted truth that no one ever has deductively sufficient reasons for believing anything about the unobserved he is said to conclude immediately that no one has *any reason at all* for such beliefs. And that is simply to assume without argument that all reasons for believing must be deductively sufficient. It is arbitrarily and quite unreasonably to lay down ridiculous and impossibly strict conditions for justified belief in matters of contingent fact. So the complaint against Hume is that to require that inferences from the observed to the unobserved be shown to be reasonable in the sense of being deductively valid is simply to require that one thing (non-demonstrative inference) be shown to be something else (demonstrative inference) which it is not. No wonder the demand can never be met. But it is a mistake to think it must be met if our beliefs about the unobserved are to be shown to be reasonable. So Hume's general sceptical conclusion does not follow from what he actually establishes.

This is a very attractive diagnosis of Hume's alleged failure, and it has actually attracted many commentators. It makes what he says clearly and importantly true while saving us from the unpalatable scepticism he thought he had proved. But I find it unsympathetic in ascribing to Hume a quite arbitrary and unjustified assumption with no explanation why he might have found it convincing. For that reason alone it would be desirable at least to supplement it with some plausible motivation for Hume. Also, it makes it difficult to see why and how so many able philosophers since Hume should have thought that his argument, if successful, would have just the sceptical implications he claimed for it.[13] Either they completely missed some rather obvious point in Hume, or else they unknowingly share his assumption about reasons. Since the latter possibility is scarcely credible in the case of recent philosophers who take seriously the problem of 'the justification of induction', it follows that they have simply misread Hume. But how? Is there any other interpretation or defence of Hume's scepticism that makes it more plausible?

Why does Hume believe that we must have some reason to believe the uniformity principle if we are to be justified in making an inference from the observed to the unobserved? At one point in explaining or defending the claim that all inferences from experience 'suppose, as their foundation' the uniformity principle, Hume says:

> If there be any suspicion that the course of nature may
> change, and that the past may be no rule for the future,
> all experience becomes useless, and can give rise to no
> inference or conclusion. (E, pp. 37–8)

This might suggest that without some reason to believe that the course of nature will not change, our past experience does not provide a basis for any inference about the future. And that is just the first step of Hume's argument, according to which no one of whom statements of the form of PE and PI are true is justified in believing FE unless he is justified in believing the uniformity principle. If that step were implied by the passage just quoted, then I think Hume's argument and its sceptical conclusion would be correct, since what that passage says seems to me to be true.

If, on a particular occasion, someone of whom statements of the form of PE and PI are true was also justified in believing that in this case the uniformity principle is false, then I think he would not be justified in believing FE on the basis of the evidence then available to him. A somewhat fanciful example which nevertheless accords with Hume's theory might bring this out. I stand on the street opposite a door marked 'Misogynists Society: Members Only', and see people coming out the door. I find a constant conjunction, holding in 499 cases, between coming out of that door and being male, and when I hear someone else coming down the stairs, according to Hume, I infer that it is a man too. But suppose I then get unimpeachable evidence, say from some members I trust, that there are 500 members altogether, and that one of them is a woman, and that no one but members is allowed in the building. Although it is still true that every person coming out that door in my past experience has been male I no longer have good reason to infer or believe on that basis that the next person to come out of the door will be male. I have extremely good grounds for believing that the uniformity principle, at least with respect to the properties of coming out of that door and being male, is not true.[14]

Consequently I am not justified in believing that the next person will be male even though in my past experience all observed persons have been male, and that is because I am justified in believing that in this particular case the relevant form of the uniformity principle is false.

So what Hume says in the above passage seems to be correct, and its correctness does not depend on the assumption that all reasons or justification must be deductively sufficient. Nothing has been said about *why* I no longer have reason to believe that the next person will be male, but whatever the explanation might be, it surely does not involve the fact that my reasons are not deductively sufficient. I did not have deductively sufficient reasons before I got the additional information either, but there was no suggestion that I had no reason then.[15]

But although the example supports what Hume says and does so without our having to assume that all reasons are deductively sufficient, what he says does not establish the first step of his sceptical argument. All that Hume says in the quoted passage, and all the example shows, is that if anyone of whom statements of the form PE and PI are true is to be justified in believing a statement of the form of FE then it cannot be the case that he is justified in believing that the uniformity principle is false. But that is not strong enough in itself to establish Hume's claim that if anyone of whom statements of the form of PE and PI are true is to be justified in believing something of the form of FE then he must be justified in believing that the uniformity principle is true. This second statement says much more than the first. Not being justified in believing that the uniformity principle is false (as the first requires) is not the same as, nor does it imply, being justified in believing that the uniformity principle is true (as the second requires). One might have no justified beliefs either way about the truth-value of a certain proposition, and hence lack justification for believing it false, without having any justification for believing it true.

It is fully in accord with what might be called 'common sense' to say that we are often justified in believing many things about the unobserved, and that we are so justified on the basis of past and present experience. As long as we have no evidence to the contrary, constant conjunctions of phenomena in our past experience are thought to give us good reason to believe things about the unobserved. But it also seems to agree with 'common sense' to say that if we *do* have evidence to the contrary, then those constant conjunctions do not give us good reason, or at least not to the same degree. So 'common sense' would seem to accept the weaker principle Hume expresses, but not the stronger one he needs for his sceptical argument. One must not be justified in believing that the uniformity principle is false if one is to be justified in believing things about the unobserved, but 'common sense' does not appear to require that we also have some *positive* justification for believing the uniformity principle to be true, if we are ever to be justified in believing anything about the unobserved. Hume's stronger principle does require that, and so, therefore, does his sceptical argument, since the stronger principle is the first step of that argument. If we must have such positive justification, and if, as Hume shows, we can never get it, then it follows that we are never justified in believing anything about the unobserved.

Only the weaker principle has been shown to be true so far. Did Hume mistakenly infer the stronger principle from the weaker one? And if so, did his alleged demand that all reasons or justification be deductively sufficient somehow lead him to make that faulty inference? Is that the only source of the plausibility of Hume's first and crucial step? The standard interpretation I have been considering would suggest that the answer to all these questions is 'Yes'. Of course, it is not a matter of what went through Hume's mind, but of how his argument is to be most plausibly reconstructed and understood.

I have suggested that Hume's negative or sceptical arguments are directed against the claims of a certain traditional conception of reason or rationality. The standard interpretation I have been considering holds that Hume shares that conception at least in assuming that all reasoning must be deductive, or that one has reason to believe something only if one has reason to believe something that logically implies it. Then it is a short step to the conclusion that no beliefs about the unobserved are reasonable, since there are no deductively valid arguments with premises only about what has been observed and conclusions about what has not been observed.

But Hume might well be exploiting another aspect of what I have called the traditional conception of reason, and in a way that leads him to a truly sceptical conclusion without having to assume that all reasons must be deductively sufficient. I do not mean to suggest that he tries explicitly to deny that assumption, but only that perhaps he could be led to his sceptical conclusion without explicitly or implicitly having to make it. I can just sketch a natural and seductive pattern of thinking along such lines.[16]

Suppose someone has observed a constant conjunction between As and Bs and is currently observing an A. Suppose also that he believes that a B will occur. Now Hume is interested in whether that belief is, or can be, a reasonable one. And it is easy to see that, for all that has been said so far, it might not be. The man might believe it for some very bad reason, completely unconnected with his past and present experience of As and Bs. Or he might just find himself believing it for no reason at all. He might have made a lucky guess. So something else must be true of him as well. It would seem that, if he is to be reasonable in believing that a B will occur, he must somehow take his past and present experience with respect to As and Bs as good reason to believe that a B will occur. His 'premisses' must in some sense be taken by him as grounds for believing his conclusion. If that were not so, then in believing that a B will occur the man would be no better off, his believing what he does would be no more worthy of positive rational appraisal, than if he had simply made a lucky guess.

If his past and present experience of As and Bs in fact gives him good reason to believe that a B will occur, but he does not believe[17] that it does, then although in one sense he has good reason to believe what he does, still his believing that a B will occur has not yet been shown to be reasonable or justified. It would be true that, among all the things he believes there is something that is good reason to believe that a B will occur, viz. that observed As have been followed by Bs and an A is observed now, but that alone does not imply that if he believes that a B will occur (as he does) then he does so reasonably. A detective might have rounded up everyone who could possibly have murdered the victim, and so in that sense have the culprit before him, but he will not yet have caught the guilty one. That involves more than having before him someone who in fact is the murderer. Similarly, believing reasonably that a B will occur involves more than believing that a B will occur and also believing something else which is in fact good reason to believe that a B will occur. It would seem that reasonable belief also requires that one see or take that something else *as* good reason to believe what one does.

But then this kind of thinking about the conditions of reasonableness or rationality will tend to continue. It seems clear enough that, even if the man does believe that what he has experienced is good reason to believe that a B will occur, and even though that belief is true, it does not yet follow that the man's belief that a B will occur is reasonable or justified. He might have no good reason for believing that what he has experienced is good reason to believe that a B will occur. He might believe that for some very bad reason, or for no reason at all. Or he might have made a lucky guess. So something else must be true of him as well.

It would seem that, if his believing that a B will occur is to be reasonable or justified, and his believing that what he has experienced is good reason to believe that a B will occur is to be part of his reason for believing it, then his believing that what he has experienced is good reason to believe that a B will occur must itself be reasonable or justified. It cannot be just something he happens to believe, for no reason at all. If it were, then his belief that a B will occur would not be reasonable. He would not be making a reasonable or justified inference from the observed to the unobserved at all.

This 'self-conscious' and therefore potentially regressive aspect of the notion of reason or justification might well be what Hume is focusing on in the traditional conception. A fully rational agent is not one who proceeds rationally only at the last step, so to speak, and who does not bother to arrive at earlier steps by any reasonable or justified process. This conception is certainly one of the sources of the quest for the alleged foundations of knowledge, for an indubitable basis from which all reasoning can start.[18] Once we try to see our beliefs as reasonable in this way, and realize that everything we appeal to must itself be shown to be reasonable, it is difficult to stop short of something we could not fail to be reasonable in believing, if there is such a thing. By concentrating on this aspect of reasonableness Hume could find support for his claim that a reasonable belief in something unobserved requires more than certain kinds of past and present experiences. It requires as well that one reasonably believe that what one has experienced is good reason to believe what one does about the unobserved. And then Hume's question, which he thinks leads to scepticism, is how one can ever get a reasonable belief to that effect.

If that question does in fact lead to scepticism, it is not because Hume implicitly assumes that all reasons must be deductively sufficient. The reflections about reasonable belief that I have just sketched do not depend on that assumption at all. They purport to show that an experienced constant conjunction between As and Bs and a currently observed A are not enough in themselves to make someone's belief that a B will occur a reasonable or justified one. One must also believe that an observed conjunction of As and Bs, along with an observed A, is good reason to believe that a B will occur. But clearly this more complicated belief, when added to what was originally believed, still does not provide the person with a deductively sufficient set of premisses for the conclusion that a B will occur.

If to the two premisses:

(PE) All observed As have been followed by Bs.

(PI) An A is observed now.

we add the further statement:

(R) PE and PI are reason to believe that a B will occur.

we still do not have a deductively valid argument to the conclusion that a B will occur.[19] If PE, PI, and R are all true, it is still possible for a B not to occur. There can be, and one can have, very good reason to believe what is in fact false.

So if the reflections I sketched were to show that a justified belief in something like R is needed in addition to PE and PI in order for one's belief that a B will occur to be reasonable, it is not because R is needed in order to provide a deductively valid argument to the conclusion that a B will occur. The additional requirement does not find its source in an arbitrary assumption about the deductive nature of all reasoning.

One serious difficulty in the line of interpretation I am suggesting is that, although it gives some plausible support for something like the first step of Hume's argument, it does not support that step in precisely the form in which I originally represented it. I have suggested that what is needed for a reasonable belief that a B will occur, in addition to an observed constant conjunction between As and Bs and a currently observed A, is a reasonable belief that what is and has been observed is good reason to believe that a B will occur. And that is not equivalent to the claim that a reasonable belief in the *uniformity principle* is what is required, since the uniformity principle says that 'those instances of which we have had no experience, must resemble those, of which we have had experience', or that 'the course of nature continues always uniformly the same' (p. 89). That principle appears to say or imply nothing about one thing's being good reason to believe another.

That is true, and might well be sufficient to discredit the interpretation I am suggesting. But it is perhaps significant that Hume sometimes expresses the additional requirement for a reasonable inference from the observed to the unobserved by saying that it requires the principle that 'instances of which we have had no experience, *must* resemble those, of which we have had experience', or that the past is a '*rule* for the future' (*E*, p. 38, my italics). And that comes close to the claim that one must reasonably believe that what is and has been observed can be relied on as a guide to the future, or that it gives one good reason to believe certain things about the unobserved, and not just that the observed *is* actually like the unobserved. To say that the murderer *must* have only four toes on the left foot is to indicate that what you already know is good or conclusive reason to believe that about the murderer, and not just that he does have only four toes on the left foot.

In any case, it is plausible to argue that no one who has observed a constant conjunction between As and Bs and is currently observing an A will reasonably believe on that basis that a B will occur unless he also reasonably believes[20] that what he has experienced is good reason to believe that a B will occur. But, Hume asks, how could one ever come reasonably to believe that? How is one to get a reasonable belief that a past constant conjunction between As and Bs, along with a currently observed A, *is* good reason to believe that a B will occur?

It might be thought that this question presents no difficulty at all, and that therefore there is no regress or circularity involved in trying to answer it. To believe that a B will occur when you have observed a constant conjuncntion between As and Bs and are currently confronted with an A might be thought to be the very height of reasonableness. What better reason could one possibly have for believing that a B will occur—especially if the constant conjunction between As and Bs has been observed to hold in a large number of instances in a wide variety of circumstances over a long period of time?

If that is the best reason one could possibly have, surely it would be absurd to say that even in that case one has no reason to believe that a B will occur. And this thought can easily lead to the conclusion that anyone who even understands anything at all about reasonable belief, and about what it is to have a reasonable belief in something unobserved, will thereby know that a past constant conjunction between As and Bs and a currently observed A are a good reason to believe that a B will occur.

So it might be thought that even if Hume, on the present interpretation, is right in saying that one must have some reason to believe that one's past and present experience's having been a certain way is reason to believe that a B will occur if one is to have a reasonable belief to that effect, there is still no threat of scepticism. One *can* know such a thing. In fact, this suggestion goes, everyone who understands the meaning of 'reason to believe' does know that already. To have observed a constant conjunction between a great many As and Bs under a wide variety of circumstances over a long period of time, and to be currently observing an A, is *just what it means* to have reason to believe that a B will occur. So what Hume claims is a necessary condition of having a reasonable belief that a B will occur is sometimes easily fulfilled.[21]

This is really an appeal to a bit of *a priori* knowledge about one sort of thing being a reason, or good reason, to believe another. The idea is that, solely by understanding the concept of being a reason for, or being reasonable, or solely by knowing the meanings of certain words, one knows that having observed a constant conjunction between As and Bs and being currently confronted with an A is good reason to believe that a B will occur. It is 'analytic' that one has good reasons in that case. Strawson puts the point as follows:

> It is an analytic proposition that it is reasonable to have
> a degree of belief in a statement which is proportional to
> the strength of the evidence in its favour; and it is an
> analytic proposition, though not a proposition of mathematics,
> that, other things being equal, the evidence for a generalization
> is strong in proportion as the number of favourable
> instances, and the variety of circumstances in which they
> have been found, is great. So to ask whether it is reasonable
> to place reliance on inductive procedures is like asking
> whether it is reasonable to proportion the degree of one's
> convictions to the strength of the evidence. Doing this is

what 'being reasonable' *means* in such a context. (Strawson (1), pp. 256–7)

One could know that one had good reason solely on the basis of knowing what reasons are, or what 'having a reasonable belief' means, only if it were analytically and therefore necessarily true that a past constant conjunction and a present A are reason to believe that a B will occur. That is a condition of the success of this strategy—all analytic propositions are necessary. But in fact that condition is not fulfilled. That proposition is not necessarily true. This is not yet to say, with Hume, that it is not true; that one in fact never *does* have reason to believe that a B will occur. It is to say only that it is not true that, *necessarily*, if one has observed a constant conjunction between As and Bs and is currently observing an A, then one has reason to believe that a B will occur. And if that is not necessarily true, then it is not analytic, and so one cannot know it simply in virtue of understanding certain concepts or knowing the meanings of certain words.

It is quite possible for two sorts of things always to be found together for a long time without the presence of a thing of one of the kinds affording us any reason in itself to believe that a thing of the second kind will occur.[22] I have never drawn a breath in the state of Mississippi; there has been a constant conjunction between being a breathing by me and being outside Mississippi. But that alone is no reason to believe on a particular occasion that the breath I am about to draw will not be in Mississippi. Suppose I am standing on the border. Or if I wake up somewhere and find myself breathing, that alone, even with the past constant conjunction, does not give me reason to believe that I am not in Mississippi. And if I definitely am in Mississippi, that alone does not give me reason to believe that I am not breathing.

Similarly, having found nothing but silver coins in the pocket of a certain pair of trousers over a long period of time is no reason to believe that the small but unseen coin I now feel in my pocket is silver. The admitted correlation between being a coin in that pocket and being silver is merely 'accidental'. Now our world is such that many accidental correlations get broken in time—especially when we ourselves interfere and break them. I run, panting, over the Mississippi border, or I finally receive a penny in change and put it in my pocket. But there is no *necessity* for all accidental correlations to break down. In fact the notion of 'historical accidents on the cosmic scale'[23] makes perfect sense.

But if it is *possible* for two sorts of things to be merely accidentally correlated in different circumstances over a long period of time, then a constant conjunction's having held in the past is not *of necessity* reason to believe that it will continue into the future. There being some reason to believe that it will continue does not follow logically from the fact that the correlation has held up till now. But the view under discussion to the effect that having observed a constant conjunction between As and Bs in the past and being confronted with an A now, is just what it means to have reason to believe that a B will occur, is committed to saying that that does follow. So that view must be rejected as incorrect.

Again, it is important to see that this by itself does not imply Hume's sceptical conclusion that there *is* no reason to believe, of any constant conjunction, that it will continue into the future. Nor is it meant to suggest that any of the long-standing correlations we are interested in are in fact accidental. It is intended to show only that, if we believe of a particular observed correlation that it does give us reason to believe that it will continue, then we cannot support that belief purely *a priori*, by appealing to nothing more than the meanings of words or the concept of having a reason to believe.

Incidentally, my defence of the empirical character of Hume's question does not really involve ascribing *to Hume* the distinction between accidental and law-like generalizations. That distinction is one he never makes, to the detriment of his own positive theory, as we shall see in Chapter IV. But I invoke the distinction here only to oppose those who would try to forestall Hume's regress in a certain way. Since he is convinced at the outset that it is always a matter of fact whether one thing is a reason to believe another, he never contemplates that particular way of stopping the regress at all, and so he does not rely on the 'accidental/law-like' distinction in order to meet it.

So we are still left with Hume's question of how one is ever to have any reason to believe that a constant conjunction's having held in the past is reason to believe that a currently observed A will be followed by a B. Any support there could be for it would have to come at least partly from experience. If it cannot be supported in that way, then no one could have a reasonable belief that a B will occur. That is just the first step of Hume's reconstructed argument: no one who has observed a constant conjunction between As and Bs and is currently observing an A will reasonably believe on that basis that a B will occur unless he also reasonably believes that what he has experienced is good reason to believe that a B will occur. The sceptical conclusion that no one could ever reasonably believe that would then be argued for as follows.

Since having observed a constant conjunction between As and Bs and being presently confronted with an A does not logically imply that one has reason to believe that a B will occur, any support for that conclusion must consist of a reasonable inference from observed instances to the truth of 'observed instances provide good reason to believe that a B will occur'. But *every* inference from the observed to the unobserved is such that it is reasonable or justified only if one has reason to believe that observed instances provide reason to believe a certain statement about unobserved instances. And therefore in particular the inference from observed instances to the conclusion 'observed instances provide reason to believe that a B will occur' is reasonable or justified only if one has reason to believe that observed instances provide reason to believe a certain conclusion about unobserved instances. But, as before, that would be 'evidently going in a circle, and taking that for granted, which is the very point in question' (*E*, p. 36). So no one could ever have any reason to believe that observed instances provide reason to believe that a B will occur. And since that in turn was seen to be a necessary condition of having a reasonable belief about the unobserved, it follows that no one ever has a reasonable belief about the unobserved.

So there might well be more in Hume's negative argument than what has come to be the standard interpretation would allow. Perhaps not all the sceptical force, or apparent sceptical force, of that argument is derived from an arbitrary requirement that all good reasoning be deductive. In any case, it seems to me that the subject is still open.

IV

Belief and the Idea of
Necessary Connection:
The Positive Phase

Great standing miracle! That Heav'n assigned
Its only thinking thing this turn of mind.

Whatever the merits of the negative phase of Hume's discussion of causality, the point of it is clear. It is an attempt to show both:

That there is nothing in any object, consider'd in itself, which can afford us a reason for drawing a conclusion beyond it; and, That even after the observation of the frequent or constant conjunction of objects, we have no reason to draw any inference concerning any object beyond those of which we have had experience. (p. 139)

Hume concludes that the inference from the observed to the unobserved is therefore not a transition that 'reason determines us to make', and so its source must be sought elsewhere.

He finds it in what he calls 'the imagination', or certain 'natural', 'primitive' dispositions of the mind. And his search for those dispositions or principles is a straightforward empirical or 'experimental' investigation. There is no doubt that we do make an inference or transition from the observed to the unobserved. And Hume finds that we make it only after we have observed a constant conjunction between two sorts of things, and are presented with a thing of one of those sorts. We always come to believe something about the unobserved in those circumstances because there is operative in the human mind a 'principle of union among ideas' to the effect that:

When ev'ry individual of any species of objects is found by experience to be constantly united with an individual of another species, the appearance of any new individual of either species naturally conveys the thought to its usual attendant. (p. 93)

The observation of a constant conjunction between As and Bs has the inevitable effect of creating a 'union in the imagination' between the

68

idea of an A and the idea of a B. Whenever an idea of a thing of one of those kinds appears in the mind, its 'usual attendant' follows immediately, without any intervening reflection or reasoning being required. We have already seen that no reasoning leads us to make the transition. We just 'find' the idea of a B in our minds when we get an idea of an A. In fact, we cannot easily prevent that idea from occurring in such a situation.

Hume thinks that most cases of relying on past experience are like this. When we come to the edge of a cliff we do not deliberately reflect on whether or not we will go downwards if we step over the edge. We stop. And we do so 'immediately' and 'automatically'. But that is not to say that we would still have stopped even if we had had no experience of unsupported bodies falling and of human beings being injured when striking solid objects with great force. Past experience is what makes us believe and behave as we do, but not by providing us with premises from which we reasonably infer our beliefs or our actions. It does so automatically in conjunction with certain principles or dispositions of the mind.

So far only one such principle has been invoked. It explains why the idea of a B appears in the mind whenever the idea of an A appears there in terms of a 'union in the imagination' between As and Bs. But there is more to explain. When we get an *impression* of an A we do not just get an *idea* of a B—we actually come to *believe* that a B will occur. That is just the inference Hume wants to explain. All that has been explained so far is why the idea of a B comes into the mind. Hume's further explanation of how an actual belief arises is primarily an explanation of how believing something differs from merely having an idea of it.[1] Believing involves having an idea, but it is also something more.

That there is a difference between thinking or conceiving or having an idea of something and believing that such-and-such is the case is obvious from the existence of disagreements. In a dispute with someone I do not believe what he says—in fact, I might believe the opposite—but I do understand or conceive of what he says. Only if I do is there a real disagreement. We can think or conceive of both sides of a question, although we *believe* at most one of them to be the case. What is the difference between 'simple conception' and belief? Hume thinks he is one of the first philosophers to see the enormous difficulties in answering this question (pp. 623, 628).

He argues that believing something cannot be a matter of adding to one's idea of it a further idea—perhaps the idea of reality or existence. First, we have no idea of reality or existence distinguishable and separable from the ideas we form of particular objects. To think of God and to think of God as existing are one and the same. There is no difference *in idea* between them. This is not to say that to think of something is to believe that it exists. It is only to say that to think of something is to think of it as it would be if it existed, or to think of it as existing; and it is perfectly possible to do that without believing that the thing exists. So there is no separate idea that we could add to the idea of a thing in order to change simple conception into belief (p. 623).[2]

Furthermore, Hume argues, the mind has control over all its ideas. We can call up, unite and separate our ideas at will. But if believing differed from merely having an idea simply in the addition of some idea of reality or existence to the original idea, then we could believe whatever we want, at will. We would just have to put one of our ideas together with another one. But we cannot believe whatever we want, at will. So the difference between believing and conceiving does not consist in the addition of an idea of reality or existence to the original idea (pp. 623–4; *E*, p. 48).

With that wrong answer out of the way, Hume treats the problem of the nature of belief, and its difference from simple conception, 'as a question in natural philosophy, which we must determine by experience and observation' (p. 101). Because of what is observed to occur, he thinks belief must be understood to be a certain sort of thing. Given a 'union in the imagination' established by the observation of a constant conjunction between As and Bs, whenever one of those ideas appears in the mind, the other will follow. But it is obvious that the mere *idea* of an A produces only the *idea* of a B; it alone is not enough to make us *believe* that a B exists or will occur. If I am looking at two motionless billiard balls on a table and suddenly think of (i.e. have an idea of) the white ball's striking the red one, I do not then come to *believe* that the red one will move. I merely think of its moving. In order to get a belief I must have an *impression* of an A. An actual belief in the unobserved arises only when we make a transition from something observed or perceived. Hume thinks this is a simple observable fact about the circumstances in which beliefs in the unobserved actually arise.

He concludes that what distinguishes an idea or simple conception from a belief is therefore whatever it is that distinguishes an impression from an idea. And an impression differs from an idea only in its degree of 'force and vivacity'. So Hume feels he has no alternative but to say that a belief is 'a more vivid and intense conception of an idea, proceeding from its relation to a present impression' (p. 103), or, in his most common formulation, 'a lively idea related to or associated with a present impression' (p. 96).

Once belief has been so characterized, there is an obvious principle or disposition of the mind that will explain why beliefs arise when they do.

I wou'd willingly establish it as a general maxim in the science
of human nature, *that when any impression becomes present
to us, it not only transports the mind to such ideas as are
related to it, but likewise communicates to them a share of
its force and vivacity.* (p. 98)

Only because this is true of the mind does a present impression
produce a belief in the unobserved. So two different principles are
needed to explain the occurrence of beliefs: the principle that an
observed constant conjunction creates a 'union in the imagination'
between things of two kinds, and the principle of the transmission of
force and vivacity from a present impression to an associated idea.

It is clear that the second principle is thought to be needed only
because of Hume's peculiar conception of the nature of belief. If a
belief differed from a simple conception in some way other than in its
degree of force and vivacity, this principle would not help explain why
beliefs arise when they do.

Hume suggests that his account of belief is actually borne out by
common experience, but the example he gives can hardly be said to
support that contention.

If one person sits down to read a book as a romance, and
another as a true history, they plainly receive the same ideas,
and in the same order; nor does the incredulity of the one,
and the belief of the other hinder them from putting the very
same sense upon their author. His words produce the same
ideas in both; tho' his testimony has not the same influence
on them. The latter has a more lively conception of all the
incidents. He enters deeper into the concerns of the persons:
represents to himself their actions, and characters, and
friendships, and enmities: He even goes so far as to form a
notion of their features, and air, and person. While the
former, who gives no credit to the testimony of the author,
has a more faint and languid conception of all these
particulars; and except on account of the style and ingenuity
of the composition, can receive little entertainment from it.
(pp. 97–8)

It is certainly a matter of common experience that there is some
difference between believing what you read and taking it as fiction.
But whatever that difference might be, it is clear that Hume has not
captured it here. What he says is almost completely untrue in every
respect, and he must have known that as well as anyone. Does a person
knowingly reading fiction have a 'less lively conception' of the
incidents described than one who takes what he reads as true? Does he

71

fail to 'form a notion' of the 'features, air, and person' of the characters described? This looks like a clear case of Hume's denying the obvious under the pressure of what he thinks his philosophical theory requires.

But he feels he has no alternative. And although in the Appendix to the *Treatise* (pp. 628–9) he expresses great dissatisfaction with that part of his theory of belief, he finds nothing satisfactory to put in its place, either there or in the *Enquiry*. But it is important to see that his dissatisfaction is not total.

Since belief differs from simple conception, believing must add *something* to the original idea. But it cannot consist in the addition of a new and different idea, so what is added must be only a different 'manner of conceiving' the original idea. Any other change would change the idea conceived, and so it would be impossible to conceive of and believe in the very same thing. About that part of the theory Hume never expresses the slightest doubt.

Then, under pressure from the theory of ideas and from a rather restricted conception of his philosophical task, he is led by the obvious facts about when beliefs arise to an unrealistic and unworkable account of what that difference in 'manner of conceiving' really consists in. We know that, given a union in the imagination between As and Bs, a belief that a B will occur arises only when an *impression* of an A is present, and not if only an idea of an A is present. But:

> as the different degrees of force make all the original
> difference betwixt an impression and an idea, they must of
> consequence be the source of all the differences in the
> effects of these perceptions, and their removal, in whole or
> in part, the cause of every new resemblance they acquire.
> Wherever we can make an idea approach the impressions in
> force and vivacity, it will likewise imitate them in its
> influence on the mind; and *vice versa*, where it imitates them
> in that influence, as in the present case, this must proceed
> from its approaching them in force and vivacity. Belief,
> therefore, since it causes an idea to imitate the effects of the
> impressions, must make it resemble them in these qualities,
> and is nothing but *a more vivid and intense conception of
> any idea*. (pp. 119–20)

This explicitly argues that since the difference in degrees of force and vivacity between an impression and an idea is the *source* of all the differences in the effects those two kinds of perception have, and since an impression differs from an idea in having *beliefs*, and not mere conceptions, as its effects, therefore a belief differs from an idea only in its degrees of force and vivacity. The difference between an idea and a belief is the same difference as that between an idea and an impression.

The inference is not obviously a good one. Hume cannot deny the observable fact that a belief arises only when an impression is present; that a mere idea is not enough to produce it. But that still leaves open the question what a belief *is,* and how it differs from mere conception. He thinks that difference has to be the same difference as that between an impression and an idea, and since he thinks force and vivacity is the only difference there, he is led into his unsatisfactory theory of belief.

All that strictly follows from the facts is that beliefs, as opposed to mere ideas, are caused in part by whatever it is that distinguishes impressions from ideas. It is somehow because of the greater force and vivacity of an impression that a belief arises. But that is a fact about the cause or origin of a belief, not about what a belief is. Hume takes the further step of *defining* the difference between an idea and a belief in terms of force and vivacity because he thinks that is the only way to explain the occurrence of beliefs by means of general principles that cover more than the particular phenomenon being explained. The principle of the transmission of force and vivacity explains it simply and is also confirmed by other phenomena (p. 627).[3] But it commits Hume to the theory that a belief is just a more lively or vivacious idea.

If he gives up that theory his 'explanation' of the origin of beliefs will shrink to the straightforward observation that beliefs arise only when an impression is present. He feels he will have no account of *why* that is so. For a genuine explanation to be possible he thinks belief must be analogous to other things that are also explained by the same principles.

> For if it be not analogous to any other sentiment, we must
> despair of explaining its causes, and must consider it as an
> original principle of the human mind. If it be analogous, we
> may hope to explain its causes from analogy, and trace it up
> to more general principles. (p. 624)

So his search for the simplest and most general principles within the theory of ideas leads him astray. Belief must be in some respects like other mental phenomena, but he cannot find a definition in terms other than those of force and vivacity because he thinks that is the only difference in the 'manner of conceiving' one and the same idea that the theory of ideas allows (p. 96).

Although Hume undoubtedly feels these pressures of theory, he also expresses serious misgivings about what he thinks the theory dictates. He thinks that 'greater force and vivacity' does not really capture the difference between a belief and a mere conception, but that there is a difference in *feeling* between them that is very difficult to describe:

> this different feeling I endeavour to explain by calling it

a superior *force*, or *vivacity*, or *solidity*, or *firmness*, or *steadiness*. This variety of terms, which may seem so unphilosophical, is intended only to express that act of the mind, which renders realities more present to us than fictions, causes them to weigh more in the thought, and gives them a superior influence on the passions and imagination. . . . I confess, that 'tis impossible to explain perfectly this feeling or manner of conception. We may make use of words, that express something near it. But its true and proper name is *belief*, which is a term that every one sufficiently understands in common life. And in philosophy we can go no farther, than assert, that it is something *felt* by the mind, which distinguishes the ideas of the judgment from the fictions of the imagination. It gives them more force and influence; makes them appear of greater importance; infixes them in the mind; and renders them the governing principles of all our actions. (p. 629)

Hume's talk of believing as a feeling must not be misunderstood. He is not saying simply that a belief differs from a conception or an idea solely in the addition of a certain mental item, viz. a feeling, to the original idea. There would then be a difference in the items that are before the mind when someone believes something and when he merely thinks about it, and that is what Hume wants to deny. It is rather in its *effects* on the mind that an idea that is a belief differs from a mere idea—it is said to 'weigh more in the thought', to have a 'superior influence on our passions and imagination', and to be 'the governing principle of our actions'.

Hume seems never to have entertained the idea that this connection between belief and the passions and the will might constitute the very difference he seeks between belief and mere conception. That is not to say that he simply missed something obvious. No adequate theory of the nature of belief has been given to this day, and that is probably because it has been investigated in virtually complete independence from the notions of passion, desire, will and action.[4]

Hume claims that the question of the nature of belief had not been seriously considered by philosophers before his time. But he tries to answer it within the confines of an impossibly narrow theory. The theory of mind he uncritically inherited leaves no room for what has been called the 'intentional'[5] character of thought or psychological phenomena generally. Thinking for him is just a matter of there being a certain entity 'before the mind'. But in distinguishing conceiving from believing he seems to be aware that one and the same idea can be involved in different mental acts or 'modes of thinking'. The same idea is present in each case, and surely Hume is right in thinking that the difference between them must somehow be understood in terms of the different 'manner' or 'mode' in which that idea is before the mind. But there are many more mental acts or modes of thinking than the two he considers.

For example, one 'manner of conceiving' an idea that Hume should have considered is denial. Although he speaks of disagreement, disbelief and dissent, he never tries to say what they are, perhaps because he thinks his theory of belief, such as it is, accounts for them. But that is not so.

If assent or belief is just a matter of having a lively idea before the mind, what is dissent or denial? It would seem to be either a matter of having that idea before the mind in some different 'manner', or else assenting to or believing the opposite of the original idea. But in the case at least of existential beliefs it makes no sense to Hume to talk of 'the opposite of the original idea'. If to think of God is to think of God as existing, or as He would be if He existed, then it is not possible to have the idea of God's not existing. And therefore it is not possible to have the belief that God does not exist by having 'in the assenting or believing manner' the idea of God's non-existence. Of course, it might be said that I believe that God does exist by having 'in the assenting manner' the idea, not just of God, but of God's existence; and therefore I believe that God does not exist by having 'in the assenting manner' the idea, not just of God, but of God's non-existence. But that could be true only if we had a separate idea of existence (and perhaps of non-existence as well) to add to our idea of God; and that is what Hume explicitly denies.

So we must look to the other alternative—to denial or dissent as another 'manner of conceiving'. On this view we have only the one idea, that of God, or of God as existing, and we can conceive it either by assenting and thereby believing that God exists, or by denying and thereby believing that God does not exist. And both of those 'attitudes' are to be distinguished from simple conception, in which one need not have an opinion one way or the other. But if denial is to be a completely different 'manner of conceiving' from both belief and mere conception, and if all differences among 'manners of conceiving' are just differences in degrees of force and vivacity, then denial will be just a matter of having an idea before the mind with yet a third degree of force and vivacity. Will it be stronger, or weaker, than belief? And how will it differ from a belief held with less than the highest degree of conviction? Will there be no difference between an atheist and a man who fairly strongly believes that God exists?

It is clear that, once we think not just about belief and conception, but about all the rest of the great variety of 'attitudes' we can take with respect to a single idea, there is no plausibility at all in saying that they differ only in their degrees of force and vivacity. For any idea representing some state of affairs p, we can conceive of or contemplate what it would be like if p obtained, imagine that p obtains, hope that p obtains, wonder whether it obtains, ask whether it does, believe that p obtains, and so on. But there is no temptation to suppose that wondering or asking is just conceiving something more faintly or more weakly than believing it.

Hume wants one important consequence to survive from his theory of belief. The belief in the unobserved arises completely naturally, like any other phenomenon in nature. It arises by 'custom', as a result of repetitions in our experience. We do not decide to believe what we do; we are not free not to believe those things that are most fundamental for us. That is part of what Hume wants to emphasize when he calls belief a feeling or sentiment. Because of the inevitability of beliefs, it is impossible to put into practice a 'total scepticism', or even a Cartesian 'suspension of belief'. But such a state of mind is not Hume's aim. The scepticism he defends is put forward for a particular positive purpose, and it is no objection to say that scepticism is impossible to live by.

> Nature, by an absolute and uncontroulable necessity has
> determin'd us to judge as well as to breathe and feel; nor can
> we any more forbear viewing certain objects in a stronger and
> fuller light, upon account of their customary connexion with
> a present impression, than we can hinder ourselves from
> thinking as long as we are awake, or seeing the surrounding
> bodies, when we turn our eyes towards them in broad sunshine.
> Whoever has taken the pains to refute the cavils of this
> *total* scepticism, has really disputed without an antagonist,
> and endeavour'd by arguments to establish a faculty, which
> nature has antecedently implanted in the mind, and render'd
> unavoidable. (p. 183)

The sceptical denigration of the role of reason and the consequent elevation of the importance of the primitive or natural dispositions of the imagination lead to the conclusion:

> *that all our reasonings concerning causes and effects are
> deriv'd from nothing but custom; and that belief is more
> properly an act of the sensitive, than of the cogitative part
> of our natures.* (p. 183)

This view is intended to break down the alleged difference in kind between men and the other animals. Hume thinks his naturalistic theory of man is actually confirmed by the fact that animals too act simply on the basis of past experience and their present impressions. We are not inclined to suppose that they do so by deliberately weighing evidence, considering the arguments on both sides, and then deciding to adopt a certain conclusion. We are willing to agree that they just 'find' themselves with certain beliefs or expectations. But they obviously are capable of thought or reason at least in the sense that they are intelligent beings who can learn from experience and profit from it.

Hume thinks that animal behaviour confirms his theory of man because the same kinds of explanations are available for behaviour that is observationally the same. Descartes' claim that animals have no souls was taken to imply that a science of animal behaviour is possible. But he thought that men, being spiritual substances whose essence is to think, are not amenable to the same kind of scientific treatment. Hume's theory denies that Cartesian claim. Both men and animals are objects in the natural world; both are subject to the same forces, and to influences of the same general kind. And those forces and influences are open to empirical investigation and discovery.

If Descartes were right in saying that animals have no souls, then Hume's arguments would show that men have no souls either. In order to explain their beliefs and actions there is no need to invoke a metaphysically detached faculty of 'reason' or 'will' operating independently of those causal chains that make up the natural world.

Hume does not deny that there is such a thing as reason, or the will. He denies only the traditional Cartesian conception of it.

> To consider the matter aright, reason is nothing but a
> wonderful and unintelligible instinct in our souls, which carries
> us along a certain train of ideas, and endows them with
> particular qualities, according to their particular situations and
> relations. This instinct, 'tis true, arises from past observation
> and experience; but can any one give the ultimate reason,
> why past experience and observation produces such an effect,
> any more than why nature alone shou'd produce it? Nature
> may certainly produce whatever can arise from habit: Nay, habit
> is nothing but one of the principles of nature, and derives
> all its force from that origin. (p. 179)

The long discussion of the inference from the observed to the unobserved is supposed to be a detour on the road to discovering the source of the idea of necessary connection. We find no impression of necessary connection in any particular instance of causality, so the origin of the idea remains obscure. In explaining why he plans to concentrate on the inference from the observed to the unobserved, rather than searching directly for the source of the idea of necessary connection, Hume hints that:

Perhaps 'twill appear in the end, that the necessary connexion depends on the inference, instead of the inference's depending on the necessary connexion. (p. 88)

That is just how it turns out.

By the end of Section 8 of Part III of the first Book of the *Treatise*, and the end of Section V of the first *Enquiry* Hume has already identified and explained a pervasive and fundamental feature of the human mind. He has shown how and why we come to have beliefs about the unobserved, and he has indicated how important it is for human life that we do so. But however important it might be, he does not think it exhausts what is meant by 'having the idea of causality or necessary connection', and so the origin of that idea has yet to be accounted for. He goes on in each case to a long section 'Of the Idea of Necessary Connexion'. But what remains unexplained, and why does Hume think that what has been said so far is not enough?

One reason for his dissatisfaction is his commitment to the official theory of ideas. On that view, to have an idea is to have a certain item in the mind, and so to explain the source of an idea is to explain how that item gets into the mind. So far in the discussion of inferences from the observed to the unobserved no mental item has been identified that could plausibly be called the idea of causality or necessary connection. And according to the theory of ideas, for every idea in the mind there must be an impression, or impressions, from which that idea is derived, and we have found no such impression so far either. So Hume returns to the search for impressions from which the idea of necessary connection is derived, partly because the architectonic of the theory of ideas must be served. Without such a search his 'first principle' of the science of human nature would remain undefended.

But there is another reason. The phenomenon to be explained is not just our getting expectations on certain occasions. We come to believe, not just that a B will occur, but that it *must*. We have the idea, not just of an event of one sort always following an event of another sort in certain circumstances, but of there being a *necessary connection* between events of two sorts in certain circumstances. Of course, it is not immediately obvious what that belief and idea come to. What is the difference between observing an A and coming to believe that a B will occur, and observing an A and coming to believe that a B must occur? What is the difference between having the idea of Bs always following As and having the idea of a necessary connection between As and Bs? Hume thinks there are such differences. And he thinks he can explain how we come to have such beliefs and ideas. As we shall see, the two questions are connected. We must have a clear understanding of what is to be explained in order to tell whether a putative explanation of it is successful. Hume concentrates more on the explanation than on the characterization of what is to be explained.

The observation of a constant conjunction of phenomena is what leads us to infer from cause to effect. Without that we would never get the idea of causality or necessary connection. But in each instance of causality we simply observe one thing following another, and we get no impression of any necessary connection. Only after repeated observation of Bs following As do we have the idea of necessary connection. But mere repetition obviously cannot reveal something in the instances that was not there to begin with, nor can it produce anything new in the objects or events in question. Each instance is independent of all the others, and would be what it is even though none of the others existed. How then can the repeated observation of Bs following As ever give rise to the idea of necessary connection, as it does?

Hume thinks it can do so only by producing something new *in the mind*, not in the instances observed. We know, Hume says, that repetition produces the idea of necessary connection in minds that originally lack it. And from the theory of ideas it follows that something else must be produced in the mind, and that that thing is an impression from which the idea is derived. That impression is not an impression of sensation, since we get no impression of necessary connection from any one of the instances. Therefore it must be an impression of reflection, or 'an internal impression of the mind'. The argument is expressed briefly as follows:

> For after we have observ'd the resemblance in a sufficient
> number of instances, we immediately feel a determination of
> the mind to pass from one object to its usual attendant, and
> to conceive it in a stronger light upon account of that relation.
> This determination is the only effect of the resemblance;
> and therefore must be the same with power or efficacy, whose
> idea is deriv'd from the resemblance. The several instances
> of resembling conjunctions leads us into the notion of power and
> necessity. Those instances are in themselves totally distinct
> from each other, and have no union but in the mind, which
> observes them, and collects their ideas. Necessity, then, is
> the effect of this observation, and is nothing but an internal
> impression of the mind, or a determination to carry our
> thoughts from one object to another. (p. 165)

This passage, as well as others like it, is extremely obscure and confusing. Part of what Hume wants to say is fairly clear, but he is led into grave difficulties. He says that the only new thing that occurs in the mind after the repeated observation of Bs following As is a 'determination of the mind to pass from one object to its usual attendant, and to conceive it in a stronger light upon account of that relation'. That means that, whenever we have observed a constant conjunction between As and Bs and are currently observing an A, we are led to get an idea of, and a belief in, a B. To say that we are 'led' is to say that the first complex mental event (having an impression of an A after observing a constant conjunction between As and Bs) causes the second (believing that a B will occur). When that happens we get the idea of a necessary connection between As and Bs; that explains how and why that idea arises in the mind. Hume confuses matters by saying that that 'determination' is 'the same with' power or necessity, the idea of which we are trying to explain. He even says that necessity *is* 'an internal impression of the mind' *or* 'a determination to carry our thoughts from one object to another'.

The puzzling identification of the determination of the mind with an *impression* needs to be explained. Hume seems to be arguing that, since the idea of necessary connection comes into the mind only as a result of one mental occurrence's causing another, and since according to the theory of ideas the cause or source of every idea is an impression, therefore the one event's causing the other *is* the impression from which the idea of necessary connection is derived. But this seems incoherent. One event's causing another cannot *be* an impression, even if the events in question are mental events, and we are aware of their occurrence. We might well have an impression *of* their occurrence, but the one event's causing the other could scarcely *be* that impression, or any impression.

Hume does sometimes say that 'we immediately feel a determination of the mind', and this suggests that we feel, or are aware of, the one mental event's causing the other. To have that feeling or awareness would be to have an impression, so it would seem to follow that we have an impression of the causal or necessary connection between two mental events. This is not a line Hume can comfortably take. It implies that there is in fact a causal or necessary connection between two mental events, and that we get an impression of that connection by 'feeling' it, presumably by introspection. There would then be at least some instances of two things being related causally in which we can and do get an impression of the necessary connection that holds between them, and that is something Hume explicitly denies. He goes out of his way to argue that we cannot get an impression of necessary connection by observing the happenings in our own minds any more than we can by observing happenings in the outer world (*E*, pp. 64–9). So Hume cannot mean that we get an impression *of* the necessary connection between two events; that is perhaps why he slides into saying that one mental event's causing another *is* an impression, rather than that it is what the impression is an impression *of*.

It is perhaps more plausible to suggest that we not only get an idea of, and a belief in, a B in the appropriate circumstances, but also that that idea appears in the mind *accompanied* by a certain feeling—a feeling of something like determination or inevitability. Of course, no such impression accompanies the first few instances of As and Bs we observe; the feeling begins to accompany the idea of a B only after repeated observations, so it is not literally an impression *of* something that is present in each individual instance. It is an impression that arises only from the repeated occurrence of certain kinds of ideas in the mind, and therefore it must be classified as an impression of reflection. But what does it mean to say that it is an impression or feeling *of* the inevitability with which something occurs? It is presumably to say more than that it is simply an impression of the occurrence of something, but how, if at all, can Hume explain what that extra element is? As we have seen, he cannot say that it is an impression *of* that occurrence's being caused, or *of* the necessary connection between that occurrence and whatever caused it.

This problem of explaining the content of the perception arises for the *idea* of necessity as well, as we see when we try to understand why Hume tends to identify necessity itself with a determination of the mind.

In a famous passage which has led to much criticism and misunderstanding Hume says:

> Upon the whole, necessity is something, that exists in the mind, not in objects; nor is it possible for us ever to form the most distant idea of it, consider'd as a quality in bodies. Either we have no idea of necessity, or necessity is nothing but that determination of the thought to pass from causes to effects and from effects to causes, according to their experienc'd union. (pp. 165–6)

In saying that necessity is something that exists only in the mind, Hume does not mean that causality only operates in the 'inner' mental world, and that in the rest of nature there is no such thing as causality. Nor does he mean that things happen in inanimate nature only as a result of something happening in our minds. He means, in part, that we have the idea of necessity only because of the occurrence of certain events in our minds when our experience exhibits certain features. Contiguity, priority and constant conjunctions between things of two kinds hold or fail to hold completely independently of thought or sensation, and they are the only relations we can observe to hold among objects themselves. We also ascribe to objects an additional property of power, efficacy or causal necessity, but we get the idea of that power only from 'what we feel internally in contemplating' the objects around us (p. 169). If it were a condition of having the idea of necessity that we get it from discovering the 'real' causes or the 'secret springs' of the correlations we observe, then we could never have the idea. But we do have an idea of necessity, so its origin must be accounted for solely in terms of happenings in our minds.

We have already seen what mental happenings produce the idea of necessity. Once we have that idea, we ascribe necessity to objects or events around us, or at least to the connections between them. Our tendency to ascribe necessity in this way is explained by appeal to another general human disposition.

> 'Tis a common observation, that the mind has a great propensity
> to spread itself on external objects, and to conjoin with them
> any internal impressions, which they occasion, and which always
> make their appearance at the same time that these objects
> discover themselves to the senses. Thus, as certain sounds and
> smells are always found to attend certain visible objects,
> we naturally imagine a conjunction, even in place, betwixt the
> objects and the qualities, tho' the qualities be of such a nature
> as to admit of no such conjunction, and really exist
> nowhere . . . the same propensity is the reason, why we
> suppose necessity and power to lie in the objects we consider,
> not in our mind, that considers them; notwithstanding it is
> not possible for us to form the most distant idea of that
> quality, when it is not taken for the determination of the mind,
> to pass from the idea of an object to that of its usual
> attendant. (p. 167)

Hume's way of putting this subtle point is confusing, but it is not obvious that there is any completely satisfactory way of making it.[6]

The analogy with secondary qualities should reinforce the point that necessity is not something that actually resides in objects or the connections between them. Just as we ascribe redness to certain things in the world only because something happens in our minds when we observe things that, according to the traditional theory, actually possess no redness, so we ascribe necessity to certain things in the world only because something happens in our minds when we observe things (viz. correlations or conjunctions) that possess no necessity. Sounds and smells, Hume says, 'really exist nowhere', and the same holds for necessity.

Why, then, does Hume say that necessity *is* a determination of the mind, and that we cannot form any idea of necessity if we take it to be anything else? For one thing, if necessity literally *is* a determination of the mind to pass from the idea of one object to that of its usual attendant, then necessity *does* exist after all. It exists in those minds in which that determination exists, and for Hume that includes all minds that have the appropriate experiences. That is perhaps why he finds himself saying that necessity exists only in the mind. But we already saw that that remark cannot be taken strictly literally.

Furthermore, if necessity just *is* a determination of the mind, then that is what our idea of necessity is an idea *of*. But if our idea of necessity is an idea of a determination of the mind, then in ascribing necessity to the connections between things we are simply saying something about our own minds. We are saying that our minds do, or would, expect a thing of one kind after having observed a thing of another kind. This would commit Hume to the subjectivistic or psychologistic view that every causal statement we make, whatever its putative subject-matter, is at least partly a statement about us. Rather than expressing a belief that something is objectively true of the connection between two objects or events, we would merely be asserting that something is happening or will happen in our minds when we observe certain objects or events.

This seems implausible as an account of the content of our ordinary causal beliefs about the world, and it is one that Hume should wish to avoid. He started out to explain how we come to believe that events are causally connected, or that a certain event must occur, given that another has already occurred. Even if there is nothing in reality which our belief adequately represents, still we do seem to have the belief that the connections between things are necessary in themselves, and would remain so whatever happened to be true about us. Of course, Hume argues that there is no necessity residing in objects—our belief that there is is actually false—but the psychologistic view denies the very existence of that belief. If we can have no idea of necessity as something residing in objects, and our only idea of it is as something that occurs or exists in the mind, then we cannot even have the false belief that necessity is something that is objectively true of the connections between objects or events in our experience. To have that false belief we need at least an *idea* of necessity as something true of the connections between events. But if we have no such idea then we do not, and cannot, have that belief.

The trouble stems from Hume's tendency to conflate the question of what our idea of necessity is an idea *of*, or what is our idea of necessity, and the quite different question of how that idea ever gets into the mind, or why we ever ascribe necessity to certain things we find in the world. He thinks he knows that our idea of necessity could arise only from certain happenings in our minds as a result of our observing constantly conjoined phenomena. Since he regards no other origin of the idea as possible, he tends to conclude that therefore the idea we get from that source is an idea *of* those happenings in our minds. The inference is quite explicit in both the *Enquiry* and the *Abstract* where, having explained only how the idea of necessity arises, he concludes:

> When we say, therefore, that one object is connected with another, *we mean only* that they have acquired a connexion in our thought, and give rise to this inference, by which they become proofs of each other's existence: (*E*, p. 76, my italics)

> Upon the whole, then, either we have no idea at all of force and energy, and these words are altogether insignificant, or *they can mean nothing but* that determination of the thought, acquired by habit, to pass from the cause to its usual effect. (Hume (2), p. 23, my italics)

The arguments preceding these conclusions mention nothing about the content of the idea of necessity, or what 'necessity' means. They treat only of the origin of that idea in our minds, so Hume appears to be inferring a conclusion about the meaning or content of an idea directly from some facts about its origin.

He is probably led to make this inference by the application of his 'first principle' about impressions and ideas. Explaining the origin of an idea will serve to explicate its content because:

> We have establish'd it as a principle, that as all ideas are deriv'd from impressions, or some precedent *perceptions*, 'tis impossible we can have any idea of power and efficacy, unless some instances can be produc'd, wherein this power *is perceiv'd* to exert itself. (p. 160)

Or, as he puts it in the *Enquiry*:

> It seems a proposition, which will not admit of much dispute, that all our ideas are nothing but copies of our impressions, or, in other words, that it is impossible for us to *think* of any thing, which we have not antecedently *felt*, either by our external or internal senses. (*E*, p. 62)

Since Hume has already argued that we can never perceive the necessary connection between two things in any particular instance, it would seem to follow from this principle that we can have no idea of necessity. Or at least, that we can have an idea of necessity only as something we can and do perceive in particular instances. But we have already seen that Hume does not think that we actually *perceive* the necessity of the connection between any two events, even events that occur in our minds. If we did, then we could get the idea of necessity directly from one of our internal experiences, and we would not have to wait for the repetition of a number of instances.

The principle as stated, however, is obviously not true, nor is it what Hume established earlier. It is quite possible to have an idea of, or to think of, a unicorn, although we have never perceived one or had an impression of one. So the principle holds only for simple ideas, and not for all ideas. Therefore, if the application of the principle to the idea of necessity is to have the consequences Hume wants, he must regard the idea of necessity as a simple idea. And he does in effect acknowledge its simplicity.[7] But he sometimes also says he wants to explain our idea of necessity; to say what it is an idea *of*.[8] And if it is a simple idea, that is a hopeless task.

But even if the idea of necessity is simple, and all simple ideas are derived from their corresponding impressions, does it follow that we can never have an idea of necessity as something that objectively resides in objects, but only as something that exists in the mind? If it does follow, then Hume is indeed committed to psychologism, and thereby to the disappearance of the very belief in the objectivity of necessary connections that he originally wanted to explain. Does that disappointing conclusion really follow from Hume's explanation of the origin of the idea of necessity? I think not.

If the idea of necessity is a simple idea, then it must be derived from its corresponding impression. It is important to remember that, according to Hume, there is no impression of the necessity with which two events are connected, so whatever our simple impression of necessity might be, it is not an impression that arises when we are directly perceiving some feature of the world (viz. necessity) that presents itself to us. This holds just as much for the 'inner' mental world as for the 'outer' world of objects and events.

Hume isolates two different candidates as possible causes of the idea of necessity—a determination of the mind to pass from the idea of one object to that of its usual attendant, and an impression or feeling of determination. If he says simply that the determination of the mind is what causes us to get the idea of necessity, then his 'first principle' would be violated, since he would have found an idea which is caused by something other than an impression. Therefore, he should say that the idea is caused by the impression or feeling of determination. But that impression or feeling cannot be understood as a direct perception of something that is objectively true of the connection between two events in the mind, since that would violate his fundamental contention that we never get any impression of necessity from observing a particular instance.

The impression or feeling of determination from which the idea of necessity is derived must therefore be understood as just a certain feeling that arises in the mind whenever a certain kind of mental occurrence causes another. The impression or feeling is not an impression *of* that one event's causing the other, or *of* the necessary or causal connection between them; it is just a peculiar feeling that accompanies, or is simultaneous with, the occurrence of that second event in the mind. That it always occurs there when it does is a fundamental fact about the human mind that Hume does not try to explain.

On this interpretation Hume is not committed to subjectivism or psychologism. For simple ideas, an idea is an idea of whatever its corresponding simple impression is an impression of. We get a 'feeling of determination' or necessity, and thereby get our idea of necessity. But once we repudiate the suggestion that the impression or feeling of necessity is a direct perception *of* the causal necessity holding between two mental events, or a direct perception *of* anything else happening in the mind, there should be no temptation to say that our *idea* of necessity is an idea of certain happenings in our minds. Our idea of necessity, which admittedly arises from a certain internal impression, will simply be an idea of whatever it is we ascribe to the relation between two events when we believe them to be causally or necessarily connected. And for the moment we can say only that it is *necessity* that we so ascribe.

Although that is perhaps disappointing, it is important to see that we are in no better position with respect to any other simple idea. We get our simple idea of red from an impression of red, but if we ask what our idea of red really is an idea of, we can say only that it is an idea *of red*. It is an idea of whatever it is we ascribe to a ripe apple when we believe that it is red. And there still seems to be nothing to say if we ask why that impression from which the idea of red is derived is an impression *of red*, or why the impression that arises when we see a ripe apple is an impression *of red*. Again, there seems to be nothing to say. But that does not imply that we have no idea of red, or that it is only an idea of something that happens in our minds.

So I am suggesting that Hume can allow that it is really *necessity*, and not just something that happens in the mind, that we project onto the relations between events in the world. In believing that two events are necessarily connected we believe only something about the way the world is, and nothing about our own minds, although we believe what we do only because certain things occur in our minds. And so it can be said after all that we really do believe (albeit falsely, according to Hume) that necessity is something that 'resides' in the relations between objects or events in the objective world.

The analogy with secondary qualities is helpful, although there too Hume usually fails to make the necessary distinctions. We say and believe that some apples and books are red—we ascribe redness to objects. We do so only because an impression of red appears in the

86

mind when we perceive those objects. According to the theory of secondary qualities, there is no redness in the objects. But it would be absurd to say that redness just *is* the impression in the mind, or that our idea of redness is just the idea of that impression, since when we ascribe redness to an apple we are not saying that that *impression* is in, or belongs to, the apple.[9] We suppose redness, not the impression, to be in the apple. Although, according to the theory, that supposition is wrong, its falsity does not force us to conclude that we do not really suppose redness to be something that resides in the apple after all. It is only because we do that we have the false belief about where redness 'resides'.

I am suggesting that Hume could give an exactly similar story about necessity. We say and believe that there are necessary connections between events in the world. We do so only because a certain impression—a 'feeling of determination'—arises in the mind when we observe constant conjunctions between events of two kinds, and not because we ever actually perceive any necessary connections between events. But it would be absurd to say that necessity just *is* an impression in the mind, or an occurrence in the mind, or that our idea of necessity is just the idea of something in the mind, since when we ascribe necessity to the connection between two events we are not saying something about our own minds. We suppose necessity, not something in our minds, to characterize the relation between two events. Although, according to Hume, that supposition is wrong, its falsity does not force us to conclude that we do not really suppose necessity to be something true of the connections between events after all. It is only because we do suppose that that we have a false belief about where necessity 'resides'. Because of the mind's natural tendency to 'spread itself' on external objects, when we get a 'feeling of determination' we then come to project necessity onto the objective relations between events in the world,[10] and thus come to believe, mistakenly, that there are objective necessary connections between events.

This suggestion might be thought to be unsatisfactory because it precludes us from saying anything illuminating about the content of our idea of necessity. When asked what is involved in our idea of necessity, or what it is an idea of, we can say nothing that helps explain or define it, even though we purport to know a great deal about its origin. That is perhaps as it should be if the idea of necessity is a simple idea. Because such terms as 'efficacy', 'power', and 'productive quality' are 'nearly synonimous'[11] with 'necessity' or 'necessary connection', Hume rejects out of hand all the 'vulgar definitions' as providing no real explanation of the content of the idea (p. 157). That is why he concentrates on explaining its origin.

But it is not just that we cannot say anything illuminating or helpful about what necessity *is*, or what 'necessity' *means*. That is true of 'red' and all other simple ideas. In the case of necessity, however, it is difficult even to say anything illuminating or helpful about what it is to have the idea of necessity, or how having that idea differs from not having it. And that is precisely what Hume is trying to explain. He wants to discover how we come to have the idea of necessary connection. I said earlier that he concentrates more on the explanation than on what is to be explained, and that is probably because of the theory of ideas. He does not see the problems involved in saying what it is to have the idea of X. I can try to suggest some of the difficulties in the case of necessity.[12]

If we ask why the idea of necessity comes into the mind, Hume's answer is that it is caused by a certain impression. Even if we grant that there is an impression that gives rise to that idea, we are still faced with the question of why that impression produces the idea of *necessity*. That, after all, is what was to have been explained. Hume's answer again is that that impression produces the idea of *necessity*, as opposed to some other idea (say, the idea of −1 or the idea of a golden mountain), because it is an impression *of* necessity or determination. But it looks as if he can say that only because he knows that impression is in fact the one that produces the idea of necessity.

In general, Hume deliberately says nothing about the causes of our impressions—his theory of the mind simply starts with them.[13] So in general he ignores the question of why some particular impression is said to be an impression of X. But in the case of necessity he does not simply ignore the question, he is precluded from answering it, since he cannot say that its being an impression of necessity consists in its being an impression derived from an instance in which necessity is exhibited. There are no such instances. So the impression and the idea of necessity simply live off each other. The idea is known to be an idea of necessity only because it is derived from an impression of necessity, and the impression is known to be an impression of necessity only because it gives rise to the idea of necessity.

In the *Treatise* Hume tries to give what he calls 'a precise definition of cause and effect' (p. 169), and in fact he gives two different 'definitions'.

> We may define a CAUSE to be 'An object precedent and contiguous to another, and where all the objects resembling the former are plac'd in like relations of precedency and contiguity to those objects, that resemble the latter.' (p. 170)

This is a 'definition' of causality 'as a philosophical relation'. It describes all the objective relations that hold between the things we designate as causes and effects.

Two things are related by what Hume calls a 'philosophical' relation if any relational statement at all is true of them. So causality is a 'philosophical' relation. All relations are 'philosophical' relations. But according to Hume there are also some 'natural' relations between things. One thing is 'naturally' related to another if the thought of the first naturally leads the mind to the thought of the other. If we see no obvious connection between two things, e.g. my raising my arm now in California and the death of a particular man in Abyssinia 33,118 years ago, we are likely to say 'There is no relation at all between those two events.' We would then be using 'relation' in something like the sense of 'natural relation'. Of course there are many 'philosophical' relations between those two events—spatial and temporal relations, for example. What we mean when we say there is no 'natural' relation between them is that the thought of one of them, if we had it, would not naturally lead to the thought of the other. Things that resemble each other, or are contiguous with each other, or are related causally, are 'naturally' related, according to Hume. That is to say that the thought of one thing naturally leads the mind to the thought of something resembling it, contiguous with it, or causally related to it. He usually expresses this by saying that resemblance, contiguity and causality are both natural and philosophical relations. They are the only relations that have this dual status.

As a natural relation, then, causality can be 'defined' thus:

A CAUSE is an object precedent and contiguous to another,
and so united with it, that the idea of the one determines
the mind to form the idea of the other, and the impression
of the one to form a more lively idea of the other. (p. 170)

It is quite clear that these two 'definitions' are not equivalent, and that neither one implies the other, and yet they purport to 'define' the very same notion by 'presenting a different view of the same object' (p. 170). How can that be? Not more than one of them could be correct as a definition.[14]

Confusion, but perhaps not obscurity, can be avoided if we see that neither of them, strictly speaking, is a definition, or is intended by Hume to be an equivalence which expresses the full and precise *meaning* of 'X causes Y'. In the *Treatise* he expresses reservations about the adequacy of either 'definition', and in the *Enquiry* he explicitly confesses that 'it is impossible to give any just definition of cause, except what is drawn from something extraneous and foreign to it' (*F*, p. 76), although in that later book he nevertheless offers what are in effect the same two 'definitions' once again (*E*, pp. 76-7).

But even if neither is an adequate definition, or is intended to be, I think we can understand why Hume puts them forward, and why he offers two different accounts. The relation between them is something like this. Any events or objects observed to fulfil the conditions of the first 'definition' are such that they will fulfil the conditions of the second 'definition' also. That is to say that an observed constant conjunction between As and Bs establishes a 'union in the imagination' such that the thought of an A naturally leads the mind to the thought of a B. That is just a fundamental, but contingent, principle of the human mind.

Furthermore, things could fulfil the conditions of the first 'definition' even if there were no minds at all, or if minds were very different from the way they actually are. The existence and precise nature of minds is irrelevant to the question whether members of one class of things are regularly followed by members of another class. But it is only because there are minds that any things at all fulfil the conditions of the second 'definition', and it is only because those minds are the way they are that things fulfil the conditions of the second 'definition' whenever they are observed to fulfil the conditions of the first. Only if there are minds will there be ideas of those things, and only if those minds are like ours will the idea of a member of one of those classes naturally give rise to an idea of a member of the other. And Hume thinks he has shown that it is only because things fulfil the conditions of the second 'definition' that any things in the world are thought to be related *causally* or *necessarily* at all. We get the idea of necessary connection only because of the passage of the mind from the thought of something to the thought of its 'usual attendant'. That is perhaps why he feels constrained to include something like the second 'definition' in any attempt to characterize our idea of causality. It is only because causality is in fact a 'natural' relation that we ever manage to get the idea of it at all. And that is a very important part of Hume's theory.

Since it is a contingent fact that we get the idea of necessity in the way we do, or that we get it at all, Hume's account of the origin of that idea leaves open the possibility of there being people with minds very like ours who do not have the idea of necessity at all.[15] They might be such that, although they can observe constant conjunctions between As and Bs, and thus acquire a 'union in the imagination' between As and Bs, so that the thought of an A naturally leads the mind to the thought of a B, that transition of the mind does not actually give them an idea of, and thus a belief in, a necessary connection between As and Bs. If there could be such people, they would have all the same beliefs about the course of their actual experience as we would have, and they could hold those beliefs with the same degrees of certainty as we do. In those respects they would be just like us. But we have an idea of necessity which, by hypothesis, they lack. They do not believe, as we do, that a B *must* occur, or that given an A a B must occur, but only that a B *will* occur, or that if an A occurs a B will occur.

Such people could observe and then come to believe that certain things fulfil the conditions of Hume's first 'definition' of causality. But by hypothesis they do not believe everything we believe when we believe that two events are causally or necessarily connected, because they lack the idea of necessity. Therefore there is a sense in which what they believe does not fully match what we believe when we believe that two events are causally connected. But since what they believe is fully expressed in the conditions of Hume's 'definition' of causality as a 'philosophical' relation, it follows that what *we* believe when we believe that two events are causally connected is not fully captured by that 'definition'. We believe something more. That 'definition' does not completely express *what* we ascribe to the relation between two events we regard as being causally related. But Hume feels constrained to include something like the first 'definition' in an attempt to characterize our idea of causality because it expresses all the objective relations that actually hold between events we regard as being causally related. That is to say, necessity is not something that 'resides' in the objects, or in the relations between them. And that also is a very important part of Hume's theory.

But if the 'definition' of causality as a 'philosophical' relation does not quite capture all that we ascribe to the relation between events we regard as causally connected, can we say that the second 'definition' does capture it? I have argued that we cannot, since that would be to accept subjectivism or psychologism. On that view, when we believe that the first billiard ball's striking the second caused the second one to move, we would believe no more than that the striking was contiguous and prior to the movement of the second ball, that the idea of the first ball's striking the second leads the mind to the idea of the second ball's moving, and that the impression of the one leads the mind to a belief in the other. And, except for the talk of contiguity and priority, that is all about happenings in our own minds. It is not a belief about any apparently puzzling relations between events in the world. So the psychologistic interpretation would deny that we have the very belief whose origin Hume is trying to explain.

I have tried to suggest a way for Hume to avoid psychologism while saying as much as can coherently be said about necessity. Admittedly, there is not much to be said about what it *is*, and nothing Hume says can be taken as a strict definition of the notion, but that is as it should be for a simple idea all of whose potential *definienda* are 'nearly synonymous' with it. The two 'definitions' are intended to help us get as close to it as we can, but it is an idea that we cannot be given by

91

definition or explanation at all. All that can be said is that we either have it or we don't, and that we get it only after having the appropriate kind of experience. I think that is what Hume is responding to when he acknowledges that any putative definition of causality will have to be 'drawn from something extraneous and foreign to it' (*E*, p. 76).

A great many objections have been made over the years to Hume's account of causality and the inference from the observed to the unobserved, and I want briefly to mention a couple that bring out something interesting and important about Hume's theory. I have argued that that theory is itself causal; it is a causal explanation of how and why we come to think of things in our experience as causally connected.

It might be objected that that puts Hume, like all sceptics, in an especially embarrassing position. He has claimed that, since we have no reason to believe anything about the unobserved, we have no reason to believe in the existence of any causal connections between things. But if that is so, then in particular we have no reason to believe Hume's causal theory about the origin of our beliefs in causality or in the unobserved.[16] The sceptic cannot have his cake and eat it too.

I think Hume would not be bothered by this objection. He holds the theory he does because of what he has observed in human behaviour. He finds that whenever someone has observed a constant conjunction between two kinds of things, and has an impression of a thing of one of those kinds, then he gets a belief in the existence of something of the other kind. In other words, Hume claims to have observed a constant conjunction between two mental phenomena: (C) the occurrence of an impression of an A in a mind that has already observed a constant conjunction between As and Bs, and (E) that mind's getting a belief that a B must occur. Whether or not such a conjunction holds in human minds is a straightforward matter of observable fact. The objection to Hume presumably does not deny that fact. It says only that, on Hume's own sceptical grounds, those 'data' give us no reason to believe Hume's theory to the effect that (C) causes (E). That goes beyond the 'data', and for Hume no inference from the observed to the unobserved is reasonable.

But if Hume's theory is true, then anyone who agrees that there is in fact a constant conjunction between phenomena (C) and (E) will come to believe Hume's theory. That theory says that when we have found a constant conjunction between two sorts of phenomena (C) and (E), we will inevitably believe that phenomena of the (C) sort are the causes of phenomena of the (E) sort. So the objection comes to nothing more than a kind of pedantic bad faith. The critic believes the theory while trying to condemn it as unjustified.

This is a comfortable position for a theorist to be in. If any one objects that although the 'data' are as he says they are, still they give no reason to believe the theory, the theory predicts that the objector, granting what he has granted, will in fact come to believe the theory. His objection is in that sense idle. If the theory is true, its being open to sceptical objections will have no effect at all on its being accepted by everyone who has made the observations on which it is based. So Hume's sceptical arguments do not prevent him from pursuing the science of man. That is just Hume's point about scepticism. Although there is a clear sense in which it is true, and its being true is important, its truth does not and could not prevent anyone from doing what he naturally and unquestioningly does. I have tried to show that Hume's scepticism has a quite different aim.

Hume begins his discussion of causality by distinguishing causality from what I called 'mere coincidence'. Two events can be related by contiguity and temporal priority without being thought of as causally connected. But when we have observed a number of events of the same kinds and found them to be constantly conjoined, he says we will come to believe that they are related causally. The repeated observation of similar phenomena precludes our thinking of them as occurring together merely coincidentally.

Is that an accurate description of our thought about causality? This is to raise the question whether the 'data' actually are as Hume claims. Do we in fact think it is impossible for a recurring pattern of phenomena—events of one kind constantly happening contiguous with and just after events of another kind—to continue for all time, but merely coincidentally? Hume's theory implies that any such pattern we observed would lead us to believe that the phenomena were causally connected, and so it would be impossible for us to see it as merely coincidental. We could never believe in 'historical accidents on the cosmic scale' (Kneale (2), p. 229). But surely we acknowledge such 'accidents' as at least a possibility. Of course, any correlation we found to hold for a long time under varied circumstances would lead us to suspect that there was a causal connection of some sort in the offing, but after repeated failure to find any connection mightn't we suspect that the correlation is merely accidental? On Hume's theory we could not. We would inevitably be led to believe there is a causal connection.

Hume's central empirical claim, from which this controversial implication springs, is that observed constant conjunctions always lead us to generalize from those observed conjunctions onto the unobserved, or always lead us to believe that things of the two conjoined sorts are causally connected. But that does not seem to be true. In fact, if Hume's theory as it stands were true and complete, then we would have no expectations at all—or what comes to the same thing, we would expect everything. That is because one and the same correlation between two sorts of things can lead to conflicting, even contradictory, expectations. The argument is due to Nelson Goodman (Goodman (1), pp. 74–83).[17]

After we have observed a number of emeralds and found each of them to be green, Hume says we would be led to believe that the next emerald we observe will be green, or perhaps even that all emeralds are green. And the only thing that leads us to that expectation is the observed constant conjunction. Now let us define a new predicate 'grue' as follows: X is grue if and only if either X is first observed before 2000 A.D. and X is green, or X is not first observed before 2000 A.D. and X is blue. Obviously, every emerald observed so far has been grue. Hume's theory predicts that, given the observed constant conjunction between being an emerald and being grue, we will come to believe that the next, or perhaps every, emerald is grue. But there is no doubt that we do not get that expectation in those circumstances, especially if we are examining emeralds on the eve of 2000 A.D. Hume says nothing about why we do not get it. His theory, in the absence of further qualifications, implies that we would.

This is not just an example of our getting two incompatible expectations when some of our evidence points towards one conclusion and some of it points towards another. For example, we might think that a murder suspect would have benefited greatly from his alleged victim's death, so he probably did it, but on the other hand, he spent the weekend in Milwaukee, so he probably did not. We have conflicting bits of evidence. In the case of 'grue' and 'green', however, the very same objects lead to two incompatible expectations if Hume's theory is applied equally to both. If our observation of emeralds can lead us to expect both that the next one will be green and that it will be blue, then it is easy to see that the same observations could be shown to lead us to expect anything at all, and therefore everything. We need only introduce a new predicate with something even more bizarre in the place of 'blue' in the definition of 'grue', and then by applying Hume's theory it would follow that we would get any bizarre expectation that can be mentioned.

The key point in this criticism, and one that Hume says nothing about, is that a prediction based on a number of instances described as belonging to a certain class can conflict with predictions based on those very same individuals described as belonging to another class. The way the individual events are described or classified is crucial. We do get the belief that the next emerald will be green; we do not get the belief that it will be blue. So what distinguishes those correlations we do generalize into the future from those we do not must have something to do with the terms or classes under which the instances in question are described. This is enough to show that not just any constant conjunction is sufficient to make us expect a member of the second class, given an impression of a member of the first.

This suggests a possible line of defence for Hume. He always speaks of our getting expectations from *observed* constant conjunctions. Obviously, the mere existence of a constant conjunction would not give us any beliefs if we were not aware of it. If we are the sorts of beings who perceive the world in terms of classes or kinds like 'green' rather than 'grue', that would help explain our generalizing into the future in terms of the former, but not the latter, predicate. There is no doubt that, in some sense, 'green' is a natural predicate for us in a way that 'grue' is not, although of course we understand both of them. So the real difficulty that now arises is what can be said about the difference we all recognize between those two types of predicates. In what sense, and why, does 'green' stand for a 'natural kind' for us, one on the basis of which we generalize into the future, whereas 'grue' does not? That is the fundamental question to which this profound criticism of Hume inevitably leads.

It is not that Hume is completely wrong in his account of the origin of our beliefs in the unobserved, but only that what he says, even if correct, cannot be the whole story. I have tried to suggest what more is needed, but I have no idea how the distinction between 'good' and 'bad' predicates is to be drawn. That is the problem Nelson Goodman has called 'the new riddle of induction' (Goodman (1), p. 80). It is a problem in the naturalistic spirit of Hume, but an adequate solution would inevitably lead far beyond the strict confines of his theory of ideas. That is not the least of the considerations in favour of pursuing that line of investigation.

V

The Continued and Distinct Existence of Bodies

With too much knowledge for the Sceptic side,
With too much weakness for the Stoic's pride,

According to Hume, our beliefs in the unobserved are not restricted to beliefs about what *experiences* we will have in the future. We also believe in the existence of bodies; and that is not just a belief about the course of our experience. Philosophers have been especially interested in the epistemic credentials of what they call our belief in the 'external world', but Hume does not concern himself with the truth or reasonableness of that belief at all. He does not begin by asking whether there are bodies or not, or whether we know or reasonably believe that there are. As a scientist of man, he asks why we have the belief, or how we come to have it. 'What causes induce us to believe in the existence of body?' (p. 187). Man, not bodies, is his primary concern.

The question whether there are any bodies or not is perfectly idle; Hume thinks ''tis in vain' to ask it. He might have said the same thing about the question whether a particular billiard ball will move, asked when we have observed a constant conjunction between billiard balls being struck and their moving, and are currently observing a ball about to be struck in normal circumstances. We cannot help believing that it will move, so any alleged 'argument' to show that it will not move could not possibly carry any conviction. The same is true of the question of the existence of bodies. Whether or not to believe in bodies is not something that has been left to our choice; it is 'an affair of too great importance to be trusted to our uncertain reasonings and speculations' (p. 187), so asking the question with the aim of determining what to believe is idle.

Although Hume is not primarily concerned to establish or defend the startling sceptical conclusion that we do not know or have any reason to believe that there is an 'external world', he is very interested in that sceptical conclusion and in the source of its obvious appeal. He sees the belief in bodies as a natural human phenomenon that the science of man should be able to explain. His attempt to explain it in the *Treatise* is very complicated and difficult, and, I think, unsuccessful. Almost all the details, and even the very question itself, are dropped without a trace from the *Enquiry*. But the *Enquiry* does carry over from the *Treatise* Hume's examination of the philosophical concern with the external world, and of the philosophical scepticism that is its inevitable consequence. He sees them both as in certain respects 'natural' human phenomena. Human beings cannot help philosophizing, and when they reflect on their relation to the world around them Hume thinks they cannot avoid a completely sceptical conclusion. That too is something the science of man should be able to explain. Hume does not have as elaborate a 'pathology' of philosophy as Kant was to develop,[1] but the little he says on the subject does help to illuminate his attitude towards philosophical scepticism and its implications, if any, for our ordinary beliefs and reasonings in everyday life.

But in the *Treatise* Hume thinks he can actually explain the origin of our belief in a world of enduring bodies. It is a belief in both the *continued* and the *distinct* existence of things. We believe that things continue to exist when they are not being perceived, and that they exist independently of their being perceived by anyone.[2] Since we have such a belief, we must have an idea of an enduring, independent world, and so there must be some intelligible way in which we come to have that idea and that belief. The general structure of Hume's explanation of its origin is similar to that of his account of the origin of the idea of necessary connection. We must get the idea and the belief either from the senses, or from reason, or from the imagination. He shows that they cannot arise from the first two, so the imagination wins by default.

The senses are certainly necessary for our getting the idea (as they are for getting any ideas), but they alone are not enough. Obviously, we cannot get the idea of *continued* existence directly from the senses, since that would require that we perceive something continuing to exist when it is not being perceived. So the senses alone can give us at most the idea of *distinct* existence.

In order to get that idea directly from the senses we would have to perceive something distinct from ourselves, and that would require that we be aware of something, aware of ourselves, and aware of the distinctness of the two. But can we ever be aware of ourselves? Do we even understand what the self is? Hume thinks the common man and perhaps everybody else as well, has no answer to this abstruse metaphysical question, but if we ignore it for the moment and take 'ourselves' to be our bodies, it might seem easy to get an impression of something distinct from our ourselves. For example, I now have an impression of my hand and of the desk beyond it and distinct from it. But this will not do, because:

> properly speaking, 'tis not our body we perceive, when we regard our limbs and members, but certain impressions, which enter by the senses; so that the ascribing a real and corporeal existence to these impressions, or to their objects, is an act of the mind as difficult to explain, as that which we examine at present. (p. 191)

All we are ever aware of in perception are our impressions, and to say that we perceive something distinct from our limbs and members is already to ascribe external existence to those limbs and members. But the origin of the idea of external existence is just what we are trying to explain. It is not simply 'read off' our impressions.

There is another quite general argument for this conclusion. All the impressions of the senses are usually divided into three classes. There are impressions of (a) figure, bulk, motion and solidity of bodies ('primary qualities'); (b) colours, sounds, smells, tastes, heat and cold ('secondary qualities'); and (c) pains and pleasures produced by the application of objects to our bodies. We all think that the qualities listed under (a) have distinct and continued existence; the vulgar, or non-philosophical, also think those in (b) continue to exist unperceived; but nobody thinks that the pains and pleasures we feel when affected by objects really exist in the objects themselves. It is not a question of whether we are right or wrong in our ascriptions. Hume's point is only that we do distinguish between these various classes of impressions, and so the distinctions are not made on the basis of the senses alone. All these classes of impressions are on a par *as perceptions*. They are all we are aware of by means of the senses alone, so we must be relying on something else when we attribute continued and distinct existence only to some, but not to all, of them.

Nor is reason the source of the idea of and belief in the continued and distinct existence of objects. Certainly the elaborate arguments concocted by philosophers in support of that belief are not operative on the majority of mankind; they have never heard of them. In fact, the vulgar think that what continue to exist independently of the mind are the very same things that they see and feel,[3] so there is no question of their making an inference from the one to the other. And if we follow the philosopher in distinguishing perceptions from the objects they are perceptions of, we find that there is no way of reasoning from the undoubted existence of the perceptions to the objects they 'represent'. We can infer from one thing to another only by means of the relation of cause and effect. And that requires that we observe a constant conjunction between two sorts of things. But since only perceptions are ever present to the mind, we can never observe a conjunction between perceptions and objects that are not perceptions. So we could never arrive by reasoning at the belief that objects continue to exist independently of being perceived.

Only the imagination is left. There must be some features of our experience which interact with certain features of the mind or imagination to produce the belief in continued and distinct existence. We have seen that we do not attribute such existence to everything we perceive. The search for the distinction between the situations in which we make such attributions and those in which we do not is analogous to the search for the circumstances in which we come to believe that two events are causally connected. Hume tries to identify the occasions on which we come to attribute continued and distinct existence to something, and then to explain how the belief actually arises on those occasions.

Descartes and Berkeley thought we tend to believe in independently existing objects because some impressions come to us independently of our will. We find some perceptions 'imposed' upon us, whether we want them or not—if I turn my head in a certain direction with my eyes open, I have no choice but to get certain perceptions—and so we naturally take those perceptions to represent something outside ourselves. This was the crucial step in Descartes' defence of his belief in the external world. But Hume easily shows that it is not enough. Pains and pleasures come to us independently of our will, but we do not suppose that they reside in external objects. Not everything that 'imposes' itself upon us, or everything that 'strikes the mind with greater force and violence' leads us to believe in the continued and distinct existence of something. Only some of our impressions have that effect.

Hume finds that those series of impressions that lead us to believe in the continuous, independent existence of something exhibit one or the other of two distinct observable features he calls 'constancy' and 'coherence'. There is a certain uniformity, or uniformity of recurrence, in our experience.

> Those mountains, and houses, and trees, which lie at present
> under my eye, have always appear'd to me in the same order;
> and when I lose sight of them by shutting my eyes or turning
> my head, I soon after find them return upon me without the
> least alteration. My bed and table, my books and papers,
> present themselves in the same uniform manner, and change not
> upon account of any interruption in my seeing or perceiving
> them. This is the case with all the impressions, whose

objects are supposed to have an external existence; and is the case with no other impressions, whether gentle or violent, voluntary or involuntary. (pp. 194–5)

But this 'constancy' shades off by degrees into 'coherence'. Many familiar objects change slightly during the intervals when they are not perceived, but still we suppose that something has remained in existence the whole time.

When I return to my chamber after an hour's absence, I
find not my fire in the same situation, in which I left
it: But then I am accustom'd in other instances to see a
like alteration produc'd in a like time, whether I am present
or absent, near or remote. This coherence, therefore, in their
changes is one of the characteristics of external objects, as
well as their constancy. (p. 195)

There is no doubt that Hume here identifies important features of our experience of an objective world, but in order to do the job required of them 'constancy' and 'coherence' must be much more precisely characterized. He is trying to explain the origin in the mind of the idea of the continued and distinct existence of objects, so those features of our experience that lead us to get that idea must be features that can be recognized or can affect us without our having the idea of continued and distinct existence in the first place. Hume is not careful on this point. He describes constancy and coherence in terms of objects—mountains, trees, books and papers—that return to him after an interval in his perception of them. But strictly speaking what he is calling 'constancy' and 'coherence' must be directly observable features of series of impressions themselves, not of the objects we suppose to exist unperceived. We do not simply 'find' that certain enduring objects return to us in our experience—that would be to 'find' the continued and distinct existence of objects within our experience itself. Rather, it is on the basis of some features we do find in our experience that we then come to believe in such objects. Those observable features are what Hume misleadingly calls 'constancy' and 'coherence', but according to the explanation he gives true constancy and coherence *of objects* is something we impose on our experience in virtue of believing in an enduring objective world.

Since Hume admits that 'coherence' plays only a supplementary role—it 'gives us a notion of a much greater regularity among objects, than what they have when we look no farther than our senses' (p. 198)—I will concentrate on the efficacy of that feature he calls 'constancy'.[4] It is what is responsible for our getting the belief in the continued and distinct existence of objects in the first place. As Hume explains it, the perception of the sun or moon is sometimes interrupted, but it often returns to us exactly as it was before, and we are therefore led to take these different perceptions to be 'individually the same' (p. 199). But we are also aware of the interruption, and we see that it is contrary to the 'perfect identity' of the different perceptions. This throws us into a conflict from which the mind naturally seeks relief; it is pulled in two different directions. On the one hand, the perceptions seem the same, but on the other, they are obviously different, since there is an interruption. We resolve the conflict by 'supposing that these interrupted perceptions are connected by a real existence, of which we are insensible' (p. 199). This supposition gains added force and vivacity from the memory of the interrupted perceptions, and from the propensity we have to think of them as the same. Having this conception with a high degree of force and vivacity is just what it is to believe in the continued existence of body, and so the origin of that belief is accounted for.

This is a very brief statement of an extremely complicated explanation. The 'constancy' in our experience puts the mind into a certain conflict or contradiction, and the belief in the continued and distinct existence of objects serves to resolve the conflict. Put strictly in terms of the theory of ideas, 'constancy' might be described as follows. When we have an *un*interrupted series of impressions of the sun, our perceptual experience is like this:

(1) AAAAAAAAAAAAAAAAAAAA

But if we turn our head or close our eyes for a few seconds in the middle our experience would look like this:

(2) AAAAAAAAABBBAAAAAAAAA

And with still more variety in our lives experience would be much more complex. For example:

(3) AAAAABBBBCCCCDDDDEEEEFFAAAAA

Situation (2) is what Hume has in mind when he talks of 'constancy'. He says that in situation (2) we suppose the two A-perceptions on either side of the Bs to be 'individually the same' even though there is an obvious interval between them which is filled with different perceptions. Despite the interval, we are inclined to ascribe to them a 'perfect identity' (p. 199). What is the source of that inclination? He says it is our tendency to confuse situations like (2) with situations like (1), where there is no interruption. An interrupted series of exactly similar impressions places the mind in almost the same disposition as an uninterrupted series of exactly similar impressions— especially if the interruption is short. And it is a fundamental fact about the human mind 'that whatever ideas place the mind in the same disposition or in similar ones, are very apt to be confounded' (p. 203). That is just what happens here.

But confounding (2) with (1) does not merely lead us to believe that there is no difference between (2) and (1). Confounding or not distinguishing between the two situations also makes us think the two A-perceptions on each side of the interruption in (2) are 'individually the same'. According to Hume, that happens only because we confuse (2) with (1) and we take situation (1) to be 'a continu'd view of the same object'. That is how our confusing (2) with (1) leads us to think of (2) as a 'continu'd view of the same object'. We tend to think we are perceiving the same thing as we were before the interruption. And that is one side of the conflict the mind finds itself thrown into.

Of course, the passage of the mind along an interrupted series of impressions is *not* exactly the same as its passage along an uninterrupted series. It only seems to be. We are mistaken in thinking that the two kinds of series have exactly the same effects on us, but Hume thinks the mistake is easily made because the two sorts of effects are very similar. The transition in (2) is 'almost the same disposition of mind' (p. 204) as that in (1), so it is very natural for us to confound them. Not only do we take the resembling, but different, perceptions to be the same, we also take the resembling, but different, acts of the mind in the two cases to be of the same sort.

Despite our strong inclination to regard (2) as a 'continu'd view of the same object', we cannot ignore or forget the obvious interruption in the middle of it. So we tend to think it cannot be the same thing. And that is the other side of the conflict the mind finds itself thrown into.

> The smooth passage of the imagination along the ideas of
> the resembling perceptions makes us ascribe to them a perfect
> identity. The interrupted manner of their appearance makes
> us consider them as so many resembling, but still distinct
> beings, which appear after certain intervals. (p. 205)

The 'act of the mind' at the heart of this conflict is that of confusing or confounding two distinct but similar perceptual situations. We wrongly take an interrupted series of resembling impressions to be just like an uninterrupted series, and thus to be a 'continu'd view of the same object' or a case of 'perfect identity'. But in order to make that mistake we would already have to have the idea of 'the same object' or 'perfect identity'. We must understand what it is for a thing existing at one time to be identical with itself existing at another. How do we get that idea in the first place?

According to Hume, we do not get it directly from the senses. Our experience is in fact nothing but a sequence of momentary, internal impressions, so even when we have an uninterrupted series of exactly similar impressions we are not actually surveying an identical object.

Therefore, in order to be in a position to make the mistake that produces the conflict we must first make the earlier mistake of taking an uninterrupted series of exactly similar impressions to be a 'continu'd view of the same object'. We do so only by means of a 'fiction of the imagination' (p. 201).

The identity of an object with itself is not the same as mere unity, Hume says, since identity involves time. The idea of identity is a combination of the ideas of unity and of multiplicity; it is the idea of *one* object's existing at *several* different times. If we think of one object existing at just one instant we have only the idea of unity. If we think of a different object existing at each different instant we have nothing but the idea of a multiplicity of objects, a different object for each different moment. But if, 'conceiving first one moment, along with the object then existent, [we] imagine afterwards a change in the time without any *variation* or *interruption* in the object' (p. 201), we get the idea of one thing remaining in existence through several different moments of time. We only 'imagine' or 'suppose' that the object remains invariable and uninterrupted. There is nothing in our experience that actually answers to that idea, so the idea of identity is nothing more than a 'fiction of the imagination'.

It is again because of the disposition of the mind in receiving its impressions that we are led to this 'fiction'. During an uninterrupted series of exactly similar perceptions the mind, by a kind of inertia, slides so easily from one moment to another that 'we suppose the change to lie only in the time' (p. 203). No 'different direction of the spirits' is required in order for the series to continue, and so we do not distinguish among the various members of the series. Of course, there is not any single, identical perception which does remain in existence. If there were, we could get the idea of identity directly from the senses, just from having that perception, and there would be nothing 'fictitious' about the idea of identity at all. Rather, we do not *notice* any variation or interruption in the series. 'The passage from one moment to another is scarce felt', and so we mistakenly 'suppose' the change to lie only in the time and not in the perceptions themselves. We thereby take the uninterrupted series to be a 'continu'd view of the same object'.

It is difficult, to say the least, to see how this explains how we originally get the idea of the identity of an object through time. We get it, Hume says, by 'conceiving' of a moment of time and an object existent at that time, and then 'imagining' a change in the time without any variation or interruption in the object. But how are we able to 'imagine' such a thing unless we already have the idea of the invariableness and uninterruptedness of an object through time?

Imagining or conceiving of X requires that one already have the idea of X; we cannot think of something of which we have no idea. In particular, therefore, we could not 'imagine . . . a change in the time without any *variation* or *interruption* in the object' unless we already had the idea of the invariableness and uninterruptedness of an object. But that is just the idea of identity for Hume. It follows that we could not perform that act of the mind that is said to produce the idea of identity in us unless we already had the idea of identity to begin with. Hume seems to 'explain' our acquisition of the idea only on the assumption that we already have it, and so he does not explain it at all. But without an explanation of the source of the idea of identity his explanation of the origin of the idea of continued and distinct existence cannot get off the ground. He would not have explained how we get into the conflict which the idea of continued existence is intended to resolve. But even if he had, his account would still run into difficulties.

If we had the idea of identity, and thus the idea of a 'continu'd view of the same object', and if the imagination had the properties Hume ascribes to it, then we would presumably get into the conflict he mentions. We would be inclined both to attribute identity to the resembling perceptions and to deny that identity because of the interruption.

> . . . there being here an opposition betwixt the notion of the identity of resembling perceptions, and the interruption of their appearance, the mind must be uneasy in that situation, and will naturally seek relief from the uneasiness. Since the uneasiness arises from the opposition of two contrary principles, it must look for relief by sacrificing the one to the other. But as the smooth passage of our thought along our resembling perceptions makes us ascribe to them an identity, we can never without reluctance yield up that opinion. We must, therefore, turn to the other side, and suppose that our perceptions are no longer interrupted, but preserve a continu'd as well as an invariable existence, and are by that means entirely the same. But here the interruptions in the appearance of these perceptions are so long and frequent, that 'tis impossible to overlook them; (p. 206)

This conflict or uneasiness is naturally intolerable to the imagination, and:

> In order to free ourselves from this difficulty, we disguise, as much as possible, the interruption, or rather remove it entirely, by supposing that these interrupted perceptions are connected by a real existence, of which we are insensible. (p. 199)

This 'supposition' or 'fiction' saves the appearances while resolving the conflict. Although the notion of continued existence is a 'fiction', it is something we need to cure the perplexity the mind would inevitably find itself in without it.

It is very important to notice that on this account we get the idea of identity and hence get into the perplexity in the first place only because we also indulge in another kind of 'fiction', or at least because we fail to realize certain facts about the nature of perception. In actual fact, according to Hume, all we ever perceive are perceptions, which are 'internal and perishing existences, and appear as such' (p. 194), but if we realized that fact and kept it firmly in mind we would never be led to the idea of identity or to a belief in continued and distinct existence. We would have to be content simply to form beliefs about the passing show of our 'momentary and fleeting' perceptions. This is something Hume emphasizes more than once. He insists that although philosophers distinguish their 'internal and perishing' perceptions from the objects those perceptions represent or are perceptions of, the vulgar ('that is, all of us at one time or another' (p. 205)) 'confound perceptions and objects, and attribute a distinct and continu'd existence to the very things they feel or see' (p. 193). They 'suppose their perceptions to be their only objects, and never think of a double existence internal and external, representing and represented' (p. 205). And it is the ordinary, non-philosophical belief in a world of external objects that Hume is trying to explain.

> Whoever wou'd explain the origin of the *common* opinion
> concerning the continu'd and distinct existence of body, must
> take the mind in its *common* situation, and must proceed
> upon the supposition, that our perceptions are our only
> objects, and continue to exist even when they are not
> perceiv'd. Tho' this opinion be false, 'tis the most
> natural of any, and has alone any primary recommendation
> to the fancy. (p. 213)

The question arises whether Hume can give a coherent description of that '*common* situation' while still explaining the source of the idea of continued and distinct existence. Precisely what position does he think the vulgar are in, and does he explain how they get there?

He says that the vulgar 'take their perceptions to be their only objects, and suppose, that the very being, which is intimately present to the mind, is the real body or material existence' (p. 206). This means at least that the vulgar think they perceive chairs and tables, trees and stones, and that they think the very things they see and feel remain in existence when not perceived. This in itself does not imply that they hold the philosophical thesis that the things they perceive are 'internal and perishing' existences. Hume says, paradoxically, that the vulgar 'suppose their perceptions to be their only objects' because for him perceptions are in fact the objects of perceiving, and are directly present to the mind. But if that is taken to imply that the vulgar believe the philosophical thesis that all they ever perceive are perceptions which are dependent upon the mind, then Hume would seem to be precluded on his own grounds from explaining the origin of the belief in the continued and distinct existence. He explicitly argues that if they believed that thesis from the outset they would never arrive at that belief at all.

So Hume would seem to be saying only that the vulgar are originally in the position of making no distinction between perceptions and enduring objects. It is not that they have the philosophical concept of a perception, and then apply it to trees, stones and other objects, but simply that they think they see and feel trees and stones and other objects, and do not think of them as 'perceptions' in the philosophical sense at all. But what does that come to? Thinking we see and feel trees and stones presumably involves thinking that the very things we perceive continue to exist unperceived. So our being in the vulgar position, so characterized, would require that we already have the idea of continued, unperceived existence. We need that idea in order to have that belief. If Hume is to explain the origin of that idea in minds that originally lack it, he must show how it arises in the vulgar consciousness, but on the present suggestion that consciousness would contain the idea already. He provides no description of the state of the vulgar consciousness before the acquisition of the idea of continued and distinct existence, out of which that idea could naturally arise. What he needs is a description of the way the vulgar take things to be that attributes to them neither a belief in the continued and distinct existence of what they perceive nor the philosophical view that all they perceive are 'internal and perishing existences'. But rather than providing such a description Hume tends on the contrary to ascribe to the vulgar *both* of those beliefs, thus attributing to them an explicit inconsistency and also leaving the origin of the belief in continued and distinct existence unexplained. No account which implies that the vulgar have that belief from the outset can explain how they originally come to have it.

In an attempt to save the vulgar view from outright contradiction Hume is almost forced to attribute to them another highly sophisticated thesis about the nature of the mind, as well as the view that all they perceive are perceptions in the philosophical sense. Since the vulgar think that the very thing they perceive is 'the real body or material existence':

106

'Tis also certain, that this very perception or object is
suppos'd to have a continu'd and uninterrupted being, and
neither to be annihilated by our absence, nor to be brought
into existence by our presence. (pp. 206–7)

And it might look as if the vulgar are simply inconsistent in supposing
that a perception could be absent from a mind without being
annihilated. Hume tries to save them from contradiction by
distinguishing between the *existence* of a perception and its
appearance before the mind. The distinction is made possible by his
theory of the mind. Since every perception is distinguishable from
every other, there is no contradiction involved in supposing, of some
particular perception, that it exists separately from every other
perception which belongs to the same bundle. For a perception to be
perceived or felt is just for it to be present to a mind, but since
according to Hume a mind is nothing but a bundle or collection of
perceptions, it is possible for a perception to exist independently of any
mind, and therefore possible for it to exist unperceived. So there is
nothing to prevent the vulgar from believing in the unperceived
existence of the very things they see and feel. An interruption in the
appearance of a perception does not imply an interruption in its
existence, so the vulgar can account for the interruptions in their
experience by supposing that the very thing that is intermittently
present to the mind is nevertheless continuously in existence. At least,
according to Hume, there is no absurdity in that supposition.

Here Hume appears to be attributing to the vulgar a belief in his
philosophical theory of the mind and personal identity, whereas earlier
in the same section he points out that the question of the nature of
personal identity is so abstruse, and requires such profound
metaphysics to answer it, that it is clear that the vulgar have no very
fixed or determinate idea of self or person. He might be arguing only
that the idea of a perception existing independently of a mind is not in
fact contradictory, whatever the vulgar might happen to think about
it, so there is no actual inconsistency in their thinking that their very
perceptions continue to exist unperceived. He would then be showing,
in effect, that their view is, perhaps unknown to them, philosophically
perfectly respectable, and so he would disarm a potentially conclusive
objection to the vulgar view. But the threat of contradiction would
arise only if the vulgar already believed that what they perceive are
perceptions in the philosophical sense, and Hume thinks they could
never start from that belief and arrive at the idea of continued and
distinct existence. And if they lacked that belief there would be no
need to invoke the theory of mind on their behalf, and therefore no
need to ascribe to them any sophisticated philosophical theories at all.

But still, the origin of the idea of continued and distinct existence would not have been explained. It is not enough for Hume to show only that the vulgar position is free from contradiction. He must explain how we come to have the idea of continued and distinct existence in the first place. There seems little doubt that if we already had the idea of continued, unperceived existence, and we noticed the conflict in our experience that Hume describes, then it would be very natural for us to adopt the hypothesis that it was a case of continued, but unperceived, existence. That would be the most obvious and easiest way to accommodate all our inclinations on that occasion. Hume often speaks as if he wants to explain how we are led to adopt that 'hypothesis' on such occasions—what leads us to *'suppose that'* our perceptions continue to exist unperceived, how we can *'assent to'* that proposition, or how the mind *'forms such a conclusion'* (p. 206, my italics). But coming to have a certain belief on a particular occasion, once one already has the ideas that form the content of that belief, is much easier to explain than coming to have a certain very complicated idea in the first place. Acquiring a new idea cannot be explained as simply a matter of selecting, among a number of antecedently intelligible alternatives, the one that best squares with all the available data, since in acquiring a new idea we come to find something intelligible or to understand something that we did not understand before. Hume is aware in general that in accounting for the origin of a belief he must first explain the origin of the ideas of which that belief is composed, but in this case he tends to minimize the difference between the two tasks and to suggest that the origin of the idea is much less difficult to account for than in fact it seems to be.

This tendency also reveals itself in a curious tension in Hume's account.[5] He wants to emphasize that the belief in continued and distinct existence finds its source in the imagination, not the understanding; that it is not arrived at by reasoning from experience, but by the natural operation of certain primitive principles of the mind. That is characteristic of his general strategy throughout the science of man. The imagination is thought of as the home of the 'sensitive' or 'passionate', rather than the 'cogitative', part of our nature, but that contrast seems to be forgotten here. The 'acts of mind' that are said to occur in the imagination to produce the belief in continued existence have a very strong 'intellectual' or 'cognitive' flavour. The belief is represented in effect as an elaborate hypothesis we somehow think up in order to resolve a conflict in the mind. In fact, the idea of continued existence is said to come into the mind solely as a result of our 'feigning' or 'supposing' the continued existence of our perceptions. And Hume says nothing about how 'feigning' or 'supposing' something differs from believing it. We know that a belief requires an idea of what is believed to be true. How, if at all, is it possible to 'feign' or 'suppose' something of which one has no idea? In the absence of an answer Hume has done little towards explaining the origin of the idea of continued existence. His 'explanation' amounts to nothing more than the claim that we get the idea of the continued existence of bodies by feigning or supposing the existence of bodies that continue to exist when unperceived. That is how we resolve an otherwise inevitable conflict in the mind. Not only is that no explanation, it does not help Hume establish the dominance of the imagination over the understanding.

The fact that what Hume says so transparently fails to explain the origin of the idea of continued existence might make it plausible to suppose that he is not primarily concerned with the origin of the idea at all. H. H. Price has argued that Hume is not asking the 'straightforward question of Empirical Psychology' (Price (1), p. 13) he seems to be asking, but rather something like: *given what characteristics of sense-impressions do we assert material-object propositions?'* (Price (1), p. 15). According to Price, this is neither a psychological nor a causal question, but is about 'the meaning of material-object words and material-object sentences, and about the rules of their use'; it is a question belonging to 'the inquiry which is now called "philosophical analysis"' (Price (1), p. 15). And according to Price, Hume answers it by showing that we assert material-object propositions only when our sense-impressions exhibit constancy and coherence.

If that were Hume's aim, then almost the whole section of the *Treatise* entitled 'Of Scepticism With Regard to the Senses' would be superfluous. He points out in two short paragraphs that 'the opinion of the continu'd existence of body depends on the COHERENCE and CONSTANCY of certain impressions' (p. 195), but he does not leave it at that. He goes on for about fifteen more pages trying to explain 'after what manner these qualities give rise to so extraordinary an opinion' (p. 195). He wants to show precisely how those features of our experience operate on us to produce the idea of, and belief in, continued existence. This puts his discussion of continued existence on all fours with that of causality or necessary connection; in each case he is primarily interested in the causes and effects of various operations of the mind.

Furthermore, it is not clear how the question Price attributes to Hume is to be understood, if not causally. Hume thinks that the belief in continued and distinct existence cannot be supported by reason on the basis of experience, so the question *given what characteristics of sense-impressions do we assert material-object propositions?'* cannot be taken as asking what characteristics of our sense-experience *justify* us in asserting material-object propositions. Hume thinks nothing justifies us at all. But to take it as a question about what *leads* us to, or *makes* us, believe in the existence of body, is to take it as a causal question, or at least a quest for an explanation, after all. That is not to deny that Hume is concerned with what might be called 'the meaning of material-object words and material-object sentences'. He is asking about the origin of the idea of, and belief in, continued and distinct existence, and that is to ask how we come to understand and believe *any* material-object words or sentences at all, or how they come to have the meaning they have for us.

If Hume were not primarily concerned with the origin of the idea of continued existence, his treatment of this topic would not serve his general philosophical aims. He has a theory of human nature according to which every idea we ever have in our minds is ultimately derived from simple impressions by means of certain natural or primitive operations of the mind. The theory must therefore be able to explain how the idea of the continued existence of bodies ever gets into the mind of someone who originally lacks it. If any ideas were innate in the sense of being in our minds from birth, or being put there by God, and thus not derived from experience, that theory would be false. But even if the idea of continued and distinct existence were innate in that sense, it would still make sense to ask Price's question about when we assert material-object propositions, and to answer it in terms of constancy and coherence. Our experience could then be said to lead us to employ one of our innate ideas in making assertions on various occasions. Hume asks a question that is prior to Price's. He is committed to showing that the idea of continued and distinct existence is not innate, and that he can explain its presence in the mind completely naturalistically. So however inadequate his answer to the causal question might be, we must understand him to be asking precisely that question in the section of the *Treatise* called 'Of Scepticism With Regard to the Senses'.

In the *Enquiry* there is no attempt at all to explain the origin of the belief in the continued and distinct existence of objects. Rather, it is described as a 'universal and primary opinion of all men' to which they are carried 'by a natural instinct or prepossession'.

> It seems evident, that . . . without any reasoning, or even almost before the use of reason, we always suppose an external universe, which depends not on our perception, but would exist, though we and every sensible creature were absent or annihilated. Even the animal creation are governed by a like opinion, and preserve this belief of

external objects, in all their thoughts, designs, and
actions. (*E.,* p. 151)

The 'naturalness' of the vulgar belief is very important for Hume. It
provides an essential contrast to the contrived, artificial philosophical
distinction between perceptions and objects, and represents the only
source of whatever plausibility that philosophical view can muster. But
an emphasis on the primitive or original character of the belief leaves
little or no room for an explanation of its origin along the lines Hume
recommends for the science of man.

The view Hume attributes to the vulgar to the effect that the things
that continue to exist unperceived are the very perceptions that are
sometimes present to the mind does not hold up well if we subject it to
the slightest scrutiny. 'A very little reflection and philosophy' is
enough to convince us of its falsity. A number of very familiar facts
about perception, when we think about them even for a moment,
easily convince us that our perceptions 'are not possest of any
independent existence', but 'are dependent on our organs, and the
disposition of our nerves and animal spirits' (p. 211). For example, we
see double when we press one eye with a finger; the size things look
depends on their distance from us; the colours and other qualities they
appear to have change in 'sickness and distempers'; and so on. But if
our perceptions are not fully distinct from, or independent of, us, then
they cannot have a continued existence either. So the view that our
perceptions continue to exist independently of us must be
mistaken—it cannot withstand the slightest critical examination.

The 'experiments' that are said so easily to refute this position are
not very fully described. And the most they can be said to show is that
what we perceive on a particular occasion depends in part on the state
of our bodies and sense-organs. It of course does not follow from this
that what we perceive is a 'momentary', 'fleeting', 'internal and
perishing' thing which depends for its existence on the mind that
perceives it. But I pointed out at the outset that Hume never seriously
considers any evidence for or against the theory of ideas. He simply
takes it for granted that the familiar facts about perception must be
described in terms of that theory. It is a view philosophers easily and
naturally arrive at as soon as they reflect at all on the nature and objects
of perception.

Although philosophers conclude that their perceptions do not
remain in existence during interruptions in their existence, they do
think that *something* continues to exist in those intervals. This they call
an 'object', which has a continued, uninterrupted existence and
identity completely independently of its being perceived. So the
philosophical system placates both urges we inevitably feel when

reflecting on the nature of perception.

> The imagination tells us, that our resembling perceptions
> have a continu'd and uninterrupted existence, and are not
> annihilated by their absence. Reflection tells us, that even
> our resembling perceptions are interrupted in their existence,
> and different from each other. The contradiction betwixt
> these opinions we elude by a new fiction, which is conformable
> to the hypotheses both of reflection and fancy, by ascribing
> these contrary qualities to different existences; the *interruption*
> to perceptions, and the *continuance* to objects. (p. 215)

Thus the philosophical system feigns 'a double existence', and thereby claims to provide a more satisfactory resolution of the conflict the perceiving mind inevitably finds itself in.

Although he expresses little sympathy for this full-blown philosophical theory, Hume thinks it is the inevitable outcome of reflecting on our perception of the world, and he even tries to explain how and why it recommends itself to us. However 'monstrous' and artificial it might be, we are led to accept it only because of the natural and irresistible appeal of the vulgar position from which we all begin. Certainly we are not convinced of the philosophical theory solely by reasoning or reflecting on the facts of perception. Starting from the hypothesis that our perceptions are momentary, fleeting and the only things immediately present to our minds, we cannot reasonably infer the existence of something else they 'represent'. For Hume, any such inference would have to be based on an observed constant conjunction between perceptions and the things they represent, but since nothing but perceptions is ever present to the mind the required conjunction could never be observed.

If philosophers arrived at their theory directly by reasoning from familiar facts of perception alone, then, as soon as 'a little reflection and philosophy' had reminded them that 'the independent existence of our sensible perceptions is contrary to the plainest experience' (p. 210), one would expect them to conclude that there is no such thing as continued, unperceived existence. But they do not. They retain the notion and invent another kind of entity to attribute it to. Even in our most philosophical moments we cannot escape the force of our tendency to believe that something continues to exist unperceived. It is one of those 'opinions . . . we embrace by a kind of instinct or natural impulse, on account of their suitableness and conformity to the mind' (p. 214), so no amount of abstract metaphysical reasoning can dislodge it for more than a moment. The natural, primitive appeal of the vulgar position is too strong for the abstract reasonings behind the philosophical view.

Nature is obstinate, and will not quit the field, however
strongly attack'd by reason; and at the same time reason
is so clear in the point, that there is no possibility of
disguising her. Not being able to reconcile these two
enemies, we endeavour to set ourselves at ease as much as
possible, by successively granting to each whatever it demands,
and by feigning a double existence, where each may find
something, that has all the conditions it desires. (p. 215)

Without the natural and irresistible inclination to believe in continued
existence, the philosophical view would never have recommended
itself to anyone. That is what Hume means by saying that 'the
philosophical system acquires all its influence on the imagination from
the vulgar one' and 'has no primary recommendation to reason or the
imagination' (p. 213).

Although the philosophical view as it were lives off the vulgar,
Hume also thinks that, paradoxically, it contradicts that vulgar
position. If the philosophical theory is correct, he says, then the vulgar
are simply mistaken. They have false beliefs about what they perceive.
Now there is no doubt that the philosophical system contradicts the
thesis that our *perceptions* continue to exist independently of their
being perceived. That is what 'a little reflection and philosophy' about
the familiar facts of perception is supposed to show. But does that
prove the vulgar position to be mistaken? It would do so if the vulgar
are in the position of actually believing that what they perceive are
perceptions in the philosophical sense, and that those very things
continue to exist when unperceived. That is what the philosophical
system contradicts. And so again it seems as if Hume must be
attributing to the vulgar that sophisticated philosophical thesis about
perception that is said to be obvious to 'the plainest experience' after 'a
very little reflection and philosophy'.

And yet he also insists on the other hand that if the vulgar were in
that position they would never have arrived at the belief in continued
and distinct existence. This negative proposition might be difficult to
prove, but Hume is in no doubt about it, and he hurls his characteristic
challenge.

Let it be taken for granted, that our perceptions are broken, and
interrupted, and however like, are still different from each
other; and let any one upon this supposition shew why the
fancy, directly and immediately, proceeds to the belief of
another existence, resembling these perceptions in their nature,
but yet continu'd, and uninterrupted, and identical; and after

he has done this to my satisfaction, I promise to renounce
my present opinion. (pp. 212–13)

His confidence comes partly from the earlier point about the vulgar
source of the philosophical view. Anyone fully persuaded that our
perceptions have no continued or independent existence would find
no conflicts or tensions in his experience of the sort Hume describes.
So-called 'constancy' would be seen as simply a case of recurring
similarity. One would know that at all times one is perceiving nothing
more than 'momentary and fleeting' items in a constantly changing
show. The belief in continued and distinct existence is said to arise only
in order to resolve mental conflicts, and so with no conflicts to resolve it
would have 'no recommendation to the fancy'.

This suggests that if Hume has any hopes of explaining the origin of
the vulgar belief in continued and distinct existence, he must see the
vulgar as not committed to any philosophical thesis about the
'dependent' nature of our perceptions. And they would be in that
position if they simply made no distinction between what they perceive
and what they think continues to exist when not perceived—they
would think that the very things they perceive remain in existence
when unperceived. But then according to the philosophical view the
vulgar are still mistaken. What they perceive is in fact 'internal and
perishing' and not independent of the perceiver. If they think they
actually perceive something that continues to exist unperceived they
are wrong, whatever they take that thing to be.

Does this philosophical theory represent the final truth about
perception? Hume's answer is complicated. He regards the
philosophical system as no more than a 'palliative remedy' that can
never really satisfy us (p. 211). We have seen that it derives its
plausibility from the vulgar view it repudiates, but it has other defects.
While we are in the grip of the theory it can seem like nothing more
than folly to believe what Hume thinks we are otherwise naturally
disposed to believe. The explanation of our belief in continued and
distinct existence appeals only to various properties of the imagination
and observable characteristics of our experience; it does not link such
properties or characteristics to anything that actually *does* continue to
exist unperceived. Nowhere in the explanation is there any appeal to
something that is perceived and actually continues to exist
unperceived. In fact, the philosophical theory explicitly denies that
there is any such thing. Hume, then, by reflecting on the nature of
perception and having won through to the philosophical theory, finds
himself inclined 'to repose no faith at all' in his senses or his
imagination, and inclined not to believe those things that come
naturally to all of us (p. 217). He sees there is nothing in the way the

114

senses and the imagination work to guarantee that we will have true beliefs about a world of enduring things, and nothing that shows our beliefs to be reasonable or defensible. And the further we pursue our philosophical reasonings, the stronger the dissatisfaction becomes.

> This sceptical doubt, both with respect to reason and the
> senses, is a malady, which can never be radically cur'd,
> but must return upon us every moment, however we may chace it
> away, and sometimes may seem entirely free from it. 'Tis
> impossible upon any system to defend either our understanding
> or senses; and we but expose them farther when we endeavour
> to justify them in that manner. As the sceptical doubt arises
> naturally from a profound and intense reflection on those
> subjects, it always encreases, the farther we carry our reflections,
> whether in opposition or conformity to it. (p. 218)

Philosophical reflection on the nature of perception inevitably leads to scepticism. It must portray our natural beliefs as unwarranted and mistaken. Even a little reflection is enough to convince us that we are much worse off in ordinary life than we unreflectively suppose.

This result, however depressing, cannot be avoided by more philosophizing. There is no antidote to scepticism within philosophy. But the conviction carried by the philosophical conclusions is at best temporary and unstable, however strong it might be on a particular occasion. 'Obstinate nature' can obliterate our sceptical doubts in a moment, and 'carelessness and in-attention' afford an easy remedy for our distress (p. 218). This is not to say that nature somehow *refutes* scepticism and shows that it is not true. Our natural instincts do not successfully meet or resolve the sceptical doubts; they simply submerge them. Man is so constituted that he must believe, for example, in the existence of bodies, even though he cannot defend that belief with any good reasons. Nor will any amount of good reasoning free him from the sceptical doubts arising inevitably out of reflection on the grounds for that belief. But we do get free from such doubts, nevertheless.

> Most fortunately it happens, that since reason is incapable of
> dispelling these clouds, nature herself suffices to that purpose,
> and cures me of this philosophical melancholy and delirium,
> either by relaxing this bent of mind, or by some avocation, and
> lively impression of my senses, which obliterate all these
> chimeras. I dine, I play a game of back-gammon, I converse,
> and am merry with my friends; and when after three or
> four hours' amusement, I wou'd return to these speculations,
> they appear so cold, and strain'd, and ridiculous, that I
> cannot find in my heart to enter into them any farther. (p. 269)

We cannot avoid seeing the results of our philosophical reflection as artificial and contrived, and we will inevitably yield to nature and accept 'the general maxims of the world' (p. 269) despite a convincing philosophical demonstration of the unreasonableness, or even the falsity, of those beliefs.

This might begin to make us wonder why we should engage in this peculiar activity of philosophizing at all.[6] It can and will depress us and alienate us from our ordinary selves for a little while, but its effects cannot be permanent and we do not remain convinced that philosophy has revealed the real truth about ourselves. Of course, we do not become convinced of the opposite either; we simply yield to the more powerful impulses towards 'action, and employment, and the occupations of common life' (E, p. 159). Nevertheless, however 'cold, and strain'd, and ridiculous' the conclusions of philosophy might look from a distance, we do have a natural human tendency towards it. It is 'almost impossible for the mind of man to rest, like those of beasts, in that narrow circle of objects, which are the subjects of daily conversation and action' (p. 271). Despite the pleasures of backgammon and good company, man has a natural curiosity about himself and the operations of his mind, feelings and actions, that he cannot always resist. Although this curiosity tends to take him out of the ordinary world, there seems no other way to satisfy him, and there is nothing behind it but fundamental human sentiments (p. 271). The 'melancholy and delirium' resulting from philosophy is not enough to prevent people from pursuing it. There is something they want and get from it that they cannot get any other way.

But again one might ask what there is of lasting value that one can get from philosophizing. It seems so far that the most one can hope for is a few moments, or with luck a few hours of conviction that one has discovered that everything one believes in ordinary life is folly and illusion—and even that conviction cannot last. But it is just the temporary, unstable nature of the philosophical 'results' that reveals the real truth Hume is interested in. Only when we realize how easily we flip back into ordinary life and leave the sterile conclusions of philosophy behind us, are we in a position to see Hume's fundamental point about human nature. We then come to appreciate:

> the whimsical condition of mankind, who must act and reason
> and believe; though they are not able, by their most diligent
> enquiry, to satisfy themselves concerning the foundation of
> these operations, or to remove the objections, which may be raised
> against them. (E, p. 160)

That is always the point of Hume's discussions of scepticism. They are intended to show that reason, as traditionally understood, is not the dominant force in human life. If it were, all belief, discourse and action would disappear, and nature would soon put an end to man's miserable existence. Contrary to the traditional conception, belief 'is more properly an act of the sensitive, than of the cogitative part of our natures' (p. 183). But that crucial fact can be brought home to us only by a clear and convincing demonstration of the impotence of reason in real life. We find that demonstration in the truth of philosophical scepticism, and only then do we achieve real insight into the foundations of human nature.

If we remain within the traditional philosophical theory we will inevitably regard ourselves as worse off in ordinary life than we would have originally supposed. But if the real discovery comes not with the philosophical conviction itself, but in an appreciation of the source of the instability and transience of that philosophical conviction, then we might no longer regard ourselves as so badly off. If we see that we simply do not, and cannot, operate according to the traditional philosophical conception of reasonable belief and action, it is just possible that our dissatisfactions will then be directed onto that conception itself, and not onto our ordinary life which is seen not to live up to it. Of course, as long as the Cartesian philosophical model is thought to embody the conception of reasonableness we actually try to fulfil in everyday life and science, that result will not be forthcoming. We will lament our ordinary 'failures' to live up to the picture, rather than the artificiality and irrelevance of the only picture we have. What is needed, then, and would be completely in the spirit of Hume's 'experimental' examinations of human nature, is an alternative description of how we actually proceed in everyday life, and what we regard as essential to the most reasonable beliefs and actions we find there. The Cartesian picture is certainly more than a mere *a priori* prejudice; there are powerful considerations in its favour. But it remains to be seen that there is no alternative that will accommodate those considerations while providing a more naturalistic and hence more palatable conception of how and why we think and act as we do. Hume does not suggest even the beginning of such a quest, probably because the theory of ideas makes it unthinkable to him, but once we escape the theory of ideas there is nothing in Hume's general picture of the proper study of man that would rule out an alternative to the traditional philosophical picture.

VI

The Idea of Personal Identity

Then drop into thyself, and be a fool!

External bodies—chairs, tables and trees—are not the only things we think continue to exist through time whether they are perceived by us or not. We also have an idea of a self, or mind or person, that continues to be one and the same thing throughout a lifetime. Each of us understands talk of himself, of Winston Churchill, and of the brothers Karamazov. How and where do we get those ideas? What makes it possible to think of a world containing a number of distinct, enduring selves?

Some philosophers have thought that we are directly or immediately aware of ourselves, that 'we are every moment intimately conscious of what we call our SELF; that we feel its existence and continuance in existence' (p. 251). If that were so, we would get the idea of the self directly from the senses, just as we get the idea of red. But Hume finds that it is not so. To get the idea of X *directly* from the senses we would have to get an impression of X. Each of us has an idea of himself as one thing that remains the same thing throughout his lifetime, so any impression that alone could give rise to such an idea would itself have to remain constant and invariable throughout a whole life. And there is no such impression. Impressions succeed one another in rapidly changing sequences, with none remaining constant for more than a moment. Even if one of those impressions were an impression of the self at a particular time, and some of the others were impressions of the self at different times, still the idea of the self as something that endures for a lifetime without interruption would not be a mere copy or correlate of any one impression. So the idea of the self is not derived directly from the senses.

'Looking into' ourselves to see what we *are* aware of, what do we find?

For my part, when I enter most intimately into what I call

118

myself, I always stumble on some particular perception or
other, of heat or cold, light or shade, love or hatred,
pain or pleasure. I never can catch *myself* at any time
without a perception, and never can observe any thing but
the perception. (p. 252)

All there is to be observed is a sequence of perceptions. There is
nothing else going on. For me to think, to see, to love, to hate, and so
on, is just for certain perceptions to be occurring. I never find anything
that is invariable and uninterrupted. All that any of us can ever find is
'a bundle or collection of different perceptions, which succeed each
other with an inconceivable rapidity, and are in a perpetual flux and
movement' (p. 252). Those are the only data present to 'inner sense' or
reflection.

The same is true of external objects as well. 'Our ideas of bodies are
nothing but collections form'd by the mind of the ideas of the several
distinct sensible qualities, of which objects are compos'd, and
which we find to have a constant union with each other' (p. 219). The
identity of an object through time is not something we ever find in our
experience. We find only collections of perceptions, but we 'regard the
compound, which they form, as ONE thing, and as continuing the
SAME under very considerable alterations' (p. 219). So the identity of
selves and of external bodies is something we merely attribute to them
as a result of various operations of the imagination; it is not something
we directly observe.

We have an idea of identity or sameness; it is just the idea of the
invariableness and uninterruptedness of an object through time. We
also have an idea of diversity—of several different objects existing
either simultaneously or in succession. We have seen in Chapter V how
easy Hume thinks it is for us to come to think that an instance of the
second of these ideas is really an instance of the first. Considering a
continuous succession of related objects is very similar to considering
an invariable and uninterrupted object, he says, and it is very natural
for us to confuse one act or disposition of the mind with another one
very similar to it. I tried to show how this mistake plays an important
role in Hume's explanation of the origin of the idea of identity.

We are so constituted that we find it natural to regard a succession of
resembling perceptions as one continuously existing thing. Yet if we
consider that succession at two distinct moments we cannot avoid
concluding that we are presented with different things, and thus with
an instance of diversity. The propensity to regard it as one invariable
and uninterrupted thing is so strong, however, that we inevitably yield
to it. Judging from the efforts of the philosophers of the past, it is very
natural to invent something that does remain constant and invariable

throughout the successive changes, something that is not directly accessible to observation (pp. 219ff). This they call a *substance*, or, in the case of persons, a *soul* or *self*. Thus the conflict between identity and diversity is apparently resolved. Everything we are aware of—the sequence of perceptions—is variable and interrupted; but there is thought to be something else—the substance—that remains invariable and uninterrupted throughout those changes. The 'accidents' that 'inhere' in the substance change, while the substance remains one and the same.

Hume regards the notion of substance as a mere philosopher's invention that is both unintelligible and unnecessary, however easy it may be for us to fall into using it when we reflect on our ideas of individual things. It is clearly an invention, since all the objects we regard as having a continuous identity are in reality nothing but a succession of parts connected together by resemblance, contiguity or causation.

> For as such a succession answers evidently to our notion of
> diversity, it can only be by mistake we ascribe to it an
> identity; and as the relation of parts, which leads us into
> this mistake, is really nothing but a quality, which produces
> an association of ideas, and an easy transition of the
> imagination from one to another, it can only be from the
> resemblance, which this act of the mind bears to that, by
> which we contemplate one continu'd object, that the error
> arises. (p. 255)

The fiction of a substance is also unintelligible, according to Hume, since it requires us to have an idea of something of which no idea can be formed. A substance is not something with which we can ever be acquainted in experience, and the only way we can represent something to ourselves is by means of ideas that are derived from experience (p. 233). Also, a substance is defined as 'something which may exist by itself', but this traditional definition does not serve to distinguish substances from those fleeting and variable perceptions which are present to the mind. Each of our perceptions is different from every other and from everything else in the universe. Every distinct thing is separable by the imagination from every other thing. Whatever is possible for the imagination is possible, so each of our perceptions can exist separately from all others, and requires nothing else to support its existence. It therefore follows from the definition of a substance that each of our perceptions is a substance, but the very point of the doctrine of substance was to have something distinct from the perceptions on which their existence depends (p. 233). This is not to say that Hume seriously believes that each of our perceptions is a substance. He has no use for the notion, and simply relies on this argument to show that the traditional distinction between substance and accidents does not help to make the notion of substance philosophically intelligible.

Furthermore, we do not need the notion of substance in order to explain how we come to attribute identity to things. We make such attributions, as we have seen, because the 'passage of the thought' along a series of related but different perceptions is so smooth and effortless that we mistake it for 'a continu'd view of the same object'. Many things facilitate that passage. If the change in what we perceive is very small and gradual we scarcely notice it. And smallness and gradualness are matters of proportion. Adding a mountain to a planet would not make us regard it as a different thing, but for many bodies, changing a few inches would destroy our belief in its identity (p. 256).

Even when we notice great changes in the succession of the parts there is an 'artifice' which still induces us to attribute identity. If all the parts are connected with 'a common end or purpose' the passage of the mind along the sequence of parts is facilitated.

> A ship, of which a considerable part has been chang'd by
> frequent reparations, is still consider'd as the same; nor
> does the difference of the materials hinder us from ascribing
> an identity to it. The common end, in which the parts
> conspire, is the same under all their variations, and affords
> an easy transition of the imagination from one situation
> of the body to another. (p. 257)

This effect is even more readily forthcoming when the parts bear to each other the reciprocal relations of cause and effect, as Hume says is the case with all animals and vegetables. Each part of one of those things has a mutual dependence on, and connection with, all the others. This makes it possible for us to allow that a particular tree, say, has undergone a total change of matter in the transition from a small sapling to a giant oak while remaining the same tree (p. 257). Such ordinary examples bring out some of the factors influencing the imagination and leading us to ascribe identity when, strictly speaking, we never observe it.

That is just what happens in the case of personal identity. There is no invariable and uninterrupted entity that is the self or mind.

> The mind is a kind of theatre, where several perceptions
> successively make their appearance; pass, re-pass, glide away,
> and mingle in an infinite variety of postures and situations.
> There is properly no *simplicity* in it at one time, nor
> *identity* in different; whatever natural propension we may

have to imagine that simplicity and identity. The comparison
of the theatre must not mislead us. They are the successive
perceptions only, that constitute the mind; nor have we the
most distant notion of the place where these scenes are
represented, or of the materials, of which it is compos'd.
(p. 253)

If we are to think of all those perceptions as constituting one mind, it
cannot be in virtue of some real connection which we observe to hold
between them. There are no such connections between perceptions,
'Even the union of cause and effect, when strictly examin'd, resolves
itself into a customary association of ideas' (p. 260). So we attribute
identity to minds only because of the effect those different perceptions
have on a mind that contemplates them. Hume's question is therefore:
'What features of the perceptions we contemplate make us suppose
that they constitute a single mind, and how do they bring about that
effect?' This is by now a familiar sort of question, and it arises here for
the same kinds of reasons as parallel questions arose about causality
and the idea of continued and distinct existence.

There are only three relations that can produce a 'union in the
imagination' between ideas: resemblance, contiguity and causation.
They are the only 'natural relations'. And here we can ignore
contiguity 'which has little or no influence in the present case' (p.
260), although Hume never really explains why.[1] Since our
attributions of identity result only from the easy transition of the mind
from one perception to another, and since resemblance and causation
are the only relations that in this case can facilitate such a transition, it
follows that resemblance and causation alone must be enough to
produce in us the 'fiction' or 'mistake' of a continuously existing self or
mind.

There are resemblances among many of the perceptions that
constitute a person primarily because people remember many of their
past experiences.

suppose we cou'd see clearly into the breast of another,
and observe that succession of perceptions, which constitutes
his mind or thinking principle, and suppose that he always
preserves the memory on a considerable part of past perceptions;
'tis evident that nothing cou'd more contribute to the
bestowing a relation on this succession amidst all its variations.
For what is the memory but a faculty, by which we raise up
the images of past perceptions? And as an image necessarily
resembles its object, must not the frequent placing of these
resembling perceptions in the chain of thought, convey the

imagination more easily from one link to another, and
make the whole seem like the continuance of one object?
(pp. 260–1)

It is not just that memory provides us with access to our past self, and
thus gives us a sense of our endurance through time. That is true, but
we think of ourselves as one enduring thing also partly *because* we
remember. To remember is for certain kinds of perceptions to occur in
the mind, so remembering actually contributes to the bundle of
perceptions some members which then come to facilitate the transition
of the imagination along the series making up the bundle. To
remember is to have a perception which represents, and therefore
resembles, the past perceptions it is a memory of, and so one result of
the fact that we remember our past experiences is a greater degree of
resemblance among those perceptions that constitute our mind. And
resemblance is a relation that leads the imagination to slide more easily
from one member of the series to another, and hence to think of it as 'a
continu'd view of the same object'.

But we do not remember all, or even most, of our experiences. We
do not conclude that we did not exist at those post-natal times we no
longer remember, so there must be something else that enables us to
think of those now forgotten perceptions as also belonging to our
enduring self. And that is where causality comes in.

the true idea of the human mind, is to consider it as a
system of different perceptions or different existences, which
are link'd together by the relation of cause and effect, and
mutually produce, destroy, influence, and modify each other.
Our impressions give rise to their correspondent ideas; and
these ideas in their turn produce other impressions. One
thought chaces another, and draws after it a third, by which
it is expell'd in its turn. (p. 261)

When we think of ourselves as existing during the intervals we can no
longer remember we extend this chain of causes and effects into the
gaps. So causation supplements resemblance to help give us the idea of
ourselves as continuing through time. The mind slides easily along a
series of perceptions that form a single causal chain, and thereby leads
us to suppose that those intervening members we no longer remember
nevertheless existed during those forgotten intervals. Thus we come to
think of ourselves as a single, continuous thing extended through
time.

Hume's explanation is much briefer and more perfunctory here than
in his account of the idea of continued and distinct existence of objects,
and he does nothing to clear up its obscurities or to make it more

plausible.[2] In an Appendix to the *Treatise* he finally despairs of ever giving a satisfactory account. It is not easy to see why. But there is no doubt he was profoundly disturbed by the whole subject. There is no trace of it in the *Enquiry*.

There seems little doubt that the fact that we can remember our experiences is very important for our having a notion of ourselves as existing through time, but it is not clear that Hume properly explains or exploits that fact. Although we regard as belonging to one mind all those experiences that are within the scope of a single person's memory, that alone could not serve to explain the origin of the idea of a single mind or person in the first place. We could hardly appeal to the notion of 'a single person's memory' to explain how we first acquire the idea of 'a single person'. Hume, of course, sees that, and says instead that it is really the *resemblance* among our experiences caused by our remembering that leads us to think of them as constituting one mind. Because we do not remember everything that happens to us, resemblance alone is not enough—it leaves gaps—but it is supposed to be enough to lead us to think of those sequences of actually remembered experiences as belonging to, in fact partially constituting, a single mind.

But is that really true? Is it simply the resemblance in a sequence of perceptions that leads us to think of them as constituting or belonging to one mind? Hume is committed to saying that if the mind is led by the relation of resemblance to 'slide easily' along a sequence of perceptions then it will come to think of that sequence itself as one mind. But that seems doubtful; or at least it does not seem that resemblance is what does the work. Consider a bundle of perceptions composed of all and only all those actual perceptions that are perceptions of the Eiffel Tower, perhaps views of it from a particular place on the bank of the Seine. We also know that according to Hume each of those perceptions resembles every other in being about the same thing. When we consider that bundle we clearly perceive the resemblance each of its members bears to every other, but we are not for a moment inclined to think of it as constituting one mind. So resemblance alone is not enough. Of course, we also know that the members of that bundle 'belong' to different people, so even if resemblance can and does have an effect on us, it might be that the perceptions must resemble each other *because they all occur in one person's memory* before we come to think of them as constituting one mind. And then the idea of one person's memory would be doing all the work. But that, as we saw, could not be what we are going on when we get the idea of a single mind in the first place, since it uses the very notion of one person's memory.

It might look as if the relation of causality could be brought in to solve the problem created by artificially 'constructed' bundles of perceptions which we do not regard as constituting persons. If each of the members of a bundle is an effect of the previous members and a cause of the succeeding ones, wouldn't the mind then 'slide easily' along the causal chain and come to think of them all as one mind? The answer to this is not as obvious as it might seem, especially given Hume's account of causality. Even if a causal chain would 'tie' the perceptions together in our minds in a way that was missing from a bundle formed by mere resemblance, it is not clear that that would be enough to lead us to think of it as one mind.

Suppose there were long-standing regularities among perceptions of various kinds, so that whenever one of the A-sort appeared, then one of the B-sort appeared, and whenever a B, then a C, and so on. That would imply, according to Hume, that a causal chain held between particular perceptions a, b, c, and so on, belonging to those kinds. Suppose furthermore that this causal chain held even though a occurred in my mind, b occurred in your mind, c in someone else's, and so on. In other words, perceptions are to be thought of as linked causally, but not only within the history of one person; there is what we would now regard as trans-personal causation of perceptions. That is to say that constant conjunctions hold between various types of perceptions regardless of which mind those perceptions belong to.

Consider now a bundle of perceptions consisting of one of my perceptions, one of its effects, which is one of your perceptions, one of its effects, which is someone else's, and so on. In considering such a bundle, or in contemplating a world in which perceptions came that way, would we find ourselves inclined to regard them all as constituting one mind? It seems to me that the answer is 'No', but it must be admitted that the speculation is so far-fetched that we hardly know what our reactions would be if it were realized. In any case, Hume is committed to saying that if our minds remained the same as they are now, then we $would$ regard such bundles as individual minds, since all their members are related causally, and causality is a natural relation that facilitates the mind's passage along the series, thus leading us to think of the bundle as one mind.

Whatever we would be inclined to do under such bizarre circumstances, it is clear that perceptions do not come that way in this world. In fact, they do not come that way even within those bundles that we unquestionably do regard as belonging to or constituting one and the same individual. That is, if we look at a bundle of perceptions that we do think of as belonging to one person or mind, we do not find that it is 'a system of different perceptions . . . which are link'd together by the relation of cause and effect, and mutually produce, destroy, influence, and modify each other' (p. 261).

In order for each one of my perceptions to be both the effect of some and the cause of others of my perceptions, each of my perceptions would have to belong to a class of perceptions the members of which have been constantly conjoined with members of those classes of perceptions to which its immediate predecessor and its immediate successor belong. Any stretch of experience ABCDEFGHIJKL would have to be such that, for example, H is caused by G (or by every perception up to and including G). And on Hume's theory that implies that there is a constant conjunction between perceptions like G (or like ABCDEFG) and perceptions like H. Only if there were such conjunctions would we come to think of the two as causally connected. But our experience in fact exhibits no such regularities.[3] It is not true that we get an experience of a certain sort only when we have just had an experience of a certain other sort, or that experiences of the first sort are always followed by experiences of another sort. Our experience does not exhibit such uniformities. And for those who like a little novelty in life, that is a very good thing.

This is not to say that there are no causal connections among our perceptions. Obviously there are. Hume has already established, for example, that every simple idea that comes into the mind comes there only as the result of some impression, and my present point does not deny that. Much of his science of man is concerned to find other causal explanations of why our minds are filled as they are. But the causality holding between impressions and their corresponding ideas is not of the right sort to help Hume solve the problem of how we come to ascribe identity to ourselves. Those causal connections run 'vertically', so to speak, from the impression up to the idea, and then perhaps to other ideas and impressions. What Hume needs is a causal chain that runs 'horizontally', as it were, along the whole series of incoming perceptions that we get from moment to moment. That is what I am arguing does not exist. When I am having an impression of a tree I might turn my head and get an impression of a building, but the first impression is not a cause of the second.[4] The first does not belong to a class of perceptions each of which has been followed by a member of a class of perceptions to which the second impression belongs. Our impressions of sensation do not exhibit any such regularity. New experiences flood into our consciousness independently of what has just been going on there, so it is not true that each of our perceptions is caused by other perceptions of ours.

Hume is ambivalent about the origin of impressions of sensation. Here he seems committed to saying that they are caused by their predecessors in a person's mind. If that were not so, then all the perceptions that constitute a single mind would not belong to a single causal chain. But in Book I of the *Treatise* he says that impressions of sensation arise in the soul 'from unknown causes' (p. 7), and that 'their ultimate cause is . . . perfectly inexplicable by human reason' since ''twill always be impossible to decide with certainty, whether they arise immediately from the object, or are produc'd by the creative power of the mind, or are deriv'd from the author of our being' (p. 84). He does not even contemplate the possibility that they are caused by other impressions of sensation.

In Book II he puts forward the more realistic view that since 'the mind, in its perceptions, must begin somewhere . . . there must be some impressions, which without any introduction make their appearance in the soul', and that they 'depend upon natural and physical causes' (p. 275). This is closer to the facts of experience, but it implies that all our perceptions do not form a single causal chain which we then regard as a single mind because of the easy transition we make from one member of the chain to all the rest.

Of course, human experience *might* have been different from what it is. It might have been more regular and uniform, so that we would easily have come to think that each different member of the series of our perceptions is an effect of those that went before and a cause of those that come after. Such a world, however boring, would perhaps make it easier for us to get the idea of a continuing, individual self. Or the world might have been such that all our perceptions were exactly alike, and then perhaps resemblance would be enough. But it is not that way. The novelty and lack of uniformity that we find in our inner life make it difficult to see how Hume's appeal to resemblance and causality could possibly be enough to explain why we come to have an idea of an individual mind or self that endures through time. The true story must be at least more complicated than he allows.

It is difficult to say whether or not Hume was fully aware of these defects in his account. Shortly after it had been published he confessed that he found it 'very defective', but he never says exactly what he thinks its defects are. He is particularly dissatisfied with his explanation of 'the principles, that unite our successive perceptions in our thought or consciousness', and 'makes us attribute to them a real simplicity and identity' (p. 635). Those 'principles', as we saw, are resemblance and causation, but why does Hume think they fail to explain the origin of our idea of the self? It is not easy to answer this question.

His rejection of his own explanation is summed up in the following lament:

In short there are two principles, which I cannot render consistent; nor is it in my power to renounce either of them, viz. *that all our distinct perceptions are distinct existences*, and *that the mind never perceives any real connexion among distinct existences*. Did our perceptions either inhere in something simple and individual, or did the mind perceive some real connexion among them, there wou'd be no difficulty in the case. For my part, I must plead the privilege of a sceptic, and confess, that this difficulty is too hard for my understanding. (p. 636)

Precisely what difficulty does Hume think is too hard for his understanding?

It might look as if it is the difficulty of holding onto both the principles he mentions and rendering them consistent. But that is no difficulty at all, since the two principles obviously are not inconsistent with each other. In fact Hume establishes them right at the beginning and they are at the heart of his whole philosophy. There are obscurities in Hume's notion of 'distinct perceptions',[5] but he means by it at least that if two perceptions are distinct then it is possible for the one to occur without the other. But then there could be no real connection between them, since if there were it would be impossible for one of them to occur without the other. And if there is no real connection between them, the mind cannot perceive one. So the two principles are perfectly compatible, taken in the way Hume understands them.

He must mean that holding onto those two principles is inconsistent with giving an adequate explanation of the source of the idea of personal identity; that they somehow make it impossible to explain what he is trying to explain. But it is not obvious why that is so. He does not think that those same two principles make it impossible to explain the source of the idea of causality—in fact, they are an essential part of that account. The same is true of the idea of continued and distinct existence. He thinks his explanation there is 'perfectly convincing' (p. 210). And in his explanation of the origin of the idea of external objects he does not lament the absence of something simple and individual in which the changing qualities of a thing might inhere. So Hume apparently thinks there is an important difference between his account of the origin of the idea of the self and that of other fundamental ideas like causality and continued and distinct existence.

What he says about the idea of the self fits in well with Hume's general strategy. Strictly speaking, we are nothing but series or bundles of perceptions. This implies that each of us is not some invariable and uninterrupted entity that continues as one identical thing through the whole course of our lives. We only mistakenly think that we have such an existence because we are led to mistake one kind of series of perceptions for another. This is analogous to the story about causality

128

and the external world. Strictly speaking, contiguity, priority and constant conjunctions are the only objective relations we observe among things, and we get the idea of necessary connection only because the mind or imagination is affected in certain ways by its perceptions. Also, the only things we ever observe are momentary, fleeting perceptions, and we get the idea of things enduring independently of being perceived only as a result of a mistake that the mind or imagination is led to make. So Hume's plan for the science of man is to rely heavily on the operations of what he calls the imagination. He invokes various principles or dispositions of the mind according to which, when the mind is affected in certain ways, we are led to think and behave as we do. Our notions of some of the things we regard as objective (e.g. necessary connections between events, enduring objects, etc.) are thus explained in terms of fictions or operations of the mind. That is why what goes on in the mind is the key to the study of human nature.

It might look as if this general technique, which seems to work well enough for causality and the external world, becomes much less feasible when applied to our idea of personal identity. The mind or imagination is said to be mistakenly led to think that there is an individual, enduring mind; that belief is really an illusion, since we are nothing but bundles of perceptions. But if the mind is only a fiction, one might well ask *what* is mistakenly led to think that there is an individual, enduring self. To say 'the mind' or 'the imagination' is not very helpful, since strictly speaking there is no such thing; there is only a bundle of perceptions. This is a very natural criticism to make, and once it has been made it can be seen to apply equally to all parts of Hume's theory, even those that seemed convincing enough.

One might ask *what* is led to expect a B, given an A and a past constant conjunction of As and Bs. Or *what* feigns a continued existence in order to resolve a conflict that it would otherwise get into. According to Hume's theory of the self, the thing that makes all these mistakes, transitions, inferences, fictions, and so on is itself nothing but a series or bundle of perceptions. And it has seemed puzzling to many that a bundle of perceptions can mistake, feign or infer anything. What could that mean?

That there is a difficulty here is perhaps obscured by Hume's penchant for talking about other people, not himself. For example, he says that:

The identity, which we ascribe to the mind of man, is only a fictitious one . . . (p. 259)

identity . . . is merely a quality, which we attribute to [the different perceptions] because of the union of their ideas in the imagination, when we reflect on them. (p. 260)

And he raises the question:

> whether in pronouncing concerning the identity of a person,
> we observe some real bond among his perceptions, or only
> feel one among the ideas we form of them. (p. 259)

And all this is expressed in the third person. It is about our ascribing a fictitious identity to the mind of another.

But each of us is only a bundle of perceptions too, and so our ascriptions of identity to ourselves must also be mistaken or fictitious. And when we cast these same remarks in the first person, the oddity that many have felt in Hume's theory becomes more obvious.[6]

> The identity which *I* ascribe to myself is only a fictitious
> one.
> identity . . . is merely a quality, which *I* attribute to *my*
> different perceptions because of the union of their ideas in
> the imagination, when *I* reflect on them.
> whether in pronouncing concerning *my own* identity, *I*
> observe some real bond among *my* perceptions, or *I* only feel
> one among the ideas *I* form of them.

What, according to Hume, is the *I* which ascribes identity, fails to observe a real bond among different perceptions, or reflects on certain ideas? Does his theory that we are all nothing but bundles of perceptions have whatever plausibility it has only because I do not ask the embarrassing question about my own identity that seems so easy to answer along Humean lines in the case of other people? What becomes of the mind or the imagination when it too is said to be a fiction?

It is worth going into this rather vague complaint; it brings out several important points in Hume's theory of the idea of the self. One form the objection might take is to say that Hume's theory is defective because it is committed to saying that a bundle of perceptions can ascribe identity to things, can reflect on certain ideas, can infer one thing from another—in short, can perform all those 'mental acts' that Hume's account depends on so heavily. How could a mere bundle of perceptions perform any mental acts? A bundle will exist if its individual members exist, and that is all there is to it. It itself does not *do* anything.

I do not think the objection in this form raises a serious problem for Hume. For me to think, to feel, to reflect, to attribute identity to something—in short, for me to perform any of those 'mental acts'—is just for a certain perception to occur in my mind. The mind's 'activity' consists in nothing more than the occurrence of perceptions in it. Therefore, if I am a bundle of perceptions, then for me to think that p is just for the thought that p to occur as a member of the bundle that I am. For Hume, a belief is nothing more than a lively idea. So, for example, when I confuse the set of perceptions AAAAABBBAAAA with another set of perceptions AAAAAAAAA, there simply occurs in the mind the lively idea or belief (which is in fact false) that the second set is just like the first. If I am to have that belief it must occur as part of my biography; but to occur as part of my biography is just for it to be a member of the bundle that I am. The same kind of account could be given of all the other 'mental acts' Hume mentions. Of course, it sounds odd to *say* 'a bundle of perceptions confused some of its perceptions with others', but that is at best a mere impropriety of speech. What is being said, when properly understood, is perfectly intelligible, and nothing follows about the incoherence of Hume's theory from the oddness of a certain form of words.

We have seen that Hume relies heavily on what he calls 'principles' or dispositions of the mind. In fact, the search for the mind's fundamental modes of operation is the main point of the science of man. This too is not incompatible with Hume's theory of the self. If the mind is, strictly speaking, nothing but a bundle of perceptions, then talk of the mind's operations or dispositions is to be understood as conditional talk about what appears in the mind *if* certain other things appear there. To say that we are all inclined or disposed to confuse an interrupted series of perceptions with a similar but uninterrupted series is just to say that whenever an uninterrupted series of perceptions occurs in someone's mind, and then a similar, but interrupted series occurs there, that mind or bundle will also come to contain the lively idea or belief that the second series is just like the first. That does not require that the mind itself be anything other than a bundle of actual perceptions. To say that it has various dispositions is just to say that various conditional statements are true of the way in which those perceptions occur there. Nor is this to deny that there is some non-conditional, categorical explanation of why those conditionals hold. Although Hume does not claim any knowledge of such an explanation, it is perfectly compatible with the mind's being nothing but a bundle of actual perceptions. He might well say that *why* minds are as they are is something we simply do not know, and it is folly to manufacture unbased speculations about it.

But there is still a problem. The original worry was expressed in the question 'When I confuse one set of perceptions with another, *what is it* that confuses those perceptions?', and Hume's answer, with the qualifications already noted, is 'a bundle of perceptions'. Even if that answer is true as far as it goes, it cannot be enough. Let us call those bundles of perceptions that we regard as minds or persons 'personal' bundles. Then even though I am nothing but a 'personal' bundle of perceptions, we cannot say that all that is the case when I believe that p, for example, is that the lively idea or belief that p occurs in some 'personal' bundle of perceptions or other. It must occur in a certain particular bundle, viz. the bundle that I am, in order to constitute *my* believing that p, and as long as there are at least two minds or persons in existence, not every 'personal' bundle is the bundle that I am.

We believe that there are many distinct minds or persons, and we usually have no difficulty distinguishing between them in the ordinary affairs of life. Since we think of minds or persons in this way, Hume should be able to explain why and how we come to do so, but in fact he says nothing about it at all. The problem of how in fact we distinguish one person from another or how we identify this person as the same one we saw yesterday is central to an account of personal identity.[7] One question typically asked is 'What criteria do we employ to identify persons as one and the same over a period of time?' and that is usually understood to mean 'What are the observable conditions the fulfilment of which logically implies that this is the same person as that?' Hume claims, as we saw, that there are no such conditions.[8] There are no objective relations or connections which bind perceptions together in one mind, although there are multitudes of ever-changing perceptions which, because of the operation of various principles of the imagination, we come to regard as constituting minds or persons. Therefore, there are no connections or relations, and *a fortiori* no observable connections or relations, such that, if they hold among a set of perceptions then it follows that it is one person. The very idea of a single, identical mind or person is a 'fiction of the imagination'.

Once we have that 'fictional' idea we can apply it to, or withhold it from, various stretches of our experience, but Hume says nothing about how and when we actually do that. That might well be a serious defect or gap in his account, but even if he had tried to fill that gap, he would not have specified a set of conditions of application the fulfilment of which logically implies that a single person is present, or is identical with a person observed on a previous occasion. Hume is not trying to give an 'analysis' of the concept of personal identity in the sense of an illuminating logical equivalence or synonym of 'A is the same person as B'. I have tried to suggest that he is not really engaged in such a task anywhere in his science of man. In the case of causality, for example, he does not find any conditions that can be said non-circularly to be both logically necessary and sufficient for the truth of 'A caused B'. He seeks those features of our experience that lead us to have the idea of causality and to apply it in the particular cases that we do. The gap between the objective features of our experience and what we actually ascribe to it is bridged by contingent principles of the mind. We ascribe something to the world on the basis of what we find in our experience, but what we find in experience never exhausts what we thus ascribe. Since there is no necessity in the relation between the objects, nothing objectively true of the world could ever exhaust what we ascribe to it when we say there are necessary connections, even though we say there are necessary connections only *because* certain objective features are present. So for Hume there are no objective conditions for applying the concept 'necessary connection' which are such that their fulfilment logically implies that one event is necessarily connected with another. And the same is true of the idea of personal identity.

Hume does not regard that as a defect in his theory of necessary connection—or of personal identity. It is not the 'analysis' of the notion that fails to satisfy him; he offers no analysis. His 'hopes vanish' only when he comes to 'explain the principles, that unite our successive perceptions in our thought or consciousness' (p. 636). This statement of the difficulty is ambiguous. It could mean that Hume has no hope of explaining what actually unites our successive perceptions into one mind or consciousness—what actually ties them together to make up one mind. Or it could mean that he has no hope of explaining what features of our perceptions and what principles of the mind combine to produce in us the thought or belief that we are individual minds—what ties the successive perceptions together *in our thought*, or what makes us *think* of them as tied together. Obviously these two interpretations are different.[9]

The first reading perhaps accords best with Hume's concession that 'Did our perceptions . . . inhere in something simple and individual . . . there would be no difficulty in the case.' If there were such a thing as a simple substance in which the perceptions inhered, then they would actually be bound together into one thing. But the second reading perhaps makes better sense of the other concession that 'did the mind perceive some real connexion among [the perceptions], there wou'd be no difficulty in the case', since the mind's *perceiving* a real connection among the perceptions is required in order for us to come to *think* of them as connected; we would not have to perceive a connection in order for them actually to *be* connected.

If, as on the first interpretation, Hume were lamenting his failure to find something that actually binds perceptions together into one mind, and perhaps countenancing the possibility of finding some solution to that problem in the future, he would have to repudiate his basic idea that 'they are the successive perceptions only that constitute the mind'. The bundle theory itself would have to go. And this interpretation would also imply that Hume is bothered by some question other than the one he appears and claims to be asking about the origin of our idea of the self. Even if all the perceptions belonging to a single mind were to inhere in a simple substance, that in itself would not explain how we ever *get the idea* of a mind or self in the first place. We would still need an account of how various features of our experience combine with fundamental principles of the mind to provide us with that idea.

It would therefore seem to be more in line with Hume's general theoretical intentions in the science of man to understand his complaint along the lines of the second interpretation. On that reading, he despairs of explaining how we come to have the idea of the self, or what makes us *think* of certain bundles of perceptions as constituting continuous selves. He sees his problem arise only after it has been established that 'we only *feel* a connexion or determination of the thought, to pass from one object to another', and therefore that 'the thought alone finds personal identity, when reflecting on the train of past perceptions, that compose a mind' (p. 635). But what aspects of the genetic explanation of how thought alone 'finds' personal identity is he dissatisfied with? We are back to our original difficulty. Does Hume recognize that, as I have suggested, the natural relations of resemblance and causality are not actually enough to do the job required of them, given the nature of our experience? It seems unlikely; that could easily have been said, and illustrated. The expression of his dissatisfaction carries more of a profound sense of some conflict or obstacle at the very heart of things—as if something within the theory of ideas itself renders impossible the Humean task of explaining the origin of *all* our fundamental ideas. What has seemed to work so well for the idea of causality and of the continued and distinct existence of objects is perhaps felt to be breaking down in the case of the idea of personal identity. What is the malady he expresses so poorly but feels so strongly? The question cannot really be settled on the basis of any texts.

One suggestion worth pursuing is that he senses not just an explanatory deficiency in his account of the origin of the idea of the self, but a certain vicious circularity in his whole scheme for the science of man.[10] Suppose that, contrary to what I have claimed, all of a person's perceptions could in fact be found to be linked by relations of cause and effect, so that every one of my perceptions would be believed to be an effect of those preceding it and a cause of those that follow. Still, it might be argued, Hume's theory could not explain the origin of the idea of the self. According to that theory we get the idea of the self because the mind 'slides easily' along a series of perceptions it takes to be causally linked, and so considers it as 'a continu'd view of the same object'. But in order for someone to get the idea that certain perceptions are causally linked he must have observed a constant conjunction between perceptions of two kinds. In other words, perceptions of the two different kinds must have appeared constantly conjoined *in that person's mind*. If all A-perceptions were followed by B-perceptions, but not within the mind of a single person, then no one would come to believe that As cause Bs or that this A caused this B. No one would ever be presented with the appropriate 'data' from which to get that belief.

This shows that the explanation of how a person comes to think of certain perceptions as causally connected by noticing constant conjunctions in his own mind makes essential use of the notion of one self or mind, while the explanation of how a person comes to think of certain perceptions as united in one mind by taking those perceptions to be causally connected makes essential use of the notion of causality. To explain the idea of causality, personal identity is appealed to; and to explain the idea of personal identity, causality is appealed to. So, it might then be argued, there is a kind of circularity in Hume's science of man. As long as we focus only on the explanation of the idea of causality, everything seems in order, but that is only because we are surreptitiously presupposing a prior notion of a single self or mind.

The point could also be made by concentrating on the principles, propensities or dispositions that Hume regards as fundamental to human nature. I said that talk of such dispositions could easily be construed as conditional talk about the appearance of certain kinds of perceptions in the mind under certain conditions. But it is now clear that those conditional statements must make essential use of the notion of one mind. On Hume's view it is a general truth that, if there has appeared in a particular mind a constant conjunction between A-perceptions and B-perceptions, and there then occurs in that mind an additional A-perception, then a further B-perception will also occur in that mind. That is a principle he needs for his science of man. In order to explain how people get the idea of causality, for example, it is not enough to show simply that whenever there has been a constant conjunction between A-perceptions and B-perceptions, and another A-perception occurs, then a further B-perception occurs. That might well be true, but if the different perceptions had occurred in different minds, the truth of that conditional would not contribute to an explanation of how anybody ever gets the idea of causality. There would be nobody to whom all those 'data' were presented. This is another way of bringing out the centrality or ineradicability of the idea of one self or mind in Hume's science of man. He absolutely needs a prior notion of a self or mind within which the fundamental principles or dispositions of human nature 'operate'.[11]

Now there is no doubt that Hume, in his theorizing about man, makes essential use of both the idea of causality and the idea of a single mind. And each idea plays a central role in the explanation of the origin of the other idea. But it does not follow that his theory is involved in some vicious circularity because of that. It does not follow that the human subjects about whom Hume is theorizing must themselves have the idea of causality in order to get the idea of a single mind, and must have the idea of a single mind in order to get the idea of causality. That *would* destroy the explanatory power of a genetic theory; but Hume's theory is not committed to any such consequence. And Hume can reasonably be expected to have noticed that fact.

I have already argued that there is nothing illegitimate in trying to find the cause of the idea of causality in people's minds. It is just an attempt to explain causally how and why the idea of causality arises in the minds of people who originally lack it. They are exposed to certain 'data' and, as a result, there appears in the mind a new idea that was not there before. And they do not have to have the idea of one self or mind in order to get the idea of causality either. The observed constant conjunctions that produce in a person the idea of causality must, as we have seen, all occur within the mind of that person, but on Hume's view the person himself does not have to think of them *as occurring in his mind* in order for them to do so. He need not have any idea of the mind at all in order to be 'exposed to the data' that give rise to the idea of causality. If the appropriate constant conjunctions between kinds of perceptions do in fact occur in the only series of perceptions a person is ever in fact aware of, then he will get the idea of causality. And if his thought 'slides easily' along that series of perceptions because of the causal connections believed to hold among them, then he will get the idea of himself as one mind. But he does not need the idea of one self or mind in order to get the idea of causality in the first place. The fact that the 'data' come as they do, i.e. all within the scope of his own experience, suffices, without his having to think of the 'data' as coming that way.

Even if this reply successfully defends Hume against the charge of circularity, it leaves unanswered the most important question about the self or self-consciousness, and it seems to me quite likely that Hume in the Appendix dimly realizes his inability to say anything about it. It is not just that he cannot think of the right answer, but that the theory of ideas and its consequences make an answer impossible.

I have represented Hume as avoiding the initial charge of explanatory circularity in his accounts of the origins of the ideas of causality and of personal identity by appealing to the undeniable fact that the only 'data' available to a person for the formation of his ideas and beliefs are his own perceptions. Hume must take that as simply a basic fact about perceptions—it is what enables a person to be influenced by various happenings in his own mind without having to possess the idea of his own mind at the outset. But although the fact seems undeniable, Hume has no way of accounting for it. Of course, he himself possesses the idea of a single mind, so he can *state* the fact from which his explanatory theory starts, but he cannot explain how or why that fact holds. He cannot explain how or why the 'data' from which the idea of personal identity is constructed present themselves in the way they do. And if they did not present themselves that way, his explanation would collapse. The point is elusive, and I think I can only indicate roughly what I have in mind.

Suppose the world were such that, as we would now say, all the perceptions there are occur within one mind. Suppose only one person existed. On Hume's theory that person would be simply a series of perceptions. If that series of perceptions exhibited the appropriate regularities, then according to Hume's theory of causality the series would eventually come to contain an idea of necessary connection. If and when there occurred a 'reflective' perception of all the perceptions that had already occurred, then according to Hume's theory of personal identity that series would come to contain an idea of a single, continuous mind. The idea of a single mind would be derived from a 'survey' of past perceptions, and that survey would encompass all the perceptions there had ever been. There is no circularity in that.

But now suppose that, as is actually the case, there are many different minds independent of each other, and so not all the perceptions there are fall within the scope of a single mind's experience. Surveys of past perceptions would not extend to all the perceptions there had ever been. How then could there arise an idea of a single, continuous mind? That idea could not be derived from a survey of all the perceptions there are, since there are no such surveys. And even if there were, they would be to no avail, since the class of all the perceptions there are does not exhibit the appropriate regularities. If all the perceptions there are did exhibit the appropriate regularities, and they all were open to a single survey, we would be back in the world with only one mind. So in the world as it is a non-solipsistic idea of one mind could be derived only from a survey of some, but not all, perceptions. To see himself as one mind among others a person's experience must be restricted to only a subset of all the perceptions that occur. But which ones?

Obviously it will not do to say that Jones could get the idea of one mind in the first place by noticing the resemblances and causal connections among all of, say, Smith's perceptions, since in order to do so he would have to be 'presented with' Smith's perceptions in some way, and even if that were possible it would require that he have some way of picking out the series of perceptions he identifies as Smith's from all the perceptions he is presented with. And in that case he would need a prior notion of one self or mind in order to get the 'data' he needs in order to acquire that idea in the first place. He would be involved in a real circle unless Smith's perceptions were the *only* ones he was presented with. And in that case Jones would *be* Smith. So if Jones, or anyone, is to get the idea of one self or mind he must get it from his own case.

If Jones would need a prior notion of a self or mind in order to get the idea of one self or mind from noticing features of *Smith's* perceptions, why would he not need a prior notion of self or mind in order to get that idea from noticing features of his own perceptions? The reason is that, if Jones were to try to use Smith's perceptions as his 'data' he would need some way to pick out Smith's perceptions from all the perceptions there are, and hence he would need the idea of the person or mind who is Smith, but if he uses only his own perceptions as 'data' he would need no such prior idea *if* his own perceptions are in fact the only ones that are ever presented to him. Among all the perceptions there are, his reflective gaze must be restricted to a certain series, and as long as that series in fact exhibits certain features there will eventually occur in that series an idea of a single, continuous mind. And when that idea is applied to the earlier members in the series Jones then comes to have the belief that he is a single mind with a continuous history.

It is therefore clear that Hume's explanation of the origin of the idea of the self or mind is not necessarily deficient in failing to give an account of how a certain idea arises from certain 'data', but that it leaves completely unintelligible and mysterious the fact that those 'data' are as they are. When we press on to that level of inquiry we find it simply taken as a given fact about the universe of perceptions that the range of reflective vision of any one of them does not extend to all the rest.[12] And it is only because one's gaze is thus restricted to a certain subset of all the perceptions there are that it is possible for a person to get an idea of himself.

But why is our gaze restricted in that way? What accounts for the fact that one cannot survey in the same way *all* the perceptions there are? It seems as if one's vision could be non-circularly restricted to a certain subset or series only if perceptions in fact occurred only *as* members of particular series—as if they came already tied together into bundles, as it were, so that no member of a particular series could be a perception of any perception outside that series. But how could that be, on Hume's theory? For him all perceptions are distinct existences, and so each one could exist independently of every other and independently of everything else in the universe. There is nothing in any perception, considered in itself, which implies the existence of any other perception, or of anything else whatsoever, and so there is nothing intrinsic to any perception that connects it with some particular series rather than another. So why do perceptions present themselves, so to speak, in discrete, separate bundles? There seems to be no way for Hume to explain that basic fact about perceptions, although his genetic explanation of the origin of the idea of the self relies on it. 'Having thus loosen'd all our particular perceptions' from each other and from everything else, when he proceeds 'to explain the principle of connexion, which binds them together, and makes us attribute to them a real simplicity and identity', he finds his account 'very defective' (p. 635).

If Hume were sensing his reliance on an inexplicable 'fact' about perceptions, as I have suggested, it would be natural for him to express his quandary by saying 'Did our perceptions either inhere in something simple and individual, or did the mind perceive some real connexion among them, there wou'd be no difficulty in the case.' Hence the plausibility of the first interpretation of Hume's statement of his difficulty. If there were such things as simple spiritual substances to which perceptions necessarily belonged, or if there were 'real' or necessary connections between certain perceptions, then that would perhaps explain why the field of vision of a particular reflective perception is restricted to a certain subset of all the perceptions there are. Each of us would be presented with only those perceptions that inhere in a particular spiritual substance, or with those that are necessarily connected with our present perception. Perceptions would really come in separate, discrete bundles, so we could not see over the fence into our neighbour's domain. It is not that we would need an *idea* of substance or 'real' connection in order to get the idea of the self, nor is it that if perceptions inhered in substances or were necessarily connected with certain others that alone would inevitably *give us* the idea of the self; rather, if perceptions inhered in substances or were necessarily connected with certain others that would explain why perceptions come as they do, why as things are, only a subset of all perceptions are open to the reflective gaze of a single person. In short, it would explain why the 'data' are in fact the way they must be if anything like Hume's explanation of the origin of the idea of the self is to be successful. But for Hume the theory of ideas implies the impossibility of a perception's inhering in a substance and of there being 'real' or demonstrable connections between perceptions. Hence the poignancy of his lament.

The present suggestion would also explain why Hume regrets the unavailability of a simple substance or of real connections among perceptions in his account of personal identity, but makes no corresponding plea in the case of the continued and distinct existence of objects or of causality. In those cases the theory of 'projection' outlined earlier works well enough. There is no need for perceptions or anything else to inhere in a 'material substance' in order for me to come to think of the world as containing independently existing objects. As long as my experience exhibits certain features the mind will acquire that 'fictitious' idea and then 'spread itself' onto the world. Nor is any objective connection between perceptions or objects required in order for me to come to think of things as causally connected with each other. As long as my experience exhibits certain regularities I will come to have that 'fictitious' idea as well. In both explanations the notion of 'my experience' is taken for granted. And if it is taken for granted, Hume's explanation of the origin of the idea of the self or mind works tolerably well also. But to take it for granted is to assume that the scope of one's experience does not extend to all the perceptions there are, and that is the inexplicable fact upon which Hume's explanation depends. To say it is 'inexplicable' for Hume is to say that it is inconsistent with the theory of ideas, which he takes to be the only way to make sense of psychological phenomena.

I do not mean to imply that Hume ever comes close to abandoning the theory of ideas. But it might well be that in the Appendix to the *Treatise* he half recognizes something that in fact is a fatal deficiency in that theory as he understands it. If the occurrence of mental 'acts' or events consists in nothing more than the presence in the mind of certain objects called 'perceptions', but there is no intelligible connection or relation between a particular perception and a particular mind, then the theory must treat perceptions as completely detached from the 'minds' or 'subjects' that have them. All perceptions are 'loose' and 'floating', independent of all the rest, and therefore, on Hume's view, independent of all minds. But thinking or psychological phenomena generally require that there be *someone* thinking something, or *someone* in some psychological state. The exclusive emphasis the theory of ideas places on the mental 'object'—on what is thought or felt, and not on the subject 'in' whom those 'objects' exist—must inevitably lead to distortion or mystery. And in his treatment of personal identity Hume pushes the theory of ideas up to the edge of that abyss and finds that only the unacceptable notions of substance or a real connection among perceptions would save him. It is but a short step from there back to the Kantian idea that there must be something about perceptions or representations—whether it is noticed or not—which constitutes their belonging to a particular self or subject, even if it is only the apparently weak requirement that it be possible for one to think of those representations as belonging to oneself. But by then the classical theory of ideas would have been abandoned.[13]

140

VII

Action, Reason and Passion

Yes, Nature's road must ever be prefer'd;
Reason is here no guide, but still a guard:
'Tis hers to rectify, not overthrow,
And treat this passion more as friend than foe:

Hume is a scientist of man who believes that every event has a cause. Most of us are perhaps inclined to agree, at least with respect to the happenings of brute physical nature. In any case, we do not believe that inanimate bodies have anything we would regard as freedom or liberty—that they can change the direction or speed of their motion, for example, independently of the causal forces operating on them. Hume claims that the same thing holds for those parts of nature that involve 'actions of the mind'. This includes not just 'mental events' alone, but human actions generally.

He thinks that what naturally and inevitably leads us to believe in causality in the inanimate world also leads to the same belief with respect to human actions. We come to think of certain physical events as necessarily or causally connected when we have observed a constant conjunction between events of those two types in the past. But if that is so, then it is obvious that human affairs are just as much cases of 'necessary operations' as is the behaviour of bodies. There is just as much uniformity in human affairs as in inanimate nature. The 'regular operation of natural principles' is equally obvious in both realms (p. 401).

This is not to say that every human being is the same as every other, or that everyone acts the same way in a given situation. It means only that every human action is an instance of some uniformity, just as is every event involving only inanimate objects. The principle that like causes produce like effects is equally true for both sorts of events. And the existence of uniformities is not incompatible with immense variety both in inanimate nature and in human behaviour. The world would be either a dreary or a chaotic place if it were. A certain sequence of events makes one tree bear apples and another tree bear plums, but we do not conclude that they are not caused to bear the particular fruits

141

that they do. We attribute their different products to different internal structure. Similarly there are differences in the sentiments, actions and passions of different human beings. For example, those of the members of one sex are 'distinguished by their force and maturity, the other by their delicacy and softness' (p. 401).[1]

But there also seems to be considerable evidence against the uniformity Hume claims to find in human behaviour. He himself puts the objection this way:

> For what is more capricious than human actions? What more
> inconstant than the desires of man? And what creature
> departs more widely, not only from right reason, but from
> his own character and disposition? An hour, a moment is
> sufficient to make him change from one extreme to the other,
> and overturn what cost the greatest pain and labour to
> establish. Necessity is regular and certain. Human conduct
> is irregular and uncertain. The one, therefore, proceeds not
> from the other. (p. 403)

Hume thinks this objection shows something about human behaviour, but not that it lacks causes. It shows that there is a great deal we do not know about human beings and how they operate. Although, given our knowledge of a person's character, motives, aims, and so on, his actions are often as predictable as inanimate physical events, it must be admitted that this is not always so. According to Hume that is because of the great complexity of the contributing factors in most human actions, and our insufficient knowledge of them. But there are also many occasions on which we lack the appropriate knowledge about inanimate physical objects as well. Our inability to predict the outcome of a turn of the roulette wheel, for example, does not lead us to believe that its operations are not really caused after all. There we are quite willing to attribute our failure to lack of knowledge rather than to the absence of causality, and Hume thinks the same is true of human action.

But he is not content simply to point out that there is in fact uniformity in human behaviour. He thinks that what we all say and do in dealing with other human beings shows that all of us actually believe in the uniformity as well, despite what we feel inclined to say about man's freedom. We continually form beliefs about the future behaviour of people on the basis of what we know about them—their 'motives, tempers, and circumstances' (p. 401). If we did not do this, how could we have any human contact at all? How could we rely on other people, or try to act ourselves in accord with what we expect them to do?

All politics, commerce, in fact, even simple communication

depends on our making inferences from what we know of a person to what we think he is about to do. A prince who imposes a tax on his subjects expects their compliance; a man who gives his order for dinner expects the waiter to bring it; and so on (p. 405). These expectations are acquired through inferences from what is known or believed about people, and Hume says they are all causal inferences. I think the waiter will bring my dinner because he wants to keep his job, and because he believes that bringing my dinner is required for him to keep his job. And these inferences, like all causal inferences, are made on the basis of past observations of constant conjunctions between people having particular 'motives, tempers, and circumstances' and their acting in certain ways.

Naturally, such expectations are not infallible. Many of our conclusions about what people will do are based on assumptions for which we do not always have very strong grounds, and even if we do, we sometimes turn out to be wrong. But that is no surprise, nor does it reveal anything special about human behaviour. We often make mistakes in our expectations about inanimate objects as well.

That we really believe in causality in both the human and the inanimate domains is further confirmed by the fact that we often put reasoning about human actions together with reasoning about physical events to reach a conclusion about the necessity or impossibility of certain occurrences.

> A prisoner, who has neither money nor interest, discovers the
> impossibility of his escape, as well from the obstinacy of the
> gaoler, as from the walls and bars with which he is
> surrounded; and in all attempts for his freedom chuses rather
> to work upon the stone and iron of the one, than upon the
> inflexible nature of the other. The same prisoner, when
> conducted to the scaffold, foresees his death as certainly from
> the constancy and fidelity of his guards as from the operation of
> the ax or wheel. His mind runs along a certain train of ideas: The
> refusal of the soldiers to consent to his escape, the action of the
> executioner; the separation of the head and body; bleeding,
> convulsive motions, and death. Here is a connected chain of
> natural causes and voluntary actions; but the mind feels no
> difference betwixt them in passing from one link to another.
> (p. 406)

All that is required for such inferences to be convincing is that we have observed the appropriate constant conjunctions in the past. Whether they are conjunctions involving only 'mental' phenomena, or only inanimate phenomena, or one of each, is irrelevant to our acquiring the beliefs we do.

143

So Hume thinks that if we observe human behaviour we will inevitably believe that human actions are caused, and that they arise 'of necessity' out of their antecedents. Only if that is so, he thinks, can human actions be explained. In the absence of causality there would simply be no answer to the question why a particular action occurred. That would leave the science of man with nothing to say—the action in question would be literally inexplicable or unintelligible. I have already emphasized the importance for Hume of seeing everything that happens—and especially human thoughts, feelings and actions—as part of a natural causal order. It is a condition of our fully understanding what goes on, and therefore a condition of the success of Hume's science of man.

But the idea that actions arise of necessity out of their antecedents has also been thought to conflict with another important and familiar aspect of human life—man's freedom, or liberty. Hume is not unaware of this tension in our thought about ourselves and others, and he tries to explain its source. He does so by trying to account for people's dissatisfaction with 'the doctrine of necessity' and for the attractiveness of 'the doctrine of liberty', in so far as liberty is thought to conflict with necessity.

What he says on this subject is important and famous. Hume's writings provide one of the main sources of today's widely shared belief that an action's being caused or necessitated by its antecedents is perfectly compatible with its being a free action.[2] He finds three distinct factors that lead people mistakenly to suppose that the two are incompatible.

The first, not surprisingly, is confusion or misunderstanding. In the *Treatise* Hume describes it as a confusion between two different kinds of liberty, but in the *Enquiry* he thinks it is simply a misunderstanding of what liberty is. We often think of someone as acting unfreely when he is forced 'against his will', for example by violence or the threat of violence, to do something by somebody else. Of such a person we can perfectly justifiably say 'he had to do it', 'he couldn't have done anything else' or 'he had no alternative', and these are taken as denials of his liberty with respect to that action. But in the normal course of everyday events, when for example I cross the street and buy some ice cream with no one threatening, imploring, requesting or even suggesting anything, it is very difficult to think that I had no alternative, that I had to do it or that I could not have done otherwise. It seems to be a perfect case of absence of force or constraint or whatever was responsible for the lack of liberty in the first kind of case. The implication Hume draws is that, in the absence of what makes liberty absent in the first kind of case, liberty is present.

What is present in the example of my crossing the street for ice cream is 'the liberty of *spontaneity*'—'that which is oppos'd to violence' (p. 407)—which Hume in the *Treatise* regards as liberty in 'the most common sense of the word' and the only kind of liberty 'which it concerns us to preserve' (pp. 407–8). We are concerned to minimize the power of others over us, and to structure our communities to reduce opportunities for people to impose their wills upon us in conflict with our own. Hume thinks that, somehow, because of the great importance the liberty of spontaneity has for us, we tend to confuse it with something quite different, viz. 'the liberty of *indifference*'. This latter sort of liberty *is* incompatible with necessity and causes, and so our failure to distinguish the two kinds of liberty leads us mistakenly to deny that human actions are caused. Of course, if Hume is right about our confusions then we are wrong to draw the conclusion that free human actions are uncaused, but he offers no explanation at all of exactly how our intense concern with 'the liberty of spontaneity' leads us to confuse it with the absence of causality. Recent writers have concentrated more on that aspect of the Humean diagnosis,[3] but there is a puzzling blank at that point in Hume's actual account.

In the *Enquiry*, there is no mention of a confusion between two kinds of liberty at all. The 'liberty of spontaneity' is said to be the only kind there is.

> For what is meant by liberty, when applied to voluntary
> actions? We cannot surely mean that actions have so little
> connexion with motives, inclinations, and circumstances, that one
> does not follow with a certain degree of uniformity from
> the other, and that one affords no inference by which we
> can conclude the existence of the other. For these are plain
> and acknowledged matters of fact. By liberty, then, we can
> only mean *a power of acting or not acting, according to
> the determinations of the will*; that is, if we choose to
> remain at rest, we may; if we choose to move, we also may.
> Now this hypothetical liberty is universally allowed to belong
> to every one who is not a prisoner and in chains. Here, then,
> is no subject of dispute. (*E*, p. 95)

This again does not begin to explain why people are inclined to deny causal determination of human actions in the name of liberty. It simply advances a view about what 'liberty' means, thus attributing the perennial dispute about liberty and necessity to some still unspecified confusion or misunderstanding.

The view about what 'liberty' means, or about the nature of that liberty that we are concerned to preserve, is expressed very briefly in this passage, and it can hardly be described as a subtle or profound analysis of the concept. A man from whom money is demanded with a gun at his head certainly has 'a power of acting or not acting, according to the determinations of the will'. If he chooses not to give the money, he may, and if he chooses to give it, he may. The penalties will be much greater on the one alternative than on the other, but which alternative is realized now depends on his will. So this example would seem to count as a case of liberty, given Hume's explanation of it, although it is clearly a case in which the kind of liberty Hume says it concerns us most to preserve is absent. The quest for liberty is more than an effort to stay out of prison or out of chains.

Hume is not concerned to offer a complete account of the precise nature and limits of what he calls the liberty of spontaneity. He says that it is one—or perhaps the only—sense of the word 'liberty', but he does not even begin to explain what that sense is, or how our failure to understand it properly leads us mistakenly to think it is incompatible with causality. Consequently he can hardly be said at this point to have shown, or to have established, that liberty and necessity are compatible.

He offers two other explanations of people's opposition to the idea that human actions are caused. We often have what Hume calls '*a false sensation or experience*' of the absence of necessity or determination in action (p. 408), and hence we conclude that there is no such thing. We have already seen that necessity is not an objective property of the relation between events we regard as causally connected; nor is it a characteristic possessed by any 'agent', whether animate or inanimate. The *observer* of human action believes that particular actions are caused by their antecedents when he has observed constant conjunctions between antecedents of those kinds and actions of those kinds. He then feels 'a determination of the mind' to pass from the idea of one of those things to the idea of 'its usual attendant'. But in *performing* an action, Hume says, we often do not feel any such determination; in fact, we are often 'sensible' of a certain 'looseness or indifference' (p. 408), and so we tend to regard our action as completely free or uncaused;

> as liberty, when opposed to necessity, is nothing but the
> want of that determination, and a certain looseness or
> indifference which we feel, in passing, or not passing,
> from the idea of one object to that of any succeeding one.
> (*E*, p. 94n)[4]

Why do we experience this 'looseness or indifference' in the case of our own actions? It cannot be because we lack experience of, and hence know nothing of, the conjunction between wants and beliefs of certain kinds and actions of certain kinds, since we do not feel the same 'looseness' when we observe the same kinds of actions performed by others. It cannot be a mere lack of exposure to instances of relevant generalizations that is responsible for the lack of the feeling of causality in our own case. Nor can it be our involvement in, and concentration on, the action at hand, since it is not a condition in general of having a feeling of causal determination, or of getting causal beliefs, that one explicitly rehearse and consider the past experience from which the feeling or belief naturally arises. Animals get expectations on the basis of experience just as people do—automatically, without deliberate excogitation. How then is it possible for us to be so immune to the pressures of past and present experience in the case of our own actions, especially if Hume is right about our causal beliefs arising from a 'feeling of determination'? Somehow, when we are acting, that feeling deserts us.

Hume does not give a satisfactory explanation of this phenomenon. He is mainly interested in showing that, whatever its source, it does not imply that human actions are not caused by the 'motives, temper, and situation' of the agent. He points out, quite rightly, that if we are confronted with two alternatives A and B, and we do A, we nevertheless have no difficulty in forming an idea of our having done B instead. And that is enough to persuade us that we could have done B instead of A, and hence that we were not causally determined to do A. But why are we so easily persuaded? According to Hume it is because we are confident that, if anyone challenges us to show that we really could have chosen B, we think we will have met the challenge if we set up the situation again and choose B *this* time. There seems no other way conclusively to prove the existence of a power that was not exercised. Since we could not do both A and B at the same time, it might seem that the only proof left to us is to do B at some later time, thus showing that we can do it, and then conclude that we could have done it earlier, and hence that our doing A was not causally determined.

Hume has little difficulty in showing that this 'experiment' is useless to demonstrate an absence of causality in the first action. The first time I was merely presented with two alternatives, and the wishes, desires and motives I had at the time led me to take A. But the second time the situation is quite different. For instance, the question of my liberty has arisen; I want to demonstrate my freedom, and I think the way to do so is to choose B this time. Obviously, the fact that doing B naturally issues from this second set of wants and beliefs does not imply that my doing A was not the effect of the set of wants and beliefs I had the first time. The fact that I do B the second time does not imply that the wants and beliefs I had the first time were not sufficient to cause me to do A. Hume suggests that it is only because we somehow mistakenly believe that that implication holds that our experiences in acting lead us to deny 'the doctrine of necessity'. He admits that 'we may imagine we feel a liberty within ourselves' (p. 408), but taken alone that proves nothing about whether or not we actually have that liberty. The experiences must be accompanied by some inference in order to establish our liberty, but at this point Hume does not explain how or why we could ever be led to make the particular faulty inference he attributes to us.

I think it is only when he reaches the third possible source of the attractiveness of 'the doctrine of liberty' that Hume begins to approach a more realistic account of what actually makes us regard liberty and necessity as incompatible, but even there what he says is brief and not fully satisfying diagnostically.

There seems little doubt that many people are opposed to 'the doctrine of necessity' because they think its truth would undermine religion and morality, and show them to be nothing but illusions. That would not in itself imply that 'the doctrine of necessity' is false, but it does explain why many people are not disposed to accept it.

The explanation can be made more specific. Opposition to 'the doctrine of necessity' involves more than just a taste for old things, or a fondness for the traditional ways. It is widely believed that, as Hume puts it, 'necessity utterly destroys all merit and demerit either towards mankind or superior powers' (p. 411). If the actions of a man or a god arise of necessity out of their antecedents, it is felt that that agent was not free not to perform the actions in question, and hence cannot legitimately be praised or blamed for them. Praise or blame—or responsibility of any sort—for an action is rightly ascribed only if the agent could have done otherwise. But if human actions are events which arise of necessity out of their antecedents then, if their antecedents have occurred, the actions in question *must* occur, they could not fail to occur, there is no alternative to their occurring. So 'the doctrine of necessity' is rather naturally taken to imply the absence of alternatives to what happens, and 'the doctrine of liberty' requires alternatives. Whatever might be wrong with this way of thinking, it is plausible to suggest that something like it is behind the feeling that liberty and necessity are incompatible, and therefore that the truth of 'the doctrine of necessity' would undermine morality and ascriptions of responsibility. What exactly does Hume say about this source of the apparent conflict?

I have already mentioned his suggestion that there is a confusion or conflation of two different senses of 'liberty' somewhere in our thinking about the conflict, but he does not point to any particular place at which the alleged confusion occurs, or explain why and how we are led to make it. And he does not give a very careful explanation of what 'liberty' or 'could have done otherwise' actually mean; nor does he show that they are consistently applicable to actions that arise of necessity out of their antecedents. Those are the sorts of tasks the successful completion of which would seem to have the greatest chance of resolving once and for all 'the question of liberty and necessity—the most contentious question of metaphysics, the most contentious science' (E, p. 95). And they would seem to be all that is needed for clearing away this felt obstacle to the success of the science of man. But Hume virtually ignores them, and he does so partly because he thinks we must all in fact accept 'the doctrine of necessity' in order to ascribe responsibility at all. It is not merely that liberty and the ascription of responsibility are compatible with necessity—they actually require it; they would make no sense without it. So for Hume to concentrate on establishing only their compatibility would be for him to concentrate on establishing much less than what he regards as the whole truth.

His argument for the stronger conclusion goes as follows. We only praise or blame someone for something *he* does. The action must be *his* action, not somebody else's, and it must not be something that merely happens to him but otherwise has no connection with him at all. If a man's 'actions' were not caused, they would not be the effects of anything at all, and so they would not be the effects of his character, wants, desires, motives, etc. But if an 'action' does not proceed from a man's character, wants, desires, motives, etc., then there is no connection between the 'action' and the man who is said to have done it. If an event which we regard as an action of a particular man is in fact not connected with him in any way, then the fact that it occurred 'can neither redound to his honour, if good, nor infamy, if evil' (p. 411). The event might involve the man in the sense that it is something occurring in or on or near a certain human body, but that is not enough to justify our attributing the event to the man as in some sense 'his', and therefore holding him responsible for its occurrence. Of course, we might regard it as unfortunate or bad that the event occurred, but that is not to hold a particular man responsible for it. So thinking of actions as being done by someone, or as being his, hers or theirs, requires a belief that the actions are effects of other things that are going on in, or are true of, particular human beings. Therefore, only if 'the doctrine of necessity' is true can a person rightly possess merit or demerit for his actions, since *his* actions are those that are caused by his character, wants, desires, motives, and so on. Everyone who ascribes responsibility must believe in 'the doctrine of necessity'.

This argument raises a number of issues. It seems undeniable that in order for an action to be the action of a particular agent, it must in some way issue from the motives, wants, beliefs, character or other dispositions or attributes of that particular agent. Only then does it make sense to attribute that action to that agent, and thus to hold him responsible for it. But that is a very vague admission. It leaves open the fundamental question of precisely *how* an action 'issues from' certain characteristics of the agent. Hume's view that the ascription of responsibility requires 'the doctrine of necessity' is based on the plausible idea that the wants, beliefs, character, etc., of an agent are the *causes* of his actions. But one could be wrong in taking the relation between them to be straightforwardly causal without being wrong about the weaker and vaguer, and apparently undeniable claim that the ascription of actions and responsibility to an agent requires that those actions in some way or other 'issue from' the wants, beliefs, character, etc., of that agent.[5]

Hume thinks he has good reason to believe that a person's actions are events that are caused by, or arise of necessity out of, their antecedents, such as the person's wants, beliefs and other propensities. As a scientist of man, he notices constant conjunctions between a certain sort of person's wanting and believing such-and-such and his doing certain things, and he then comes to believe that phenomena of those two sorts are causally connected. And that is why he concludes that 'the doctrine of necessity', or of the causal origin and explanation of human actions, is what is required for the attribution of those actions to particular agents.[6] Hume's causal theory of action is a natural outcome of his conception of science, and in particular of the science of man.[7]

The whole question of the nature of human action—its genesis and explanation—is very complicated, and remains in a highly unsettled state. I return in the next section to a discussion of some aspects of Hume's causal theory, in particular the nature of wants or desires and their role in the 'production' of actions. For the moment I want to concentrate on another point relevant to his treatment of the dispute about liberty and necessity.

Suppose Hume were absolutely right. Suppose that the only way we could make sense of the attribution of actions to agents was by taking those actions to be caused by the wants, beliefs or other characteristics of those agents. Then if we also were still inclined to believe that 'the doctrine of necessity' is incompatible with liberty and hence responsibility, some of the things we believe would have to be false. Both sides simply could not be true. But that is typically the beginning, rather than the end, of a philosophical problem. Hume would have provided us with a dilemma—perhaps even an antinomy—which demands solution. Our minds would be 'uneasy' in such a situation and would 'naturally seek relief from the uneasiness'. And Hume does not really offer us any relief.

We need a demonstration, and not merely an unsupported assertion, that liberty and necessity are perfectly compatible. The ascription of responsibility requires that the agent could have done something other than what he did at the time, and we need an account of what that requirement comes to, and how it could be fulfilled even though the action that occurred arose of necessity out of its antecedents. Granted, those who suspect an incompatibility here do not have an unproblematic account in clearer terms of what 'could have done otherwise' means, but one does have enough of a sense of what the requirement involves to notice deficiencies in candidates actually offered by compatibilists.

If it is causally necessary that if an A occurs then a B occurs, then if an A occurs, a B must occur. The occurrence of something other than a B is not possible if an A has occurred, given that it is causally necessary that if an A occurs then a B occurs. That is to say, given the way the world is—the causal connections which hold in it and the state of affairs that obtains when that A occurs—there is no alternative to a B's occurring. Of course, it is, in itself, *possible* for a B not to occur—that involves no contradiction or absurdity. The world might simply explode or come to an end right after the A occurs. That is simply Hume's point that no two events are such that the occurrence of one of them can be deduced from the occurrence of the other. But 'a B occurs' does follow logically from the conjunction of 'an A occurs' and 'it is causally necessary that if an A occurs then a B occurs'. So if the causally impossible, but still possible, situation in which an A occurs and a B does not occur were realized, it would follow that it is not the case that it is causally necessary that if an A occurs then a B occurs. That is to say that it is a contingent fact, which could have been otherwise, that the causal connections which hold in our world do hold. But *if* a causal connection does hold between As and Bs and an A occurs, then a B cannot fail to occur. No alternative to a B is possible in such a world after an A has occurred. If no B occurred it would follow that the world is not as the causal statement says it is.

But surely to say that, at the time of the A's occurrence, an agent in that situation could have brought about some alternative to a B, is to say at least that an alternative to a B was possible in that situation in that world.[8] And that is what 'the doctrine of necessity' denies. Some compatibilists, armed with an analysis of 'X could have done otherwise', would reject the implication from 'X could have done otherwise' to 'an alternative to what X did was causally possible at the time of X's action' on the grounds that liberty consists only in the absence of constraint, or coercion or the like, and has no implications about physical or causal possibility.

The dispute is not one I wish to enter into further. I say only that this particular denial of the implication by compatibilists seems, as it stands, clearly mistaken. It is difficult to see how someone could have done otherwise at the time of action if no alternative to what he did was causally possible at that time. But, more important for present purposes, Hume does not actually argue for any such claim, nor is he in a position to do so without a more realistic account of 'the liberty of spontaneity', or of the meaning of 'X could have done otherwise'. Consequently he is not in a position to point to the place at which a fallacy occurs in the reasoning I have roughly sketched in favour of incompatibility between liberty and necessity. I do not say that there is no mistake in the reasoning—only that Hume does not identify it and give us the relief from conflict which we all seek.

Hume sometimes betrays more of a sense of the conflict than he officially allows one can have. He realizes that he has not silenced all possible objections.

> It may be said, for instance, that, if voluntary actions be subjected to the same laws of necessity with the operations of matter, there is a continued chain of necessary causes, pre-ordained and pre-determined, reaching from the original cause of all to every single volition of every human creature. No contingency anywhere in the universe; no indifference; no liberty. While we act, we are, at the same time, acted upon. The ultimate Author of all our volitions is the Creator of the world, who first bestowed motion on this immense machine, and placed all beings in that particular position, whence every subsequent event, by an inevitable necessity, must result. (*E*, pp. 99–100)

This is an example of some theological difficulties apparently implied by 'the doctrine of necessity'—it is one of the reasons the doctrine has been thought to be dangerous to religion. Hume tries half-heartedly to deal with one of the theological problems, but he confesses a failure to resolve them all, and the tone of his remarks suggests that he regards that as so much the worse for religion and theology (*E*, p. 103). But for some reason he does not even consider a non-religious form of the same kind of determinism. If the theological version can seem plausibly to lead to the conclusion that God is the only responsible agent, as Hume admits, then a fully secularized version could equally plausibly lead to the conclusion that there are no responsible agents at all.

Leaving 'the original cause' out of the picture, it is easy to see 'the doctrine of necessity', when applied to everything that happens, as implying a description of a world in which 'there is a continued chain of necessary causes' extending from time immemorial to 'every single volition of every human creature' and thus leaving no alternatives, 'no indifference, no liberty' anywhere in the universe. Surely that is the worry of many who see 'the doctrine of necessity' as a threat to man's liberty—their opposition comes from more than an embarrassment at having to admit that God is the place where the buck stops.

And there seems to be at least some good reason for worry. Many sorts of actions for which agents were held responsible in the past are no longer so regarded. Greater knowledge of certain kinds about what makes people act as they do leads us to ascribe to them only diminished responsibility for those actions, or perhaps no responsibility at all. Our greater sensitivity to psychological factors in everyday life and the increased use of psychiatric testimony in the courts are sufficient proof of the point. And knowledge of the causes of human behaviour is growing. It is quite likely that the connection between the growth of our knowledge and the corresponding shrinking of the domain of responsibility is due at least in part to our belief that certain kinds of causal knowledge about human actions tend to show that the actions could not have been avoided, and to our belief that a person is not responsible for something he could not have avoided doing. And that seems to be genuine moral progress. It is wrong to blame or punish people for what they could not have avoided doing.

Once again, we might be extremely confused in thinking that some causal explanations of action show that the agent could not have done otherwise and so ought not to be blamed, but the fact is that we do think so, and our ascriptions of responsibility to some extent reflect that fact. I have already said that Hume does not identify and expose the source of any such confusion. Nor does he address himself in any detail to the question of exactly how certain kinds of causal explanations can and do lead us to withhold ascriptions of responsibility. That is one place to look for a resolution of the dispute about liberty and necessity. It requires a much closer scrutiny of our actual practices of praising, blaming and excusing than Hume gives us, and some explanation of how and why the domain of moral responsibility is thought to contract as we learn more about the causes of human behaviour. If we withhold blame from a psychopath, for example, not merely because his behaviour was determined, but rather because it was determined in some particular way, then what is the distinction we are using between events determined in an exonerating way and those determined in such a way that the agent remains responsible?

These are familiar, which is not to say easy, questions. I do not suggest that it is impossible for a determinist to answer them. But certainly Hume does not answer them; nor does he make much of a beginning. That is probably because they do not embody his real concerns. The general strategy of his 'reconciling project' is not new. It is found in all essential respects in Hobbes (e.g. Hobbes (1), vols 4, 5). Hume thinks his only original contribution to the dispute is his novel conception of necessity—it 'puts the whole controversy in a new light' (Hume (2), p. 31). His main aim throughout is to establish that uniformities, and therefore necessities, are present to the same degree in human affairs as in the operations of inanimate matter, since for him that is a necessary condition of there being a science of man. The possibility of such a science is what he is interested in, so 'the doctrine of liberty' is dealt with only to the extent that it might seem to count against that condition's being fulfilled. A demonstration that liberty and responsibility actually require 'the doctrine of necessity' erases any threat from that quarter. *A fortiori*, it secures the weaker point that they do not conflict, but it does so without explaining how that compatibility is possible, and therefore without fully resolving what has been felt to be the perennial dispute. But if we know that liberty and necessity must be compatible, then the 'attempt to introduce the experimental method of reasoning into moral subjects' can proceed.

Although every human action is an event that has a cause, and the science of man seeks the causes of human behaviour, it is not part of Hume's aim in any of his philosophical writings actually to explain any particular actions that have occurred. He wants only to lay the foundations for such specific investigations by showing that they are possible and that they will all have a certain general structure. Something can be said in advance about the *kinds* of causes human actions have, and the *sorts* of ways they bring about their effects, and Hume tries to sketch some general principles. What he says appeals primarily to psychological phenomena, understood in terms of the theory of ideas, but there is nothing in his general programme to exclude physiology from the total theory of man.

Just as in other parts of his philosophy, so here too there is a negative and a positive aspect to the overall plan. And here too the theory of ideas plays a large role in the negative phase. In outlining a general theory of action and morals, Hume discusses from another angle the role of reason in human life. His verdict is no more optimistic here than elsewhere. He starts by asking how human actions are actually brought about.

We do things of various sorts in all kinds of different circumstances, so it might seem very difficult to say anything illuminating in general about human action. Is there anything interesting in common between a man's tying his shoelace this morning and his choosing a certain profession or mode of life after years of experiment and deliberation? Hume thinks there is, and that it has profound implications for those who believe that man is a rational animal in the traditional sense.

When we reflect on the great variety of human actions it seems obvious that at least some of them, and often the most important ones, are the result of a great deal of thought. Thousands of hours of information-gathering, hypothetical reasoning, and deliberation went into the invasion of France on D-Day, for example, and finally the event occurred. Isn't something like that also often the case for individual human beings who deliberate and then decide what to do? They seem to be trying to determine or discover what they should do, or what is the best thing for them to do, and it seems as if they often succeed, and then, as a result of that discovery, act. In short, it seems that men often try to be as rational or reasonable in their actions as they can. They think about what they are about to do, and try to make their actions as much the result of rational, informed thought as possible.

The importance of rational or reasonable action is enshrined in the traditional moral precept that we ought to keep our emotions and passions under the control of our reason; men are thought to be virtuous in so far as they conform themselves to the dictates of reason. No man can always achieve this ideal, any more than a man can always believe only what he has the best reasons for believing—interest and passion will sometimes intervene—but in so far as a man is most human he will follow the guide of his reason. Rational men act in accord with their knowledge and informed beliefs.

Hume thinks this conception of reason and its relation to action is completely mistaken, just as he thinks the traditional Cartesian conception of how we come to believe things on the basis of reason could not possibly be right. He tries to demonstrate that by showing:

> *first*, that reason alone can never be a motive to any action
> of the will; and *secondly*, that it can never oppose
> passion in the direction of the will. (p. 413)

This is an attempt to prove that what has been thought to be an important factor in the genesis of action is never *alone* sufficient to do what it has been thought to do. If the proof is successful we will have to change our view of the role of reason in action, and also come to see more clearly those causal factors that are actually most important in the production of action.

Reasoning is a process of arriving at beliefs or conclusions from various premises or bits of evidence, and according to Hume there are only two general kinds of reasoning—demonstrative and probable. Mathematics, or demonstrative reasoning generally, is certainly useful in almost all areas of human life, but he thinks that in itself it has no influence on action, since it is always employed to achieve 'some design'd end or purpose' (p. 414). It can be used to direct our judgments concerning cause and effect, but that is all. And asking how we arrive at those judgments of cause and effect leads us to the second kind of reasoning—the 'experimental' or probable. But it too can only direct our impulses or actions; it does not produce them. If we already have an 'end' or 'purpose', then of course we can use reasoning of either kind to help us discover the best or most appropriate means of achieving it.

> 'Tis obvious, that when we have the prospect of pain or pleasure from any object, we feel a consequent emotion of aversion or propensity, and are carry'd to avoid or embrace what will give us this uneasiness or satisfaction. 'Tis also obvious, that this emotion rests not here, but making us cast our view on every side, comprehends whatever objects are connected with its original one by the relation of cause and effect. Here then reasoning takes place to discover this relation; and according as our reasoning varies, our actions receive a subsequent variation. But 'tis evident in this case, that the impulse arises not from reason, but is only directed by it. (p. 414)

As a way of showing that reasoning alone can never produce action, this is hardly a conclusive argument. It says only that when we already have a 'propensity' towards a certain end, the only role reason can play in action is to guide us in choosing the appropriate means to that end. In the cases Hume describes it is clear enough, as he says, that 'the impulse arises not from reason, but is only directed by it', because they are described as cases in which we start out with an antecedent 'propensity' and then look around for a way (or the best way) to satisfy it. If we have a 'propensity' or 'aversion' already, then perhaps there is nothing left for reason to do but 'direct' it, but it must be shown that all cases of human action are like this—that reason alone can *never* produce action.

Hume claims that there must be what he calls 'propensities' or 'aversions' present in every case of action, and so the 'prospect' of a certain end, or the 'mere' belief that it will be forthcoming, can never alone produce action. And that seems plausible when we consider that:

> It can never in the least concern us to know, that such objects are causes, and such others effects, if both the causes and effects be indifferent to us. Where the objects themselves do not affect us, their connexion can never give them any influence. . . . (p. 414)

Here Hume is saying that in order to perform any action, or to be moved to perform it, we must be 'affected' in some way or other by what we think the action will lead to; we must not be indifferent to the effects of the action. We must in some way want or prefer that one state of affairs obtain rather than another if we are to be moved to bring about that state of affairs. And that seems extremely plausible.

We often come to believe something by reasoning, and that discovery alone does not lead us to act, for just the reason Hume gives. I might find out by observation and reasoning that there is a large juicy water-melon in the next room. I also know by reasoning what I must do in order to get some—I must get up and walk into the next room, try to get someone to bring me some, or some such thing. But clearly all that knowledge, both categorical and hypothetical, is not alone sufficient to lead me to do anything as long as I do not *want* any water-melon. If I do not want any to eat, or to give to someone else, or to use as a paperweight or for anything else, then all the knowledge I admittedly have will not lead me to try to get it. Without a want or desire, or at least a preference for water-melon over its absence, I will do nothing, however much knowledge I have acquired by reasoning. This is part of what Hume has in mind when he says that no discovery of causes or effects would concern us or affect us in any way if we were indifferent to those causes or effects.

But he wants to establish a stronger conclusion. He is trying to show that reason alone is impotent in the sphere of action—that it alone can never lead to action. And he can show that only if he can show that our being concerned by, or being affected by or our not being indifferent to, a certain course of action, is itself something that cannot be the result of some process of reason or reasoning. This can be put in another way.

'Propensities' or 'aversions' are for Hume the causes of all actions. If we could arrive by reason alone at various 'propensities' or 'aversions', then, we could be led by reason alone to act, since propensities and aversions are what cause actions, and if reason alone could bring about those states that are the causes of actions, then reason alone could be the cause of action after all. So in order to establish his thesis of the impotence of reason in action Hume must show that no propensities or aversions could be arrived at by reason alone. It would seem that whether or not that could be established would depend on what sort of things propensities or aversions are. Hume calls them 'emotions' or 'passions', and thus contrasts them directly with anything that could be arrived at by reason. But that is precisely what is in question. If to call something a passion or emotion is to assign it to a different 'faculty' and thus to imply that it could not be arrived at by reason, then it must be independently settled whether or not propensities (i.e. the causes of action) *are* passions or emotions in that sense. Hume thinks they must be.

His main argument, if successful, would establish that conclusion about propensities only indirectly. That is no shortcoming in this case, since it would do so by establishing the stronger thesis about reason and action that Hume is most interested in. He claims to be able to prove that reason alone could never lead to action, and that an action could never be 'opposed to' or 'contrary to' reason. And from that it would follow that, whatever the causes of actions are, whatever 'faculty' propensities and aversions are to be assigned to, they cannot be the sorts of things that are arrived at by reason. If they were, then action could proceed from reason alone; but Hume tries to argue independently that it cannot. If that argument is successful, the propensities or aversions that produce action must be 'emotions' or 'passions', and not the sorts of things that can be arrived at by reason.

Not only do 'conclusions of reason' and the 'propensities and aversions' that are the causes of action belong to different faculties. Hume thinks it is a mistake to think of them as even possibly in conflict with each other. In order for reason to conflict with passion in the direction of the will, reason would have to be 'pushing' the agent or creating an impulse in a direction opposite to that in which passion is 'pushing' the agent. And if reason is perfectly inert, and cannot produce any impulses at all, then obviously it cannot be opposed to passion in the production of action.

> Thus it appears, that the principle, which opposes our passion, cannot be the same with reason, and is only call'd so in an improper sense. We speak not strictly and philosophically when we talk of the combat of passion and of reason. Reason is, and ought only to be the slave of the passions, and can never pretend to any other office than to serve and obey them. (p. 415)

This famous passage is the heart of Hume's theory of action, and therefore of his theory of morals as well.

His main argument for it is very complicated, and he gives it twice, in two different forms.

> A passion is an original existence, or, if you will, modification of existence, and contains not any representative quality, which renders it a copy of any other existence or modification. When I am angry, I am actually possest with the passion, and in that emotion have no more a reference to any other object, than when I am thirsty, or sick, or more than five foot high. 'Tis impossible, therefore, that this passion can be oppos'd by, or be contradictory to truth and reason; since this contradiction consists in the disagreement of ideas, consider'd as copies, with those objects, which they represent. (p. 415)

When he comes to refer back to this argument in the first section of Book III, 'Of Morals', Hume repeats it as follows:[9]

> Reason is the discovery of truth or falshood. Truth or falshood

consists in an agreement or disagreement either to the *real*
relations of ideas, or to *real* existence and matter of fact.
Whatever, therefore, is not susceptible of this agreement
or disagreement, is incapable of being true or false, and can
never be an object of our reason. Now 'tis evident our
passions, volitions, and actions, are not susceptible of any such
agreement or disagreement; being original facts and realities,
compleat in themselves, and implying no reference to other
passions, volitions, and actions. 'Tis impossible, therefore,
they can be pronounced either true or false, and be either
contrary or conformable to reason. (p. 458)

In order to try to understand what Hume is getting at, let us say that
the sorts of things that are true or false are 'propositions'. They are
'representative' entities in that they represent things to be a certain
way, and they are true if and only if things are as the proposition
represents them to be. Only propositions, so understood, are the
proper 'objects of reason'. Hume appears to be saying that the only
way something could be opposed to, or in conflict with, reason is by
being opposed to, or in conflict with, one of the 'objects of reason'.
But something can be in conflict or contradiction with a particular
proposition only if it differs in truth-value from that proposition, and
so whatever can be in conflict or contradiction with a proposition must
be something that itself has a truth-value. And the only things that
have truth-values, the only things that are either true or false, are
'representative' entities such as propositions.

But a passion or emotion is what Hume calls an 'original existence,
compleat in itself'; it is not a proposition at all. When I have a certain
passion, then I am in a particular state; I undergo a certain
'modification of existence'. And Hume concludes that passions do not
'represent' things to be a certain way; they just exist, or are felt. My
being angry is a state or condition I am in, just as is my being more than
five feet high. Therefore passions and emotions are said to be incapable
of truth or falsity, and hence incapable of being in conflict with, or in
opposition to, any of the 'objects of reason'. Those 'objects' are
propositions that are either true or false, so there could be no such
thing as a conflict or combat between reason and passion.

Of course we do speak of actions, and even passions, as being
'unreasonable', or contrary to reason, but Hume thinks that is just a
loose way of speaking and is quite compatible with his view. He thinks
an action is said to be 'unreasonable' only when it is 'accompany'd
with' some judgment or proposition which is itself 'unreasonable' or
'contrary to reason'. If we do or feel something only because we believe
that *p*, and it is in fact false that *p*, then our action or passion might be

159

said to be unreasonable. It is unreasonable for a man to be searching the swamps of Florida for the fountain of youth, because there is no such thing; it is unreasonable for a man to try to get his car to move only by beckoning it with his finger. In the first case the man has a false belief about what exists, and in the second he has a false belief about the appropriate means for achieving one of his ends. But in both cases, Hume says it is because of the falsity of the proposition believed that his action or passion is called 'unreasonable'. Strictly speaking, no actions or passions themselves can be unreasonable or 'contrary to reason'.

> 'Tis not contrary to reason to prefer the destruction of the whole world to the scratching of my finger. 'Tis not contrary to reason for me to chuse my total ruin, to prevent the least uneasiness of an *Indian* or person wholly unknown to me. 'Tis as little contrary to reason to prefer even my own acknowledg'd lesser good to my greater, and have a more ardent affection for the former than the latter. . . . In short, a passion must be accompany'd with some false judgment, in order to its being unreasonable; and even then 'tis not the passion, properly speaking, which is unreasonable, but the judgment. (p. 416)

The argument obviously turns on the contention that the only 'objects of reason' are propositions, or things that are 'representative' and can be true or false. Since only 'original existences' or 'modifications of existence' can cause something to happen, Hume thinks that the objects of reason, and therefore reason itself, can have no such influence. Now there is no doubt that the objects of reason, so understood, can never cause anything. Propositions are at best abstract entities with no location in space or time, and so they cannot themselves cause anything that happens in space and time. They are not 'original existences' or 'modifications of existence'. That part of Hume's argument is perfectly correct. What is questionable is his further assumption that reason is somehow to be understood simply as the totality of the 'objects of reason', i.e. as a set of propositions. That seems to leave out altogether the notion of reason as a faculty of the mind, or reasoning as a mental process.

Hume does say that reason is the *discovery* of truth or falsehood, and that implies that the activities of reason or reasoning involve more than just the 'objects of reason'. They involve our taking a certain 'attitude' towards some 'objects of reason', or our 'operating' with or on them in certain ways, or our 'getting into a certain position' with respect to them. To discover that something is so is to come to believe it. *What* a person believes is either true or false, but his discovering or believing it

160

is not. That is just as much a state of the person, or a 'modification of existence', just as 'non-representative' and incapable of having a truth-value, as is his being angry or his being more than five feet tall. So although the 'objects of reason'—the things that are true or false—cannot cause action, and therefore cannot be opposed to passion in the production of action, it does not follow that reason or reasoning alone cannot cause action. For all Hume has shown so far, it is possible for the discovery by reasoning of the truth of a certain proposition to lead one to act, even though that proposition itself cannot cause anything.

There are good reasons for Hume to agree with this assessment of his argument. For one thing, it seems that one belief—one 'believing'—can be in conflict with another in the same way that one passion or propensity can be in conflict with another. A mother can believe that her son is a good boy while also believing that he has just committed his seventh robbery and assault, and that good boys don't do such things. There can be conflict, or tension, even felt tension, between believings. This is not to say only that all the propositions believed cannot be true together. That is so, but the conflict I am referring to cannot be understood purely in terms of the truth-values of the propositions believed. It is a conflict or tension between two different 'original existences' or 'modifications of existence', and it is just as familiar in the case of beliefs, or believings, or inclinations to believe, as it is in the case of passions or emotions. If, as it seems, believing something can have such effects even though the propositions involved do not, and if, as Hume allows, we can discover or come to believe things by reason or reasoning, then the argument considered so far does not show that it is impossible for reason or reasoning alone to cause action.

Hume's own positive theory to the effect that 'belief is more properly an act of the sensitive, than of the cogitative part of our natures' (p. 183), supports this verdict. He describes the state of believing that p as that of having a certain *feeling* or *sentiment* towards the idea of p, or of 'holding' the idea of p in the mind with a certain sentiment or feeling. Sentiments and feelings can certainly conflict, and can cause action, so if Hume is to show that beliefs arrived at by reason or reasoning cannot cause action, he needs some independent argument for the impotence of those particular sentiments or feelings that are beliefs arrived at by reason. The admitted fact that the 'objects of reason' or the 'objects' of belief are not 'original existences, compleat in themselves', will not suffice.

Furthermore, if Hume's argument showed that no passions or actions, but only propositions, can be contrary to reason, or unreasonable, it would also show that no *beliefs* can be contrary to

161

reason or unreasonable either. Someone's believing something is not itself a proposition that is either true or false, any more than his being more than five feet tall has a truth-value. To believe something, or to be more than five feet tall, is simply to be in a certain 'state'. If the 'reasonableness' or 'unreasonableness' of a belief is solely a matter of the truth-value of what is believed, as Hume suggests, then *how* someone comes to discover or believe something—what procedures he follows, how careful and thorough he is, and so on—is irrelevant to the question of the reasonableness of his belief. But is an unreasonable belief simply one that is false? Surely a person can quite reasonably believe something that is, unknown to him and to everyone else, false, or quite unreasonably (e.g. superstitiously) believe something that is actually true. Hume never thoroughly discusses this distinction.

We saw that he puts forth the sceptical view that we have no reason to believe any of the things we believe; that we are mistaken in thinking that we have any good reasons for believing what we do. And so it might be thought that Hume can gladly accept the conclusion just arrived at to the effect that no *beliefs*, as well as actions or passions, can be contrary or conformable to reason. But that is not so. To accept that conclusion would deprive him of a way of making the very point he insists on about the role of passion or feeling in the production of action. He establishes his sceptical conclusion by showing that, contrary to appearances, the best possible reasons anyone could ever get for any of his beliefs about the unobserved are never good enough to give him any reason to believe what he does rather than its negation; the grounds for each are equal. But the consequence just deduced from Hume's latest argument is much stronger than that. It says that beliefs are simply not the sorts of things that could possibly be reasonable or unreasonable. It is not just that the best possible reasons there could be are, alas, not good enough, but that believings, not being propositions, are no more capable of being reasonable or contrary to reason than are my passions, my actions or my height.

But the whole point of Hume's discussion of the production of action is to contrast feelings or passions with discoveries by reason, and to argue that the former are always the dominant factor and that the latter alone can never cause action. And the kinds of discoveries by reason he has in mind include at least ordinary beliefs about the behaviour of things in the world around us arrived at by straight-forward causal reasoning. He wants to show that even my well-based belief that there is a large, juicy water-melon in the next room, say, can never alone lead me to do anything. Observing various things and making causal inferences from them on the basis of past experience is all part of what Hume means to include under the rubric 'reason or reasoning' when he contrasts it with passion or feeling.[10] The assumption is that to acquire a belief by reasoning is not in itself to be 'influenced' or 'affected' one way or the other. In short, it is not to have a 'propensity' or 'aversion' to any action. And without a 'propensity' or an 'aversion' no action occurs.

Hume still has not established that to acquire a belief by reasoning is not in itself to have a 'propensity' or 'aversion'. That conclusion does not follow from the fact that the 'object' of belief, the proposition that is either true or false, has no causal influence. Nor can he easily concede that believings are simply not the sort of things that could be reasonable or unreasonable, since that would put believings and feelings into the same class, and deprive him of the desired contrast between feelings and beliefs arrived at by reason. How then does he know that our coming to believe something as a result of reasoning never by itself causes us to act and that a feeling or passion is always present?

Hume finds that sometimes 'we feel an . . . emotion of aversion or propensity' (p. 414) and this might suggest that we are *directly aware* of the second and dominant factor in the causality of all action. Perhaps we notice by direct inspection, as it were, that we have the propensity, and notice that it is different from the 'mere' belief or 'prospect'. This would be the best possible evidence we could have for the presence of the two different factors, and there is no doubt that we often have such feelings. We sometimes *feel* impelled to act; we even speak of feeling 'uncontrollable' passions, and on those occasions, perhaps, we can directly find a passion which we take to be the cause of our action. But Hume's thesis is that passions or emotions—states that are not arrived at by reasoning—are *always* present in the production of action, and it is difficult to believe that I am overcome with emotion when I simply decide to cross the road or when I decide to write down something I have just found out. I am certainly not aware of any emotion or passion impelling me to act in such cases—they seem the very model of cool, dispassionate action.

Hume agrees that direct inspection or introspection does not always yield a passion as the cause of action. He thinks that although it often seems to us as if there is no passion or emotion involved, nevertheless in such cases we are wrong. There is a passion there, although it is entirely natural that we should miss it.

'Tis natural for one, that does not examine objects with a strict philosophic eye, to imagine, that those actions of the mind are entirely the same, which produce not a different sensation, and are not immediately distinguishable to the feeling and perception. Reason, for instance, exerts itself without producing any sensible emotion; and except in the more

sublime disquisitions of philosophy, or in the frivolous subtilities
of the schools, scarce ever conveys any pleasure or uneasiness.
Hence it proceeds, that every action of the mind, which
operates with the same calmness and tranquility, is confounded
with reason by all those, who judge of things from the first
view and appearance. Now 'tis certain, there are certain calm
desires and tendencies, which, tho' they be real passions,
produce little emotion in the mind, and are more known by
their effects than by the immediate feeling or sensation. These
desires are of two kinds; either certain instincts originally
implanted in our natures, such as benevolence and resentment,
the love of life, and kindness to children; or the general
appetite to good, and aversion to evil, consider'd merely as
such. When any of these passions are calm, and cause no
disorder in the soul, they are very readily taken for the
determinations of reason, and are suppos'd to proceed from
the same faculty, with that, which judges of truth and
falshood. Their nature and principles have been suppos'd the
same, because their sensations are not evidently different. (p. 417)

We do not simply *feel* 'calm passions'; their existence and efficacy is
not discovered by direct inspection.

But Hume says ' 'tis certain' that there are such passions and desires;
they feel to us just like 'determinations of reason', but he claims to
know they are not. This does not cohere very well with his fundamental
principle that we cannot be wrong about the contents of our own
minds at a given moment.

For since all actions and sensations of the mind are known to us
by consciousness, they must necessarily appear in every
particular what they are, and be what they appear. Every thing
that enters the mind, being in *reality* a perception, 'tis impossible
any thing shou'd to *feeling* appear different. This were to
suppose, that even where we are most intimately conscious, we
might be mistaken. (p. 190)[11]

Apparently we are often mistaken about whether or not a certain calm
passion is before the mind. On the basis of the feeling or sensation
alone we often think that only a 'determination of reason' is leading us
to act, but in fact, unknown to us, it is a calm passion. Hume is willing
to forget one of the foundations of the theory of ideas in order to
support his account of the role of reason in action, although, as we shall
see, his theory of action takes its shape primarily from the theory of
ideas.

He says that the calm passions are 'more known by their effects than

164

by the immediate feeling or sensation', but what are the effects by which such passions are known to exist? The only candidates would seem to be the actions or inclinations which the calm passions actually cause. But if the calm passions are known to exist from the fact that certain actions or inclinations occur, and the fact that those passions are the causes of those actions or inclinations, then there must be some independent way to discover that calm passions are the causes of those actions and inclinations. If we knew that passions were always involved in the production of every action we could infer from the occurrence of an action that a passion existed, even if it was not 'violent' enough to be felt. That is in effect what Hume does. But he still has given no such independent justification. The question of whether a separate passion is in fact involved in the causality of every action is precisely what is at issue.

There is considerable truth in the passage about calm passions just quoted, but it is not obvious that the idea that having a 'propensity' is a matter of having a certain feeling or passion is part of that truth. Even Hume's own examples of the calm 'passions' do not clearly support that idea. He says there are certain 'calm desires and *tendencies*' which are of two distinct kinds: either 'certain *instincts* originally planted in our natures' or 'the general *appetite* to good, and *aversion* to evil, consider'd merely as such'. It is quite plausible to suggest that involved in the causality of every action there must be certain *tendencies, instincts* or *appetites*. Without tendencies or urges to do something of one sort rather than another how could we ever be led to do anything at all? But Hume thinks appetites or desires are themselves passions or feelings.

For example, he speaks of kindness to children as a passion or emotion—one of those 'instincts originally implanted in our natures'. But to have that 'instinct', it would seem, it would be enough for one to be moved to act and disposed to feel certain things on certain occasions; for example, to treat children kindly, to try to prevent harm from coming to them, to feel distress when they might be harmed or in danger, and so on. Being the sort of person who tends to act and feel in those ways is what it is to be a person who is kind to children. But being that sort of person does not require any particular feeling, sensation or passion which is itself the feeling or passion of kindness to children. People who lacked the appropriate tendencies or dispositions would not be thought of as kind to children, but they would not be disqualified because there was a particular feeling or passion they lacked. But Hume says that such tendencies or propensities are passions or feelings.

He clearly thinks that to have a tendency to do a certain thing rather than some alternative is to *prefer* to do that thing, or not to be

165

indifferent as between the alternatives. We could never be led to act unless we were not indifferent to what we think the act will lead to; that is what 'being moved' to act is. And from the true premiss that we would not act unless we preferred one thing over another, or were not indifferent, Hume appears to conclude that we are always moved to act by a passion. Or perhaps it is more accurate to say that he does not carefully distinguish his conclusion from that premiss. For him they seem to be just the same. This is confirmed by the famous passage considered earlier.

> 'Tis not contrary to reason to *prefer* the destruction of the whole world to the scratching of my finger. 'Tis not contrary to reason for me to *chuse* my total ruin, to prevent the least uneasiness of an *Indian* or person wholly unknown to me. 'Tis as little contrary to reason to *prefer* even my acknowledg'd lesser good to my greater. . . . (p. 416, my italics on verbs)

and he concludes:

> In short, a *passion* must be accompany'd with some false judgment in order to its being unreasonable. (p. 416, my italics)

This is supposed to be an illustration of how it is impossible, strictly speaking, for a passion to be contrary to reason. But Hume's examples are *preferrings* and *choosings*, and so they confirm his main thesis only if preferring one thing to another, or choosing one thing over another, is a matter of having a certain *passion*. But that is just what was to have been established.

The theory of ideas is probably at work here. Hume thinks that if you want something or have a propensity towards something then there must be something that is your want or your propensity, and that that thing must be a perception in the mind.

> It has been observ'd, that nothing is ever present to the mind but its perceptions; and that all the actions of seeing, hearing, judging, loving, hating, and thinking, fall under this denomination. The mind can never exert itself in any action, which we may not comprehend under the term of *perception*. . . . (p. 456)

Wanting something is a case of what Hume calls 'the mind's exerting itself in action'; it is a certain kind of mental or psychological phenomenon, and he believes that there must be a perception before the mind if any psychological phenomenon is occurring. The perceptions involved in the case of wanting, preferring, and so on, are all impressions. In particular, they are those impressions of reflection which are emotions, feelings or passions.

I have argued that Hume does not prove, or even make very plausible, the contention that a feeling or passion must always be present for action to occur. Much of its attraction for him derives from the general framework of his unquestioned theory of the mind. But it is difficult to deny the intuitive idea from which he begins to the effect that no belief about the consequences of a certain course of action will lead me to do it unless I also want or prefer those consequences to obtain. If I am totally indifferent as between their presence or absence I will never be moved to bring them about or to prevent them from coming about, whatever I believe. So it seems that something in addition to the 'mere' belief must be present if any action is to occur. But none of this implies that the 'something in addition' is a particular mental item or event, even one that we perhaps do not notice when we 'judge of things from the first view and appearance'. And this is an important point about wants or propensities.

If one event B comes about as a result of another event A, then two things must be true: (i) A occurs, (ii) A causes B. If the first condition is not fulfilled then B does not happen as a result of A; and if the second condition is not fulfilled then B does not happen as a result of A, even though A happens. So we can distinguish two parts or aspects of the production of B, and hence say that the 'mere' occurrence of A is not alone enough to bring about B. At least one other condition must be fulfilled. But obviously none of this implies that if A occurs and B occurs then because A *could have* occurred without B, or *could have* occurred without causing B, there must have been some other event in addition to A which 'helped' cause B. In a world in which A causes B, the occurrence of A alone is enough. If that were not so, then on Humean principles it would follow that *no* event or state of affairs, however complex, would ever be enough in itself to cause any other event or state of affairs, so nothing would ever come about as a result of anything else. For any two events allegedly related as cause and effect Hume argues that it is always possible for the first to exist without the second. But if that implied that in order for the second to be brought about something else must be added to the first, then even the then-augmented 'cause', since it too *could* exist without the second event occurring, would still not be enough to bring the second about, and so on, and so on. This naïve appeal to possibility obviously proves nothing about causal insufficiency.

This shows that there is a way of understanding Hume's quite reasonable claim that no belief alone would lead me to act *unless* I also had a certain desire or preference, without taking it to imply the existence of two distinct items or events, in the mind or elsewhere. It can be quite true that there are two parts or aspects of the production of an action—belief and desire or propensity—without desires or propensities themselves being particular mental items. A 'mere' belief alone would never lead a person to act unless that person were such that, when he gets a belief of that kind, it leads, or tends to lead, to action. And being in some such dispositional state might be all that having a certain desire or propensity consists in. It need not be an additional mental item that itself produces the action.

I am suggesting that the intuitive idea from which Hume derives his theory of action is quite compatible with a non-Humean theory of desires or propensities. It might well be that to have a desire for or propensity towards E is simply to be in a state such that when you come to believe that a certain action will lead to E you are moved to perform that action. I am not interested in the details of such an account at the moment—obviously it is hopelessly crude and oversimplified as it stands[12]—but if some such theory is on the right track, then wanting, preferring or having a propensity need not be understood as a matter of a certain perception's being before the mind. Having a propensity will be nothing more than there being a disposition for certain things to occur in the mind when certain others occur there. We have seen earlier that Hume's pattern of psychological explanation must endow the mind with some dispositions or propensities which cannot themselves be understood in terms of the presence of actual perceptions, so not every psychological statement is such that its truth requires the existence of actual perceptions in the mind. The present suggestion about wants or propensities would be one further instance. If a person is not in a state such that, when he gets a certain belief he will be led to act in a certain way, then the 'mere' belief alone will not lead him to act in that way. He lacks the appropriate propensity or desire. And even if desires or propensities are understood as certain kinds of causal states, or dispositions—and not particular items felt or inferred to be in the mind—there is still a perfectly good sense in which without the desire or propensity the belief would never lead to action. If A occurs, but does not cause B, then B does not come about as a result of A's occurrence.

When Hume says that desires or propensities are passions or emotions he does not mean only that they are feelings. He is even more concerned to show that they are not arrived at by reasoning, and hence that reason alone can never produce action. And even on the non-Humean theory I have suggested, according to which desires are not feelings, he could still be right about the role of reason in action. There is not much independent argument on this point. I said that Hume does not distinguish the true premiss that we would not act unless we wanted or preferred one course of action over another from the questionable conclusion that we are always moved to act by a passion or feeling. And since for him passions or feelings are not the sorts of things that can be arrived at by reason, he thinks he has established that reason alone can never produce action. But there is at least one attempt to show more directly that reason must be supplemented by something not derived from reason if action is to occur. It is the claim that 'the ultimate ends of human actions can never, in any case, be accounted for by *reason*' (*E*, p. 293).

> Ask a man *why he uses exercise;* he will answer, *because he desires to keep his health.* If you then enquire, *why he desires health,* he will readily reply, *because sickness is painful.* If you push your enquiries farther, and desire a reason *why he hates pain,* it is impossible he can ever give any. This is an ultimate end, and is never referred to any other object.
>
> Perhaps to your second question, *why he desires health,* he may also reply, that *it is necessary for the exercise of his calling.* If you ask, *why he is anxious on that head,* he will answer, *because he desires to get money.* If you demand *Why? It is the instrument of pleasure,* says he. And beyond this it is an absurdity to ask for a reason. It is impossible there can be a progress *in infinitum;* and that one thing can always be a reason why another is desired. Something must be desirable on its own account, and because of its immediate accord or agreement with human sentiment and affection.
> (*E*, p. 293)

This is perhaps the best expression of Hume's conception of reason.[13] It does not deny that I can come by reasoning to have a certain want or propensity that I lacked before I engaged in the reasoning. Wanting good health, but not knowing how to get it, I can discover by experimental reasoning that exercise is the best way to get it, and thereby come to want exercise. Reasoning as I did is what led me to want exercise. But if I had not wanted health at the outset, the discovery that if one exercises then one stays healthy would not have resulted in my wanting exercise. A prior want, propensity or lack of indifference is always required in order for reasoning to provide me with wants. And if reasoning provides me with wants or propensities only if I have some prior want or propensity, then reasoning cannot provide me with all the wants or propensities I have. Something must be wanted on its own account, and not just as a means to, or as a way of, getting something else one wants.

Hume's examples here trace the chain of wants back to a desire for pleasure, or for the absence of pain, but there is no need for a view like his to incorporate only a monolithic doctrine of motivation. A Humean theory of the role of reason in action could be correct even if there were many different basic, underived wants. All that is required is that, for each action, there be at least one want or propensity in its causal ancestry that is not arrived at by reasoning. And that follows from the extremely plausible proposition that for every action there is a want or propensity in its production, together with the plausible principle that reasoning produces a want or propensity only if the agent also has some prior want or propensity. Those who see men as sometimes moved to act on the basis of reason alone must deny this latter principle, and also explain how considerations of reason alone can actually move someone to act. [14] They have tended to concentrate their hopes in the domain of morality.

VIII

Reason, Passion and Morality

There's not a blessing Individuals find,
But some way leans and hearkens to the kind.

Hume's discussion of human action is not meant to stand alone. It is put forward primarily to illuminate the nature of morality—one of Hume's earliest and most central interests. Understanding morality involves understanding why and how there comes to be such a thing at all, why we approve or disapprove of any of the people or actions around us, and why we take the particular moral attitudes to them that we do. The aim here, as elsewhere in the science of man, is to explain a pervasive and fundamental part of human life, or at least to lay the foundations for an accurate and detailed naturalistic explanation. And, as elsewhere, this 'scientific' goal is to be achieved partly by a negative and partly by a positive phase, with the negative task once again that of repudiating the traditional pretensions of reason.

Hume's pessimistic verdict about the power of reason in action would lead one to expect a similar conclusion about its role in morality, since he regards morality as the 'practical' study *par excellence*. And his conception of the importance of passion or feeling in the motivation of action would equally lead one to expect a positive theory of morality as based on feeling. Neither expectation is disappointed.

In fact he even thinks his treatment of morality will partly 'corroborate' his account of the understanding and the passions (p. 455), since morality will be found to be yet another sphere in which the importance of reason is denied and the 'sensitive' part of our nature emphasized. If reason really were dominant in morality, if it were possible by some rational means to determine whether an action is right or wrong, then it would be extremely puzzling to find reason so powerless in the affairs of the understanding, which has been thought to be its proper domain. A theory of man holding both views would look seriously split, and suspicious. Hume thinks his account of

171

morality bears out, and lends credence to, his general theory of human nature because it adds to that theory one more important piece that coheres well with the rest.

The theory of ideas plays its part here too, as it did in the explanation of human action. Seeing, hearing, judging, loving, hating, hoping all involve the presence before the mind of perceptions, and the same is true of our 'judgments'[1] of the moral characteristics of people or actions. According to Hume, to approve or disapprove of something is to have a perception before the mind, and so he sees the task of understanding morality as that of explaining what those perceptions are like, and how and why they get there. In fact, he begins with the question:

> *Whether 'tis by means of our* ideas *or* impressions *we distinguish betwixt vice and virtue, and pronounce an action blameable or praise-worthy?* (p. 456)

And he tries to show that to make a moral 'judgment' or 'pronouncement' is to have an impression, and not an idea, before the mind. The impressions in question are said to be feelings or passions, and so sentiment, not reasoning, is found to be the source of morality.

The negative phase repudiating the claims of reason follows a familiar pattern. If reasoning were enough to produce moral judgments, it would do so either by demonstration (or the comparison of ideas) or by means of an inference to some matter of fact. Since for Hume those are the only kinds of reasoning there are, he tries to show that neither leads us to the conclusion that a particular act or character is good, or that it is evil, and so he concludes that no reasoning at all ever leads us to a moral conclusion.

The second part of this negative phase—that concerned with reasoning from experience to some alleged matter of fact—is not completely self-contained. Hume relies on what he regards as positive facts about human nature to reach his negative conclusion. There is no doubt, he says, that morality naturally has an 'influence on human passions and actions' (p. 457). Men are often moved to do something because they think it is good or right, or moved not to do it because they think they ought not to or that it is bad. Such considerations are often completely decisive in themselves to produce or prevent action. This important fact can be noticed simply by a 'cautious observation of human life', and Hume thinks it is enough to show that we can never arrive at moral views by reason or reasoning alone.

> Morals excite passions, and produce or prevent actions. Reason of itself is utterly impotent in this particular. The rules of morality, therefore, are not conclusions of reason. (p. 457)

Given the obvious motivational influence of moral conclusions or moral judgments, they could not be arrived at by reason, since 'an active principle can never be founded on an inactive' (p. 457).

The 'inactive' character of reason or reasoning Hume takes as already established. He thinks he has proven that simply coming to believe something by reasoning is never alone enough to produce or prevent action—a propensity or aversion is also required. But if people are in fact moved to action by moral considerations alone, it would seem that in making a moral 'judgment' or 'pronouncement' a propensity or aversion is already involved. So it looks as if there are some 'judgments' in the very making of which one is moved to act. They are not 'mere' theoretical judgments about causes and effects which can be made in a state of complete indifference. Hume agrees that there are such 'motivating' judgments or 'pronouncements', that we do often arrive at them and that they alone do indeed cause us to act. But for him that is not to concede that reason alone can ever produce action, since he argues that no such judgments or 'pronouncements' are ever arrived at by reasoning. That is what the negative phase of his discussion of morality seeks to establish.

In order to discover by means of *demonstrative* reasoning alone that a certain act in a particular situation is vicious, how would we proceed? For Hume, all demonstration proceeds by the comparison of ideas, so to demonstrate that a certain kind of act in certain circumstances is vicious we would have to show that the idea of vice is included in the very idea of an act of that kind in those circumstances. Hume claims that there are only four kinds of relations between things which are such that we can determine demonstratively whether those relations hold between the things in question. They are resemblance, contrariety, degrees in quality and proportions in quantity and number. For example, from what is included in the idea of five and the idea of three we can demonstrate that five is greater than three. That for Hume is the foundation of the certainty of arithmetic.

But if vice and virtue were demonstrably true of certain acts, then vice and virtue would have to be definable in terms of one or more of those four relations. As Hume puts it: 'When we blame any action, in any situation, the whole complicated object, of action and situation, must form certain relations, wherein the essence of vice consists' (p. 464n). The 'essence' of the vice of an action in certain circumstances would have to consist in some combination of these four kinds of relations holding between the action and the circumstances. On Hume's account of demonstration, that is a condition of the action's being demonstrated to be vicious in those circumstances.

There is no hope of making any such view of moral characteristics plausible, Hume argues, since those same kinds of relations hold between inanimate objects. That would imply that inanimate objects or events are virtuous or vicious, and are to be praised or blamed.

> *Resemblance, contrariety, degrees in quality*, and *proportions in quantity and number;* all these relations belong as properly to matter, as to our actions, passions, and volitions. 'Tis unquestionable, therefore, that morality lies not in any of these relations, nor the sense of it in their discovery. (p. 464)

This is a very general and abstract argument, and it is not easy to understand. No defence at all is given anywhere for the principle that the four kinds of relations mentioned are the only ones that things can be demonstrated to bear to each other. Hume does no more than hurl his familiar challenge for someone to come up with some new relation that will secure the demonstrability of moral judgments. ' 'Tis impossible', he says, 'to refute a system, which has never yet been explain'd' (p. 464). But that hardly establishes the truth of Hume's own unexplained counter-claims, and if he had fully established those claims no such challenge would be necessary. A detailed reconstruction and examination of Hume's counter-argument, even if it were possible, would take us too far afield. It would involve speculating about, among other things, a Humean version of something like a deduction of (some of) the categories.

Some sense of what Hume has in mind can perhaps be gleaned from the particular applications he makes of the general abstract argument. He tries to illustrate the absurdity in any notion of virtue or vice that allows for their discovery by demonstration alone. Parricide is acknowledged to be one of the most horrible acts human beings are capable of committing, but it can be shown that that verdict is not arrived at by demonstration.

> To put the affair, therefore, to this trial, let us chuse any inanimate object, such as an oak or elm; and let us suppose, that by the dropping of its seed, it produces a sapling below it, which springing up by degrees, at last overtops and destroys the parent tree: I ask, if in this instance there be wanting any relation, which is discoverable in parricide or ingratitude? Is not the one tree the cause of the other's existence; and the latter the cause of the destruction of the former, in the same manner as when a child murders his parent? (p. 467)

The implication is that, as far as the general 'relations' characterizing parricide are concerned, there is no difference between the two cases. Thus, if our judgment about the viciousness of parricide were based only on those relations we ought also to think that what the sapling did was vicious. But we do not. Something must be found to be included in the 'essence' of parricide that is not true of the sapling's destroying the parent tree, if our moral judgment in the first case is to be arrived at by demonstration.

Hume of course is not arguing that there are no differences, or no morally significant differences, between the two cases. He is interested at this point only in the definition or 'essence' parricide must have if its viciousness is to be *demonstrated* from the idea of parricide alone. Hence he thinks it is to no avail to argue that the first case is different from the second in that a human will is involved, since that shows only that the cause in each case is different, while it remains true that both are examples of one thing's causing destruction of the cause of its own existence. If that is the 'essence' of parricide, and it implies that parricide is vicious, then it follows that the sapling did something vicious.

Also, it does not help to argue that the sapling is not to be blamed because it has no mind and does not know that what it does is wrong. Hume makes this point with respect to another kind of act believed to be vicious, incest. The wrongness of incest cannot be deduced from the idea of sexual intercourse with one's parents, offspring, or siblings, since that idea applies to non-human animal behaviour which we do not regard as wrong. The difference in moral judgments cannot be explained by saying that it is not wrong for animals because they are unintelligent and so do not know that it is wrong, since that implies that it *is* wrong for animals. And that is not what we believe.

> Animals are susceptible of the same relations, with respect
> to each other, as the human species, and therefore wou'd
> also be susceptible of the same morality, if the essence
> of morality consisted in these relations. Their want of a
> sufficient degree of reason may hinder them from perceiving
> the duties and obligations of morality, but can never hinder
> these duties from existing; since they must antecedently exist,
> in order to their being perceiv'd. Reason must find them,
> and can never produce them. (p. 468)

Hume concludes that any general characterization of the act in the human case that enables us to demonstrate its moral quality will also hold of the non-human case. And since that is absurd, it is impossible to arrive at moral conclusions by demonstration.

It need hardly be said that this argument is not completely decisive. But that is perhaps as it should be, given the vagueness and imprecision of the views Hume is arguing against.[2] Those who held that morality, like algebra and geometry, is 'susceptible of

175

demonstration', tended to draw their examples of successful demonstrations from those mathematical sciences, and not from morality itself. The precise way in which it is analogous to mathematical proof was never specified. Hume's unjustified restrictions on what is demonstrable would tend to rule out many perfectly acceptable demonstrations outside of morality as well, but the fact remains that his opponents did not actually present even one putative moral demonstration for him to consider.

The more important and more interesting half of Hume's negative argument is that concerned with the inference to some matter of fact. He believes not only that the vice or virtue of an action cannot be demonstrated by the juxtaposition and comparison of ideas alone, but that an action's being virtuous or vicious is not a matter of fact that can be inferred by reason from anything. Virtue and vice are in that respect like necessity. We can never observe, in any particular instance, the necessity with which one event follows upon another, and we can never make any reasonable inference from what has been observed to the conclusion that two events are necessarily connected. Similarly, we can never observe the moral characteristics of any action or character, and we can never make a reasonable inference from what we do observe to the conclusion that the act or character in question has certain moral characteristics. But we do believe that events are necessarily connected, and we do arrive at moral 'judgments'.

The passage in which Hume most directly and most forcefully makes this point about morality is as confusing and obscure, and open to as many different interpretations, as the corresponding passage about necessity.

Take any action allow'd to be vicious: Wilful murder, for instance. Examine it in all lights, and see if you can find that matter of fact, or real existence, which you call *vice*. In which-ever way you take it, you find only certain passions, motives, volitions, and thoughts. There is no other matter of fact in the case. The vice entirely escapes you, as long as you consider the object. You never can find it, till you turn your reflexion into your own breast, and find a sentiment of disapprobation, which arises in you, towards this action. Here is a matter of fact; but 'tis the object of feeling, not of reason. It lies in yourself, not in the object. So that when you pronounce any action or character to be vicious, you mean nothing, but that from the constitution of your nature you have a feeling or sentiment of blame from the contemplation of it. Vice and virtue, therefore, may be

176

compar'd to sounds, colours, heat and cold, which, according to modern philosophy, are not qualities in objects, but perceptions in the mind. (pp. 468–9)

The primary negative point about reason is that an action or character's being vicious is not something that can be observed 'in' the action or character in question, nor is it something we can reasonably infer to obtain on the basis of something we do observe. Observing or reasoning to some matter of fact is irrelevant, since for Hume morality does not consist in 'any *matter of fact*, which can be discover'd by the understanding' (p. 468). That is not to deny the obvious fact that, usually, we simply observe an action or character and immediately pronounce it to be, say, vicious. That is what happens; but when it happens we are not then reporting something we observe to be true of the action or character in question or stating the conclusion of an inference reason has determined us to make from the action or character we have observed to the conclusion that it is vicious. The same is true of necessity. In believing that two events are necessarily connected we go beyond any observed relations between the events in question, and beyond anything our experience gives us any reason to believe. But when we see one billiard ball strike another we immediately believe that the motion of the second arises of necessity out of its contact with the first.

The argument for these negative claims is not always as explicit in the case of morality as in the case of necessity, but it is quite clear what Hume has in mind. Many things can be observed or inferred to be true of a particular action we regard as vicious, but each of them is just another 'matter of fact' about what happened. In a case of wilful murder, for example, we can discover by (roughly) causal reasoning that one man deliberately and unnecessarily destroyed a human life and caused great suffering, pain and hardship both to the victim and to others. But according to Hume that is not to discover that the act is vicious. That the act has those observable characteristics and consequences is one matter of fact; that it is vicious is said to be quite another. And no process of reasoning can lead us from the first to the second.

Hume's official view is that two distinct matters of fact can be seen to be distinct from each other if we find we can conceive of the one holding without the other. He thinks that implies that the one is possible without the other. But can we really conceive of an act's leading to all that hardship and suffering without its being vicious? Hume must allow that there is a clear sense in which we cannot. According to his theory of human nature, we are so constituted that the contemplation of an act of that kind inevitably leads us to regard it as

177

vicious, so any attempt on our part to conceive of an act with those characteristics without also regarding it as vicious is bound to fail. The same is true of necessary connection. Two kinds of events' being constantly conjoined in our experience inevitably leads us to regard them as necessarily connected, so we cannot acknowledge the constant conjunction without regarding them as necessarily connected as well. But I argued in Chapter IV that Hume seems right to say that two kinds of events' being necessarily connected is not the same 'matter of fact' as their being constantly conjoined, and he makes a similar distinction in the case of morality.

What we believe when we believe that two events are necessarily connected is different from, and 'more than', what we believe when we believe they are an instance of constantly conjoined phenomena.[3] And what we believe or 'pronounce' when we regard an action as vicious is different from, and something 'more than', anything we can discover by perception of the action or by inference from its observed characteristics to other matters of fact about it. Hume grants that there are certain observable characteristics an action can be known to possess which are such that, when we know the action has them, we inevitably regard it as, say, vicious. But he quite rightly insists that that does not imply that regarding that action as vicious is simply believing that it has those observable characteristics. He thinks that 'pronouncing' an action to be vicious is something different, and that is why he says that the vice entirely escapes you, as long as you consider only the object thought to be vicious.

In the case of necessary connection Hume had little more to rely on than our intuitive recognition that to say that two kinds of events are constantly conjoined is not the same as to say that they are necessarily connected, even though we always believe the latter when we know the former to be true. In the case of morality he has what he regards as more to rely on. He takes it as an undeniable fact about human beings that consideration of the morality of an action sometimes in itself influences our conduct. If it did not, there would be no point in trying to inculcate morality in people. It is a practical, and not a merely speculative, study. But if the 'judgment' that an action is vicious is sometimes enough to lead us to avoid it, then that 'judgment' cannot be a conclusion of reason, since reason or reasoning alone can never lead us to act. We are led to act only if we are not indifferent to the act in question, and our not being indifferent, or our having a desire or aversion, is never a result of reasoning, or reasoning and observation, alone.[4]

It is therefore because of the relation between moral judgments and action that Hume thinks they cannot be solely the results of reasoning. To make a moral judgment is to be 'engaged' on one side or the other.

But is this ever to be expected from inferences and conclusions of the understanding, which of themselves have no hold of the affections or set in motion the active powers of men? They discover truths: but where the truths which they discover are indifferent, and beget no desire or aversion, they can have no influence on conduct and behaviour. What is honourable, what is fair, what is becoming, what is noble, what is generous, takes possession of the heart, and animates us to embrace and maintain it. What is intelligible, what is evident, what is probable, what is true, procures only the cool assent of the understanding; and gratifying a speculative curiosity, puts an end to our researches. (*E*, p. 172)

If moral judgments, because of their 'active' character, cannot be arrived at solely by reasoning, then no belief in any 'matter of fact' we arrive at by observation and reasonable inference from what we observe can be a moral judgment. That is the sense in which virtue and vice are not something 'in' the object. Everything 'in' the object can be observed or known by inference to be there. What we ascribe to an action when we call it virtuous or vicious is therefore something different from, and more than, what we ascribe to it when we believe any 'matter of fact' about the action discovered by observation and reasoning.

Given Hume's view that a desire or aversion is involved in the production of every action, his conception of morality has the consequence that a desire or aversion is somehow involved in the making of every moral judgment. But for Hume desires or aversions are themselves feelings or sentiments, and that is why he says you can never find the vice until you look into your own breast and find a 'sentiment of disapprobation' towards the action. That sentiment, of course, is not discovered by reasoning, but by being felt. It is a sentiment that occurs in the mind whenever we observe or contemplate actions or characters that have certain characteristics, and if we never got such feelings there would be no such thing as morality. Morality is thus based on feeling or sentiment, not reason.

I argued in Chapter VII that even if Hume is right that there is a want or propensity involved in the genesis of every action, he does not establish that a feeling or passion is always involved. His general identification of propensities and aversions with feelings remains unjustified. If having a desire is just being disposed or inclined to act in certain ways in certain circumstances, then it could be true that there is no action where there is no desire without its being true that there is no action where there is no feeling, sentiment or passion. If so, it would not follow that morality is based on feeling, or that some sentiment is somehow involved in the making of every moral judgment. Moral judgments could still be 'practical' or 'active', but they would not require the presence of a feeling in order to have those motivational effects.

But having to abandon feelings and sentiments as the causes of action and therefore as the source of morality would not force Hume to abandon his negative claims about the role of reason in action and therefore in morality. If a desire or preference is involved in the production of every action, and if reaching a moral 'conclusion' is sometimes enough in itself to cause action, then a desire or preference is somehow involved in the making of every moral judgment. According to Hume's theory of action, reason or reasoning can provide one with a new desire or preference only if one already has some desire or preference to begin with, and so reason cannot be the source of all of one's desires. In the causal ancestry of every action there must be at least one desire not produced by reason, or else no desires at all would be present, and so the action could not occur. So in the case of those actions that occur as a result of moral considerations alone there must be at least one desire not produced by reason without which the action would not have taken place. Any conclusion we arrived at by reason alone, then, without the prior existence of any other desire or preference, could not move us to act and hence could not be an 'active' moral judgment.

Hume does not distinguish having a desire or preference from having a feeling or sentiment, and so he concludes directly from his attack on the role of reason in morality that morality is based on feeling or sentiment. But what does this relation of being 'based on' come to in Hume's theory? Exactly what role do feelings play, and what is the relation between the sentiments I feel 'in my own breast' and the moral 'pronouncements' I make? Just as in the case of necessity, there are several different possible answers to this question, all of which are connected fairly closely to what Hume actually says.

Perhaps the most straightforward view is that when I say or believe that a particular action is vicious I am saying or believing that I have a feeling or sentiment of disapprobation towards it. Clearly I am not then talking about something in the action, but only about a feeling I have. I am reporting how things are 'in my own breast'. On this view, every so-called 'moral judgment' is really a statement about the mind of the speaker. The 'moral judgments' I make are about me, and when you say 'X is vicious' you are saying that you have a certain sentiment towards X. Moral talk is autobiography. This view exactly parallels what I called the 'psychologistic' account of causal statements[5]—that they are reports of happenings within the mind of the person asserting them.

This interpretation certainly emphasizes the importance of feeling in moral judgments, since such judgments would be straightforwardly false if the appropriate feelings were not present to the mind. And it also has the desired implication that moral judgments are not arrived at by reasoning. But it leaves a lot to be desired as an account of what 'X is good' actually *means*. It seems to me to have no more initial plausibility as an explanation of what we are saying of an action when we 'pronounce' it good as does its psychologistic counterpart in the case of causal necessity. In saying 'That was a vicious act, done by an evil man' we certainly seem to be saying something about an action and an agent, and not something about our feelings. Of course, appearances are sometimes deceiving, and it might be that that is all we are saying, but if so we need at the very least some understanding of how it can seem to us that we are attributing some characteristic to the action itself, even if we are not.

Hume only adds to the confusion in the way he draws the analogy with secondary qualities. Because, as he says, you cannot find the vice in the object, but only in your own breast where you find a certain feeling, he concludes that vice and virtue, like sounds and colours, are not qualities in objects, but are 'perceptions in the mind'. But that cannot be literally true. If vice were a perception or feeling in the mind, then in saying that I get a certain feeling from contemplating X I would be saying that I get vice from contemplating X. And that is incoherent.

Vice and virtue could be likened to secondary qualities, however, without holding that the very quality (viciousness or redness) is itself a perception in the mind. We could say simply that although there is no vice or redness in the object, nevertheless we ascribe such qualities to the object only because we get a certain feeling or impression when we contemplate or observe it. This does not imply that vice or redness is a feeling or impression, and so the incoherence is avoided. But similarly, the crude psychologistic view is avoided as well, since from the fact that we ascribe viciousness or redness to something only because we get a certain feeling or impression from it it does not follow that when we say 'X is vicious' or 'X is red' we are simply reporting the presence in the mind of a certain sentiment or impression. If the feeling were not present I would not speak or judge as I do, but my utterance or judgment is not thereby shown to be a report of the presence of the feeling.

One thing I might be doing in uttering 'X is good' is expressing a certain feeling or sentiment I have towards X. Now if I smile or wince or cheer I can be said to be expressing my feelings also. I do not *say* that I feel a certain way, since I assert no proposition, but I do something only because I have a certain feeling, and what I do expresses that feeling. It might be that in uttering 'X is good' I am not saying anything either, but am simply expressing in a linguistic way a certain feeling or emotion I have towards X.[6] It would be like a cheer for X; cheers are linguistic, but are typically not assertions.

This 'emotivist' view emphasizes the importance of feelings in moral 'judgments', and it also has the desired consequence that moral 'judgments' are not arrived at by reasoning. But there is no evidence that Hume even considered any such theory. He thinks of a moral conclusion or verdict as a 'pronouncement' or judgment—something put forward as true. Of course, his considered view is that moral judgments are not literally true of anything in the action in question, any more than causal statements are literally true of something in the objects said to be causally connected, but that does not imply that we do not tend to regard those statements as objectively true, and to put them forward as such. It is just that behaviour that Hume wants to explain.

Neither psychologism nor emotivism alone looks plausible as an account of what 'X is good' means, and not only because they are too simple or crude. They could be combined into a more realistic and more sophisticated kind of psychologism according to which in saying 'X is good' I am both reporting the presence of a certain feeling and simultaneously expressing that feeling—I am, as it were, cheering for X while also stating that I have a positive feeling towards it. But even a cheery report of a feeling is still a report of a feeling, and that is what seemed so implausible as an account of the full meaning of 'X is good'. Is there some intelligible alternative interpretation that avoids psychologism while retaining Hume's emphasis on the importance of feelings in moral judgments?

Hume himself sometimes suggests a view that might look more plausible, but it does not cohere very well with his general strategy. He speaks of the impression 'arising from virtue' (p. 470), suggesting that the virtuousness of an action is some objective property of it, and in the *Enquiry* even goes so far as to 'define' virtue to be '*whatever mental action or quality gives to the spectator the pleasing sentiment of approbation*' (*E*, p. 289). This 'definition' can be taken in two different ways, but either way it implies that vice and virtue are objective features of an action or character; they are the features that cause us to have certain feelings when we observe or contemplate them.

If the 'definition' is understood to be equating viciousness with that quality which in fact causes a certain feeling of disapprobation in human beings as they are presently constituted, then it would seem that we could come to discover by reasoning and observation alone whether a particular action has that quality. In fact, there would seem to be no other way to come to that conclusion. One thing Hume thinks makes us approve of an action or character, for example, is its 'utility', its tendency to contribute to the well-being or pleasure of human beings, and he thinks we can discover by reasoning which actions and characters have that quality. Therefore we could discover by observation and reasoning alone which actions and characters are virtuous, and so we could arrive at moral judgments by reason and observation alone. That is what Hume explicitly denies; it would destroy the whole point of his moral theory. Furthermore, if vice were that quality in an action that in fact gives us a certain feeling, then it would be something 'in' the object after all, and actions and characters would have it whether anyone ever actually approved or disapproved of them or not. We could stop approving of 'useful' actions tomorrow, but that would not destroy their utility. It would not make it false that those actions contribute to the well-being or pleasure of human beings. It follows from this way of taking the 'definition' that our getting certain feelings is not essential to there being such things as virtues and vices, and that is not what Hume intends.

This unpalatable consequence could be avoided by taking the 'definition' as implying only that 'X is vicious' means that X has that quality, whatever it might happen to be at the time, which actually causes us to have a certain sentiment of disapprobation towards X. This would not equate viciousness essentially with any particular objective property or characteristic, and it would have the virtue of emphasizing the importance of feelings for the very existence of such things as vices and virtues, as Hume intends. On this interpretation, if no feelings of disapprobation ever occur, or if they stop occurring, it follows that nothing is vicious. Similarly, if those feelings do occur but are not caused by any quality in the objects contemplated or observed, then nothing is vicious. This accords with Hume's contention that to explain 'the origin of virtues and vices' it is enough to explain how and why human beings get certain feelings on the contemplation of actions or characters. The feelings themselves would not *be* virtue or vice, but virtue and vice would exist only in so far as we get such feelings. 'X is vicious' would be straightforwardly true as long as actions or characters had certain properties which caused us to get certain feelings.

Hume's main interest in moral judgments, however, is not in what they mean, but in what leads us to make them, and even on this account he cannot avoid the conclusion that reasoning is what leads us to 'pronounce' X to be vicious. We might get a certain feeling on contemplating X, but that alone cannot lead us to believe that X is vicious, if 'X is vicious' means that X has some quality that causes that feeling. Having a feeling towards X is not enough in itself to lead us to believe that some property of X caused us to have that feeling. Of course we might well believe that some property of X did cause the feeling, but we will not believe that solely on the basis of the feeling alone. According to Hume's theory of causality, we will come to believe it only by making an inference from an observed constant conjunction between objects (or the contemplation of objects) of a certain kind and feelings of a certain kind. And that is a matter of reasoning, not feeling. Therefore 'X is vicious', so understood, could not be a 'pronouncement' we arrive at by feeling or sentiment alone.

We saw that it was not plausible to *define* necessity as 'that feature of the relation between events which gives to the spectator an impression of determination'. We know what that feature is, and we know how it gives rise to the impression of determination, but to say that that feature *is* necessity would imply that, contrary to Hume's intentions, necessity is indeed an objective feature of the relation between events. The 'definition' Hume offers of virtue suffers from the same defect as his 'definition' of causality. Both are 'drawn from something extraneous and foreign' to what they purport to define. They do not adequately express what we say or believe of something when we say or believe that it is vicious or that it is necessarily connected with something else, although perhaps they do adequately pick out what it is in the objective situation that inevitably leads us to say it or believe it. Perhaps they get as close to adequate definitions of such fundamental notions as we can get.

More of Hume's aims would be served by a theory of moral judgments that follows the same general lines as I suggested for the case of necessity. I contemplate or observe an action or character and then feel a certain sentiment of approbation towards it. In saying or believing that X is virtuous I am indeed ascribing to X itself a certain objective characteristic, even though, according to Hume, there really is no such characteristic to be found 'in' X. In that way virtue and vice are like secondary qualities. In saying that X is virtuous I am not just making a remark about my own feeling, but I make the remark only because I have the feeling I do. In 'pronouncing' it to be virtuous I could also be said to be expressing or avowing my approval of X. Hume thinks that approval is a quite definite feeling, so for him it would be expressing my feeling towards X.

This would avoid the pitfalls of psychologism and emotivism, and of their combination, while still emphasizing the importance of feeling in the making of moral judgments. Without the appropriate feelings there would be no such things as moral judgments, so in that sense morality is a matter of feeling, not reason, and hence moral considerations can influence the will. What I actually feel determines the moral judgment I make, and since the judgment has no other source, it is not something that could be arrived at by reasoning. The judgment is an expression of my feeling, but not a report to the effect that I have such a feeling. Rather, it is the attribution of a certain characteristic—virtue or goodness—to an action or character. Although there is in fact no such characteristic in actions or characters, the feelings we get on contemplating them inevitably lead us to ascribe it to them. The acceptance or assertion of the moral judgment is thus a reaction to or a result of the feeling, but it does not merely evince the feeling as does a cry or a cheer. We express the feeling by way of making an assertion, but not an assertion about the contents of our own minds. Our moral judgments, like our causal judgments, are 'projections'.

It must be admitted that this sketch of a view goes beyond anything explicitly stated in Hume's discussion of morality, but it is on all fours with his treatments of other central topics in the science of man, and it coheres better than any alternative with his general philosophical aims. Nor is it inconsistent or incoherent in itself.

There is superficially a difficulty in Hume's theory of moral judgments that is absent from his account of causal statements, however. In the case of necessity we are said to have an *idea* of necessity that we employ in formulating our *belief* that two events are necessarily connected, but Hume nowhere mentions a corresponding *idea* of virtue or goodness and he never talks explicitly about moral *beliefs*. The official view is that a belief is a lively idea, but we saw that Hume takes himself to be arguing that it is not by means of our ideas at all, but only by means of our impressions, that 'we distinguish betwixt vice and virtue, and pronounce an action blameable or praise-worthy' (p. 458). That is thought to be required to establish the impotence of reason in morality. But then what could a moral 'pronouncement' be? It would seem to consist only of an impression or feeling, but how do we employ that very feeling in formulating a 'pronouncement' or judgment?

It seems as if there must be some difference between having a certain feeling towards X and 'pronouncing' or judging X to be virtuous, just as there is a difference between our getting an impression or feeling of determination when observing one event following another and our believing that the two events are necessarily connected. And that distinction need not undermine the point of Hume's theory. The belief in question requires an idea, and the idea of necessity, for example, arises directly and naturally from the impression or feeling of determination. Thus we *believe* that the two events are necessarily connected, but the presence of the impression or feeling is absolutely essential for our getting that causal belief.

Although he does not do so, Hume might well have given an exactly parallel account of moral judgments. He could say that in saying or believing that X is vicious I do employ an idea of viciousness, but that I get that idea and make that judgment only because I get a certain feeling or sentiment from contemplating X. So it is still by

185

means of my impressions, and not my ideas, that I 'distinguish betwixt vice and virtue, and pronounce an action blameable or praise-worthy'. I make the distinction on the basis of my impression or feeling, but I use an *idea* of viciousness or virtuousness in making my pronouncement.

Kemp Smith has argued very persuasively that the general line Hume follows throughout the science of man—the idea that on the basis of our feeling we inevitably and quite naturally 'project' onto the world various characteristics that it does not actually possess—was first suggested to him by Hutcheson's theory of morals, and that Book III of the *Treatise*, 'Of Morals', was probably written first (Kemp Smith (2), chs I–II). If so, that would explain the relative crudity of Hume's account of moral judgments in comparison with that of causal statements. Only when he comes to articulate the rest of the 'new scene of thought' he has discovered, by generalizing the theory to all parts of man's intellectual life, and in particular to causal thinking and reasoning, does he see the importance of the notion of belief, and hence the need for *ideas* to make up the content of beliefs. The general thrust of the theory—that sentiment and not reason is the dominant factor in human affairs—remains unaltered when the importance of beliefs, judgments or 'pronouncements' has been acknowledged, and so the appropriate parts of the moral theory could have been rewritten without danger along the lines I have suggested.

But still, in morals as in the case of necessity, we might feel a residual dissatisfaction with the theory of 'projection'. For all of Hume's efforts, he does not explain in any way *what* we are attributing to an action when we say it is virtuous; he does not tell us what 'virtuous' means, any more than he tells us what 'necessary' means. That is perhaps not surprising if, as is likely, Hume regards the notion of virtue or goodness as simple. The *origins* of certain simple perceptions in the mind can be explained, but their meaning or content cannot be explicated further. Any purported definition would have to be 'drawn from something extraneous and foreign' to virtue or goodness. But the theory does enable him to explain how and why there is such a thing as morality, how and why we make the moral judgments we do. Most important of all, it shows how the very nature of moral judgments—their character as reactions to and expressions of the feelings of approbation and disapprobation we receive from actions we contemplate—precludes their being arrived at by reasoning.

The impotence of reason and the force of sentiment in morality is Hume's most important point. He clearly emphasizes it in a passage that has come to be famous by being understood somewhat differently.

186

I cannot forbear adding to these reasonings an observation, which may, perhaps, be found of some importance. In every system of morality, which I have hitherto met with, I have always remark'd, that the author proceeds for some time in the ordinary ways of reasoning, and establishes the being of a God, or makes observations concerning human affairs; when of a sudden I am surpriz'd to find, that instead of the usual copulations of propositions, *is*, and *is not*, I meet with no proposition that is not connected with an *ought*, or an *ought not*. This change is imperceptible; but is, however, of the last consequence. For as this *ought*, or *ought not*, expresses some new relation or affirmation, 'tis necessary that it shou'd be observ'd and explain'd; and at the same time that a reason should be given; for what seems altogether inconceivable, how this new relation can be a deduction from others, which are entirely different from it. But as authors do not commonly use this precaution, I shall presume to recommend it to the readers; and am persuaded, that this small attention wou'd subvert all the vulgar systems of morality, and let us see, that the distinction of vice and virtue is not founded merely on the relations of objects, nor is perceiv'd by reason. (pp. 469–70)

This is the last paragraph of Section One of Book III of the *Treatise*. Hume apparently added it as something of an afterthought he hoped would be helpful. He does not repeat it, or anything like it, in the *Enquiry*.

Although many claims have been made both for and about this passage,[7] Hume seems primarily concerned to re-emphasize the point that it is because of the special character of moral judgments that they cannot be 'perceiv'd by reason'. We undoubtedly make transitions from beliefs about the way things are to the judgment that things ought to be a certain way. That is to say, we observe actions and discover by reasoning some of their other characteristics and their consequences, and then we immediately and quite naturally arrive at moral judgments or conclusions. But if we understand the peculiar nature of these 'conclusions'—if we recognize their 'active' or motivational force—we see that the transitions by which they are reached are not ones that reason determines us to make. Once we come to have certain beliefs about the way things are, then, because of natural human dispositions we come to feel certain sentiments which we express in moral judgments.

Hume takes himself to have explained the only way in which such transitions can occur. Because of the 'active' power of moral judgments, we arrive at them from other beliefs only by the interposition of a feeling or preference, since feeling or preference must be present for action to take place. Given what he takes to be the undeniability of those facts, Hume expresses the conviction that anyone else who tries to explain how we arrive at moral judgments will come to agree with him. He has already explicitly argued against the claims of reason, and he thinks that only an unexamined faith in the powers of reason, or a failure to see the relation between moral judgments and the will, or a simple failure to investigate the question at all, could have led traditional moralists to suppose that moral judgments are arrived at by reason. That is why some 'small attention' to the question he raises would subvert all the vulgar systems of morality. He sees his 'subversive' answer to it as the only possible answer.[8]

In order to complete his positive explanation of how and why we make the moral judgments we do, Hume must describe in more detail the peculiarly moral feelings we get on contemplating actions and characters, and this leads to serious difficulties in his account of the precise role of actual feelings in the making of moral judgments. He says that the feeling or impression of virtue is pleasant or 'agreeable', and that of vice 'uneasy'. That is why we seek virtue and shun vice. But not just any feeling of pleasure or uneasiness we get from contemplating an action or character gives rise to a moral judgment concerning it. If it did, it could equally give rise to moral judgments concerning inanimate objects, since they too give us pleasant or uneasy feelings, and Hume would then be guilty of the same absurdity he found in the views of the moral rationalists. There must therefore be some distinction between the peculiarly moral sentiments and other pleasant or uneasy feelings.

It is not enough to say that moral sentiments are those pleasant or uneasy feelings we get from contemplating only *human* actions and characters, since not even all those feelings are feelings of virtue or vice. An enemy or opponent might cause us great pain or hardship, but we can still respect and even morally praise him. The pain he causes us is an uneasy sensation, but our praise or esteem must come from a sentiment that is pleasant, so not all the feelings he causes in us are moral feelings. The moral feelings constitute only some of the feelings we get on contemplating human actions or characters.

As Hume points out, it is often difficult to distinguish phenomenologically between the sentiments we get 'from interest' and those we get 'from morals' (p. 472). We often think an enemy vicious simply because he causes us pain or discomfort; we do not distinguish between 'his opposition to our interest and real villainy or baseness' (p. 472). It is an important fact about human beings that it is often difficult for them to make such distinctions, especially in the heat of the moment. But nevertheless, Hume argues, the sentiments are in fact distinct, whether we notice it or not. There is a distinction between a man's opposing our interest and his being vicious:

> and a man of temper and judgment may preserve himself
> from these illusions. In like manner, tho' 'tis certain
> a musical voice is nothing but one that naturally gives a
> *particular* kind of pleasure; yet 'tis difficult for a man
> to be sensible, that the voice of an enemy is agreeable, or
> to allow it to be musical. But a person of a fine ear,
> who has the command of himself, can separate these feelings,
> and give praise to what deserves it. (p. 472)

No doubt we can acknowledge a difference between an enemy's opposing our interest and his being vicious or a villain. And no doubt we can morally praise someone we recognize to be causing us pain by opposing our interest. These are some of the facts of our moral thinking Hume tries to account for. His theory of moral judgment as expounded so far implies that if I acknowledge on a particular occasion that a man is opposing my interest and causing me pain but that he is nevertheless virtuous, I have two quite distinct feelings at that time towards him. It follows that when we feel nothing but pain from an opponent it is impossible for us to regard him as virtuous in any way. That is an unrealistic conclusion. And to say that if we do regard him as virtuous it is because we have a feeling we are not then aware of, is to threaten Hume's general principle that all sensations 'must necessarily appear in every particular what they are, and be what they appear' (p. 190). If we cannot be mistaken about what we are feeling, and if all moral judgments are made on the basis of what we actually feel at the time, then when we judge a man to be virtuous we must be aware of some pleasant feeling his action or character produces in us. And that does not seem always to be true in real life.

So there is a serious question of the extent to which a faithful and realistic account of the conditions under which we make moral judgments can maintain that we make them on the basis of, and in proportion to, the actual feelings we have at the time of making the judgment. Hume is certainly aware of the difficulty, and although, characteristically, his attempt to deal with it is an attempt to be true to the facts of moral thinking, it puts considerable strain on his official theory of the role of feelings in morality.

Hume wants to grant that we often make moral judgments about actions or characters that do not currently engage our feelings at all, or at least do not engage them to the degree they would have to if his

189

official theory were correct. According to Hume I do not get the same lively pleasure from contemplating the acts or character of an ancient Greek as I do from those of a close friend I am enjoying myself with right now, but still I might 'esteem' the Greek more. If my actual feelings constitute, or are the source of, my moral judgments, this would seem to be impossible; my actual feelings are stronger towards my present friend than towards the ancient Greek. But in fact, Hume says, our 'esteem' does not vary with every variation in our actual sentiments; that is precisely what makes moral thinking and dialogue possible.

Because each of us is in a unique and constantly changing position with respect to every other person and thing in the universe, if we spoke only of the way things seem and feel to us from our point of view at the moment, nothing resembling human discourse and communication would even be possible. We speak of 'the size' of an object, although it appears smaller or larger depending on our distance from it. According to Hume, we soon learn to arrive at this 'more stable' judgment of things, and to describe them as they would be experienced from a 'steady and general point of view' (pp. 581–2). This is just as true of the moral sentiments as of the impressions of the senses.

> In general, all sentiments of blame or praise are variable,
> according to our situation of nearness or remoteness, with
> regard to the person blam'd or prais'd, and according to
> the present disposition of our mind. But these variations
> we regard not in our general decisions, but still apply the
> terms expressive of our liking or dislike, in the same
> manner, as if we remain'd in one point of view. Experience
> soon teaches us this method of correcting our sentiments,
> or at least, of correcting our language, where the sentiments
> are more stubborn and inalterable. (p. 582)

So our actual sentiments do vary with changes in our relations to the objects of those sentiments, and with changes in our interests and concerns, but the moral judgments or 'pronouncements' we make about those objects do not vary or change accordingly. If our actual feelings cannot be 'corrected' or altered, what we say or believe on the basis of those feelings can. And this leaves Hume with an obvious problem. If there can be alterations in our actual sentiments without corresponding alterations in our judgments of esteem, and vice versa, then the judgments or 'pronouncements' we make are not solely a function of the feelings we have at the time. How then do we come to make them?

We apply the moral epithets, Hume says, 'in the same manner, as if we remain'd in one point of view', even though we do not in fact remain in such a single point of view. Our situation and our feelings are constantly changing, as are all our impressions, and we soon learn what we *would* experience if we *were* in a certain position that we know we are not in at the moment. Although a diligent and faithful servant arouses stronger and more pleasant sentiments in us than does Marcus Brutus, we do not thereby judge the servant to be morally superior, because 'we know, that were we to approach equally near to that renown'd patriot, he wou'd command a much higher degree of affection and admiration' (p. 582). Similarly, although a beautiful countenance does not give as much pleasure at twenty paces as it does at two, we do not say that it is, or even that it appears, less beautiful at a distance, because 'we know what effect it will have in such a position, and by that reflexion we correct its momentary appearance' (p. 582). So our moral judgments, like our aesthetic judgments, are not always direct expressions of our actual feelings. Rather, they are judgments about what we, or perhaps anyone, *would* feel on contemplating the object in question from a 'steady and general point of view'. The judgments are thus 'disinterested' in that they are not a direct expression of our current feelings or interests.[9]

This complication of Hume's theory has the effect of divorcing our moral judgments from our actual feelings, but of course it does not put Hume completely in the camp of the moral rationalists. Feelings or sentiments are still of fundamental importance for morality—without some reliance on them there would be no such thing as morality at all. If not an actual feeling, then at least a possible one, is involved or alluded to in the making of every moral judgment. And, as Hume intends to show, moral thought or reasoning is really a reflection of human nature, and is not simply about some abstract 'relations' in which actions or characters are alleged to stand. So the divorce between moral judgments and actual feelings does not imply that moral judgments are arrived at by the comparison and juxtaposition of ideas alone, or that moral thought is a matter of purely *a priori* reasoning. To that extent it is compatible with Hume's general philosophical aims.

But his 'new scene of thought' would make sentiment dominant over reasoning; in particular it sees morality as 'more properly felt than judg'd of' (p. 470). And such a view would seem to require an actual feeling for every moral judgment. It is not by feeling alone that we discover that we *would* feel such-and-such *if* certain conditions were to obtain. Only by experience and reasoning can we come to such a conclusion. For example, to come to believe that something that is slightly pleasurable at a distance would give us more pleasure when brought nearer we must rely on our past experience of having got nearer to such things in the past and having recognized the need to 'correct' the judgment made on the basis of 'momentary appearance'.

The inference is not a good one in every case. And if the same holds for morality, then only by experience and reasoning could we know that Marcus Brutus, *if* he were here now, *would* give us a stronger sentiment of approbation than our diligent servant. And that implies that our moral judgment is arrived at by reasoning from experience. Without such reasoning we would make a different moral judgment, or none at all. So Hume's attempt to bring his theory of moral judgment more into accord with the facts of moral thinking commits him to the view that moral judgments are the results of certain operations of the understanding. And that is just the conclusion he wants to avoid. It is incompatible with the conjunction of his two fundamental conclusions about human behaviour—that making a moral judgment is often enough in itself to lead us to act, and that reasoning alone can never lead to action.

Hume shows no real awareness of these difficulties in his theory, probably because he was primarily concerned to emphasize the importance of feelings in morality and to repudiate the views of the moral rationalists. The rationalistic theory is weak just where Hume thinks his theory is strongest—on the relation between moral judgments and the will. He thinks it is the 'active' character of moral judgments that the rationalists cannot account for. But given his straightforward theory of the role of feelings in the production of action, Hume is in danger of breaking the connection between moral judgments and the will by arguing simply that feelings are involved or alluded to in some way or other in the making of every moral judgment. He must show precisely how a 'disinterested' moral judgment is nevertheless 'active', or how a thought or belief about merely possible feelings can lead us to act. That is something he never explains.

No doubt it is more realistic to allow that our actual feelings change and vary in intensity in a way that our moral judgments do not, so Hume seems correct to divorce the two. But when he comes to the question he is primarily interested in, viz. how and why we make the particular moral judgments that we do, or what makes us the kind of moral beings that we are, he slips back into the official straightforward theory and tries to answer it by explaining how and why we get the actual feelings we do from the contemplation of various actions and characters. As we shall see in the next chapter, he tends to forget the extent to which moral judgments ought to be divorced from our actual feelings. The attractions of the simple theory prove irresistible.

IX

Morality and Society

Forc'd into virtue thus by Self-defence,
Ev'n Kings learn'd justice and benevolence:
Self-love forsook the path it first pursu'd,
And found the private in the public good.

Men approve of certain things and disapprove of others, and Hume finds that that approval or disapproval alone can lead them to act. He also explains, with some equivocation, what making a moral judgment is, how it is related to approving or disapproving of something, and how and why it leads to action. A further, and perhaps the most important, task for the science of man is to explain why we come to approve or disapprove of the sorts of things that we do. Despite the more sophisticated version of his theory of moral judgments outlined at the end of the previous chapter, Hume usually takes this task to be that of discovering what sorts of things produce actual sentiments of approval or disapproval in us, and how they have those effects. To explain what it is in human nature that leads us to have certain sentiments when confronted with certain sorts of phenomena is for Hume to explain 'the origin of virtues and vices'. We saw that regarding something as virtuous or as vicious is not simply a matter of having an actual sentiment towards it, but Hume tends to forget that when he tries to catalogue the different sorts of things that we approve or disapprove.

Once again, a 'cautious observation of human life' is enough to provide him with his data. He seeks some features common to all those things we approve of, and something common to all those things we disapprove of, and although he does not find one simple feature in either case, he comes up with a very short list. It is important to see that Hume produces this list in his capacity as a philosopher of human nature, not as a common man engaging in moral thinking about the world around him. Observation and experimental reasoning do not themselves yield moral views about what is virtuous or vicious.

To have the sense of virtue, is nothing but to *feel* a

satisfaction of a particular kind from the contemplation of a character. The very *feeling* constitutes our praise or admiration. We go no farther; nor do we enquire into the cause of the satisfaction. We do not infer a character to be virtuous, because it pleases: But in feeling that it pleases after such a particular manner, we in effect feel that it is virtuous. (p. 471)

In everyday life, when pronouncing something to be virtuous, we make no inference; the feeling is enough. But as philosophers concerned with the phenomenon of morality we must inquire into 'the cause of the satisfaction', just as we inquire into the origin of the idea of necessity, even though the vulgar need have no views about the origin in either case.

There is a strong tendency, in thinking about human nature, to say that a man approves of only those things that are in his self-interest, or, more plausibly, those things he believes to be in his self-interest. This monistic theory finds a single feature present in every case of approval. Hume explicitly and energetically rejects any such view. As we have seen, we praise or condemn actions performed in ancient times, although we know that they cannot further or impede our self-interest in any way; and we can approve of the actions or character of an enemy who is actually thwarting us. Perhaps the difficulty of explaining how this is possible has led some people to deny that it occurs, but that is simply to fly in the face of the facts. According to Hume, there are actually four different sorts of things that we approve of, and he tries to explain the mechanism by which that approval arises in each sort of case.[1]

Most of the acts or characters we approve of are useful to society, or tend to produce the good of mankind. It is because of their 'utility' that we approve of justice, obedience to law, fidelity or trustworthiness, and allegiance, as well as generosity, charity and moderation. All of these characteristics contribute to the well-being of mankind, and that is why we feel the sentiments of approbation towards them that we do.

Some of the acts or characters we approve of do not have utility for mankind as a whole, but they contribute to the interest and satisfaction of the person possessing them. A person's temperance, prudence, frugality and enterprise do not so obviously lead to the good of society in general, but they are good or useful characteristics for a person to have. The customs prevailing where a man lives partly determine what qualities it is most beneficial for him to possess, but there is a long list of qualities that would seem to serve a man well in whatever conditions he lives.

Although it might be argued that our approval of what is useful to mankind or society is really based on self-love or narrow self-interest, because of our alleged belief that society's well-being is also our own, it is much less plausible to suggest that this second class of qualities are also approved of on the basis of self-love, or concern only for our own self-interest. We applaud enterprise, patience, discretion, perseverance and many other qualities in men with whom we could have no contact and from whom we could reap no benefits, and not because those qualities tend to promote the well-being of society. Hume thinks this proves that 'the happiness and misery of others are not spectacles entirely indifferent to us' even when that happiness or misery in no way touches our own. And, as we shall see, he is equally sceptical of the attempt to reduce our approval of the good of mankind to a species of self-love.

The great majority of the things we approve of belong to one or the other of these first two classes: they tend to promote either the good of mankind in general or the good of the particular men who have them. They are approved of for their results, of which we approve. But there are human characteristics that we simply find 'agreeable' in themselves, not for the sake of anything else, and they too fall into two classes. There are characteristics that are immediately agreeable to those who observe or contemplate them, such as wit, ingenuity, eloquence, decency, decorum and even cleanliness. Contemplating someone endowed with these features, Hume says, gives us 'a lively joy and satisfaction' whether we actually encounter the person or not (E, p. 262). And finally, there are certain qualities that are immediately agreeable, not necessarily to those who observe or contemplate them, but to those who possess them. It is not always clear what Hume thinks falls into this class. He mentions cheerfulness, serenity, contentment, self-pride and self-respect. We regard them as virtues, he says, because we recognize them as immediately agreeable to those who possess them.

The accuracy and completeness of this classification of the things we approve of is not nearly as important for our purposes as its variety.[2] Humes tries not to make a simple assumption about how men are able to feel approval for things. Rather, he observes what things people actually regard as good, and then tries to reduce the variety to as few kinds as possible without distortion. That is completely in accord with his Newtonian programme. But the classification is only part of the story; it gives only a constant conjunction between being a characteristic of a certain sort and being approved. The next question is how something's being of a certain sort actually gives rise to that approval.

According to Hume's theory, I get a pleasing sentiment of approbation from contemplating someone's possessing qualities that are immediately agreeable to him or to those who observe them. And I get a similar sentiment from contemplating someone's possessing qualities that tend to benefit him or to benefit society. In the latter two cases I get the sentiment from something that tends to promote a certain end, so it must be that I am not indifferent to that end. The well-being of particular people and the flourishing of society and mankind generally must be things which themselves give me pleasing sentiments of approbation. Only if that were so would I approve of what leads to them.

Even though the well-being of society does not necessarily lead to my own well-being, and the well-being of other individuals does not further my own interests at all, there is a fundamental property of the imagination that is responsible for my approving of them nevertheless. Without that property almost none of the things we now regard as virtues or vices would be so regarded, and the monistic self-interest theory would be correct. Hume usually calls the property in question 'sympathy', and although he is not always consistent or accurate in what he says about it, the general idea is clear enough. And some such phenomenon does, indeed, seem to play an important part in morality.

We undoubtedly have a general propensity to feel what others around us are feeling.

> A good-natur'd man finds himself in an instant of the
> same humour with his company; and even the proudest and
> most surly take a tincture from their countrymen and
> acquaintance. A chearful countenance infuses a sensible
> complacency and serenity into my mind; as an angry or
> sorrowful one throws a sudden damp upon me. (p. 317)

The passions are 'contagious'; like tightened strings, the movement of one is communicated to the rest. According to Hume this happens because of an operation of the imagination familiar in other forms. For example, we can sometimes make ourselves feel sick or afraid just by thinking about certain things; a thought leads to a feeling. In Hume's terms, an idea is converted into an impression. That is just what happens when we observe or contemplate other people who are feeling certain things, and that is how we can be affected and moved by their feeling what they do.

> When I see the *effects* of passion in the voice and gesture
> of any person, my mind immediately passes from these
> effects to their causes, and forms such a lively idea of the
> passion, as is presently converted into the passion itself.

In like manner, when I perceive the *causes* of any emotion,
my mind is convey'd to the effects, and is actuated with
a like emotion. Were I present at any of the more terrible
operations of surgery, 'tis certain, that even before it began,
the preparation of the instruments, the laying of the
bandages in order, the heating of the irons, with all the signs
of anxiety and concern in the patients and assistants,
wou'd have a great effect upon my mind, and excite the
strongest sentiments of pity and terror. No passion of
another discovers itself immediately to the mind. We
are only sensible of its causes or effects. From *these*
we infer the passion: And consequently *these* give rise to
our sympathy. (p. 576)

It is just a fact about us that the pain and suffering of others is
unpleasant to us, and that their pleasure and well-being is pleasant to
us, and that is how we can come to approve of and be moved by
consideration of the welfare of others or of mankind generally. It is
because of the operation of what Hume calls 'sympathy'.

Sympathy is to be understood as a disposition we have to feel what
others are feeling; it is not a particular feeling itself. If, as Hume
sometimes suggests, it were a particular feeling we get when
contemplating others, then the appeal to sympathy would not explain
what he wants it to explain. For one thing, if another person feels pain
and I consequently feel that special feeling that is sympathy, then I do
not feel what he feels after all—his feeling is not being transmitted to
me. He feels pain, but I feel sympathy. Furthermore, I am said to be
upset when I know someone else is feeling pain, and pleased when I
know someone is feeling pleasure. Both are examples of what Hume
calls sympathy. But clearly my feelings or reactions are quite different
in the two cases, as they must be if they are to explain the very different
ways I might act in the different situations. So it cannot be that
sympathy is a particular feeling. If it were, its presence could not
explain why I approve of some things and disapprove of others.

But if sympathy is the disposition to feel, even faintly, the very same
things that others feel, then there is some question whether there is
such a thing. Although I sympathize with the child with a bad
toothache—her suffering is unpleasant or perhaps unbearable to
me—it can hardly be said that in doing so I actually have a toothache
myself. Because another's suffering can move me to action Hume is
committed to saying that it produces some feeling in me, since only
feeling can move one to action. But he need not say that it produces in
me the very same kind of suffering as the other is undergoing. It would
be enough for his purposes to say that by means of the operation of

sympathy we get feelings of the same general affective quality as those we observe or contemplate. Unpleasant feelings in others cause unpleasant feelings in us, and pleasant feelings cause pleasant feelings in us. Only if that were so could Hume explain why we disapprove of and try to prevent unpleasant feelings in others, and why we approve of and try to promote pleasant feelings in them.

Of course, sympathy might be better described simply as the disposition to be moved to prevent pain and promote pleasure in others, or to disapprove of what tends to produce pain and approve of what tends to produce pleasure in them. It could be that our simply *believing* that pain is unpleasant to people is what moves us to disapprove of it and to try and prevent it, but Hume cannot accept such an account. If we are moved by the prospect of something, it must be because we are not indifferent to it. And for Hume, not being indifferent, or preferring one thing to another, is always a matter of having a certain feeling. A mere belief that such-and-such is the case is incapable of producing action. If that were not so, a discovery of reason could alone lead us to act.

If we were not 'sympathetic' beings then almost none of the things we now regard as virtuous or as vicious would be so regarded. Certainly the variety of things we approve of would not be as great as it is. In that sense, sympathy might be described as the foundation of morality—not as something that can provide us with, or serve as a basis for, a rational proof of the moral quality of an act or character, but as a fundamental human characteristic that is responsible for morality being what it is. It is the source of morality just as other natural dispositions are the source of causal thinking, or of the belief in the continued and distinct existence of objects. And in discovering these fundamental dispositions in each case Hume thinks he has taken his investigation as far as he can. There might well be an explanation of why we tend to share the feelings of others, or why an observed constant conjunction and an impression of a thing of one of the conjoined kinds always produces an idea of something of the other kind, but Hume does not know what the explanation is in either case, and he does not speculate. Within his theory there are fundamental facts he does not try to explain, and which he doubts can be resolved into principles 'more simple and universal'. But that is not to say they are miracles or mysteries. All explanation stops somewhere.

But Hume points out that in another way his explanation of the virtues and vices has not gone far enough. There are some things we approve of that do not obviously fall into his four-fold classification, and to make his account complete he tries to show that the apparent exceptions really are covered by his theory after all. Putting it this way might make it sound like a mere tidying-up operation, but in fact the attempt to deal adequately with the difficulty leads into a wide-ranging discussion of the origins of society.

There is no doubt that we regard such things as justice and promise-keeping as virtuous. To find that a particular act was an act of justice is to approve of it. There might be thought to be no great difficulty in explaining why we have this attitude towards justice and promise-keeping, but in fact Hume's explanation is very complicated. Complications arise primarily because, although it seems such an obviously good thing for all of us that there is justice in the world, it is not easy to show that acts of justice are regarded as virtuous solely because of their social utility. That is because there are particular acts which are certainly just, but which, considered in themselves, either do not further, or are directly contrary to, the public interest and the interests of the individuals directly involved. That makes it difficult to see why anyone would approve of them or would be motivated to perform them.

For example, if I have borrowed some money and the day agreed upon for repayment has arrived, what reason or motive do I have to restore the money? Certainly justice requires repayment as agreed, but what actually recommends that just action to me? It might be thought that it is in my own self-interest to repay the debt, since my reputation will suffer if I do not, and it will be more difficult to borrow in the future, but Hume points out that this explanation will not work in general.

> For shou'd we say, that a concern for our private interest
> or reputation is the legitimate motive to all honest
> actions; it wou'd follow, that wherever that concern ceases,
> honesty can no longer have place. (p. 480)

If I can be assured in a particular case that my reputation will not suffer from an act of injustice (as surely I sometimes can) then in that case I will have no motive towards justice at all, on the supposition that concern for my reputation is my sole motive for being just. And it can scarcely be argued that I will simply be better off repaying the loan whether my reputation is affected or not, since I will certainly have less money than I now have, and in fact might become completely impoverished by repaying it.

It is no more plausible in general to suggest that I can be moved to repay the loan or to approve of its repayment because it would contribute to the interests or well-being of the other person involved.

> For what if he be my enemy, and has given me just cause
> to hate him? What if he be a vicious man, and deserves

199

the hatred of all mankind? What if he be a miser, and
can make no use of what I wou'd deprive him of? What if
he be a profligate debauchee, and wou'd rather receive
harm than benefit from large possessions? What if I be
in necessity, and have urgent motives to acquire something
to my family? In all these cases, the original motive to
justice wou'd fail; (p. 482)

But still, Hume suggests, since repaying the loan is the just thing to do,
and justice is a virtue, we do approve of it and are moved to do it. That
fact still needs explanation.

The most promising candidate as a motive towards justice is a
concern for public interest or the welfare of society in general, but even
that cannot be seen to be straightforwardly operative in each particular
case. Sometimes the public interest is not directly affected one way or
another by a just or unjust act. A loan made in strict privacy, for
example, so that the public knows nothing about it, can scarcely affect
the public interest, but still justice requires repayment. And
sometimes the public interest is directly affected negatively by a just
act.

When a man of merit, of a beneficent disposition, restores
a great fortune to a miser, or a seditious bigot, he has
acted justly and laudably, but the public is a real sufferer.
(p. 497)

This is obviously not to say that *no* acts of justice contribute to the
public interest, but only that there are some easily imaginable, and
often actually realized, circumstances in which a single act of justice
does more harm than good for both individual and general welfare.

Hume's way of making this point is to say that 'public interest is not
naturally attach'd to the observation of the rules of justice' (p. 480), or
that justice is not a 'natural virtue'. But since we obviously do approve
of justice and regard it as a virtue, the problem is to explain what kind
of a virtue it is, or how it does in fact serve the public interest, although
not 'naturally'. Hume finds that men in the ordinary affairs of life do
not actually consider the public interest when repaying their debts or
refraining from theft; what recommends those actions to them is
simply that they are just. 'The sense of morality or duty' is often
enough in itself to lead people to act (p. 479). But although people can
undoubtedly be led to perform an action solely out of a regard for its
virtue, it still needs to be explained how the action can actually be
virtuous. Hume is interested in the 'origins' of virtues and vices, and so
far he has not shown that justice inevitably and quite generally leads to
any of the things we naturally approve of and are motivated towards.

That is the problem he sets himself, and the solution he offers is that justice must be understood as an 'artificial' virtue. The individual acts of justice that apparently do not fit into Hume's classificatory scheme are to be explained away by showing that, with the interposition of a certain artifice or convention invented by men for their own well-being, particular acts of justice do further more than they detract from the public interest after all.

To understand the sense in which justice is an 'artificial' virtue one must understand the origins of justice—how there comes to be such a thing at all. And for Hume that requires reflection on human beings and their place in nature. Man, among all the earth's creatures, is probably least equipped to satisfy his needs and wants on his own. He needs a great variety of food, most of which is often difficult to get, and he needs clothes and shelter for protection. But he is not richly endowed with the natural abilities for satisfying those needs. He is, relatively speaking, not very strong and not very fast, and he does not have as much endurance as most of the other large animals. All this makes it important for men to band together with others if they want their needs to be satisfied. With greater numbers man's strength is increased, along with his security and his ability to produce the variety he needs.

But men would not be motivated to form societies unless they believed that such advantages would actually result. Sexual instinct inevitably brings human beings together, with the inevitable children, and so groups or small societies are naturally formed. This shows men some of the advantages of living together, and it also prepares them for any larger societies they might join.

This blissful picture is complicated by a number of factors that naturally incline men away from society and make the presence of other human beings disadvantageous to them. For example, everybody loves himself more than he loves anyone else. According to Hume, men are naturally, although not exclusively, selfish. Each of us is primarily interested in promoting his own welfare and interests, and then next in line comes that of our relatives and friends. In fact, Hume says:

> This avidity . . . of acquiring goods and possessions for
> ourselves and our nearest friends, is insatiable, perpetual,
> universal, and directly destructive of society. (pp. 491–2)

It leads to conflict, which makes it even more difficult to satisfy one's needs.

Men are also naturally led away from society by the relative scarcity and instability of many of the things necessary for survival. When men live close together there are often not enough clothes, shelter, food and other goods to satisfy everyone. And those goods are easily transported, and so can be taken from one person by another without great difficulty. This might tend to convince a man that he would be better off as far away from most other people as possible. A quantity of food that is not quite enough for fifty people all looking out for their own interests would be more than enough for a family of five on their own.

Men are thus thrown into a conflict. Their natural instincts or feelings incline them both towards society and away from it. The only remedy, Hume says, is for them to invent a set of rules or procedures for guiding their behaviour with one another, so that they can secure the advantages of social living while minimizing its disadvantages. The set of rules or institutions will be 'artificial' in being somehow deliberately decided on or adopted in order to resolve the conflict men's natural propensities throw them into. Given the way men are, and the way the world is, men could not survive for long if they did not have such an 'artificial' construction to preserve society.

Hume regards it as impossible directly to oppose and repress the natural self-interestedness or 'avidity' of men, so he thinks that entering into society is at most intended to divert or channel that impulse in directions that allow for a higher chance of greater satisfaction. Men therefore enter society in the hopes of greater security in acquiring and retaining the goods they need, and they see that that end will be achieved only if others do not interfere with those goods. Since each man must recognize that fact if the prospect of society is to be attractive to him, each man will enter society with the intention of forsaking the chance to take things he wants from others whenever it is easy to do so, on the condition that others do so as well. If everyone restrains his natural impulse to take whatever he can whenever he can get it, everyone will have a greater chance of satisfying to a greater degree his own self-interest and the interests of those closest to him. So everyone will see society and justice as a good thing for themselves—in fact, as the best way of guaranteeing the enjoyment of what they have or can get. Without it, everyone would be worse off. That is why they enter into a convention or agreement:

> to bestow stability on the possession of those external goods,
> and leave every one in the peaceable enjoyment of what he may
> acquire by his fortune and industry. By this means, every one
> knows what he may safely possess; and the passions are restrain'd
> in their partial and contradictory motions. (p. 489)

Hume sees justice as almost exclusively concerned with the establishment and maintenance of property rights. It is something designed to help men peacefully retain what they have worked for or

202

inherited or otherwise come to possess. There is no mention of justice as a set of procedures for guaranteeing fairness or equity in the distribution of goods or opportunities. Questions about why this person, and not that person, should be in a particular position in society seem not to have occurred to him at all.[3] Property and possessions are the *raison d'être* of the institution of justice. In fact, without the 'artifice' of justice there would be no such thing as property at all. Simply to have something in one's hand or pocket is not necessarily to own it. Ownership involves a *right* to keep or use the goods in question. Those goods are one's property, and for Hume, property is 'those goods, whose constant possession is established by . . . the laws of justice' (p. 491). Since laws of justice do not exist before men 'agree' to form themselves into a society, there is no such thing as property outside of society. In fact, without the laws of justice there are no rights, duties or obligations at all. The virtue of being just, or acting in accord with the laws of justice, is therefore 'artificial'.

The artificiality can also be brought out by trying to imagine what it would be like if the conditions that make the institution of justice desirable or necessary did not obtain. If men were not selfish and primarily motivated by concern for their own self-interest, if they were just as concerned for the welfare of every man as they are for their own, then according to Hume there would be no need for laws of justice to regulate people's behaviour to one another. Similarly, if things were not scarce, and everything men wanted were as plentiful as the air we breathe,[4] there would be no need for laws determining ownership. I could easily get more of whatever someone took from me.

> Here then is a proposition, which, I think, may be regarded as certain, *that 'tis only from the selfishness and confin'd generosity of men, along with the scanty provision nature has made for his wants, that justice derives its origin.* (p. 495)

Justice is an invention adopted by men to meet the specific conditions they find themselves in. If those conditions were different in certain ways, there would be no need for it. As it is, it is the best possible alternative to a totally unacceptable state of nature.

The original motivation for establishing rules of justice is therefore a concern for one's own interest and, secondarily, for the interest of those one especially cares about. Each man sees that life would be intolerable without a system of rules or procedures to guarantee him a reasonable chance of satisfying his wants. The convention or agreement is therefore arrived at because each man sees that it is to his advantage to abide by it as long as others do. Once men recognize that just actions tend to preserve the stability of society they will get sentiments of approbation from those acts. Since justice is seen as necessary to promote something that benefits all, men will approve of it through their natural sympathy with their fellow men. But still justice is an artificial virtue. The system of rules of justice arises artificially or by convention; but our approval of it is not artificial. When we see the consequences of having that system we naturally approve of it and of all its applications, through sympathy.

It is important to see that to call justice an 'artificial' virtue is not to disparage it or to give it a second-class status among the virtues. Hume thinks justice will inevitably arise among intelligent human beings motivated primarily by 'avidity' in conditions of relative scarcity and instability of goods. It will arise through the conventional adoption of an invented set of principles, the need for which is clearly perceived by 'the judgment and understanding' (p. 489), and the principles will be approved precisely because they are seen 'as the best way to satisfy that need.⁵ So justice is said to be an 'artificial' virtue primarily because of the way it arises, or because of the 'oblique and indirect' way it serves the public interest, and not because it lacks a source in human nature.

> Mankind is an inventive species; and where an invention is obvious and absolutely necessary, it may as properly be said to be natural as any thing that proceeds immediately from original principles, without the intervention of thought or reflexion. Tho' the rules of justice be *artificial*, they are not *arbitrary*. Nor is the expression improper to call them *Laws of Nature*; if by natural we understand what is common to any species, or even if we confine it to mean what is inseparable from the species. (p. 484)

The question still to be faced is precisely how this account of the origins of justice and of our approval of it solves the problem Hume sets himself. In fact there is some question about exactly what that problem is. If 'the public is a real sufferer' on a particular occasion when a beneficent man repays a loan to a miser or a seditious bigot as justice requires, then why do we approve of it? It would seem that our natural sympathy with the beneficent man or with public welfare generally would lead us to disapprove. Why don't we?

Hume's answer is not easy to understand. It involves a distinction between the consequences of particular just acts, 'considered in themselves', and the consequences of the 'whole plan or scheme' of justice, considered as a whole.

> But however single acts of justice may be contrary, either to public or private interest, 'tis certain, that the whole plan or scheme is highly conducive, or indeed absolutely

requisite, both to the support of society, and the well-being of every individual. 'Tis impossible to separate the good from the ill. Property must be stable, and must be fix'd by general rules. Tho' in one instance the public be a sufferer, this momentary ill is amply compensated by the steady prosecution of the rule, and by the peace and order, which it establishes in society. And even every individual person must find himself a gainer, on ballancing the account; since, without justice, society must immediately dissolve, and every one must fall into that savage and solitary condition, which is infinitely worse than the worst situation that can possibly be suppos'd in society. When therefore men have had experience enough to observe, that whatever may be the consequence of any single act of justice, perform'd by a single person, yet the whole system of actions, concurr'd in by the whole society, is infinitely advantageous to the whole, and to every part; it is not long before justice and property take place. (pp. 497–8)

The main point is the one that all 'avid' men with limited and unstable goods can be expected to see—that without the rules of justice or property all the advantages of living in society would be lost, and so everyone would be worse off. And Hume seems to be suggesting that even if some people sometimes suffer from individual acts of justice, everyone is still much better off than they would be if there were no system of justice at all. We are said to 'ballance the account' and find that justice, even with its rare unfortunate accompaniments, is 'infinitely' better for each of us than any other alternative.

But does Hume adequately explain how and why each of us would come to that conclusion? Consider a particular man deliberating about whether to join with others to form a society founded on rules of justice. He might grant that the existence of rules of justice is essential both for the well-being of mankind, and for himself, but that in itself does not provide him with sufficient motivation actually to abide by those rules on each, or indeed on any, occasion. According to Hume, the man is primarily selfish, and is concerned for his own self-interest and the interests of those close to him. And if that natural avidity is as strong as Hume suggests, the man might easily conclude that although justice is essential to society and therefore is a good thing, society will not collapse if he alone violates its principles. He could see that he would be best off if he acted justly only when it leads to more good than harm for himself, and unjustly the rest of the time, when that is the best way to serve his own interest. He could then get all the advantages that result from justice without any of the disadvantages.

205

It might be replied that the man could not endorse a system of *justice* that allowed him to violate its principles, because the rules of justice are to be universally binding. To have rules that allowed for exceptions for particular people in particular circumstances would be to give certain people special preference, or immunity from the law, for no special reason, and that is unjust. But our man might agree that it could not be one of the rules of justice that he is to receive special treatment whenever he does not want to do what the law requires. He might agree that universal and exceptionless laws are the best things for society to have, but still ask what reason there is for him to obey those universal and exceptionless laws in those cases in which he will be a loser by doing so. His avidity, and the scarcity and instability of goods, will lead him to favour a system in which everyone respects his rights while he violates those of others for his own advantage whenever he can.

It should not be supposed that there are many people like this, or that it is a type we should try to model ourselves after. The point of the example is only to raise a challenge to Hume's explanation of the origin of justice. He says that each man, on the basis of virtually self-interested motivation alone, would see the advantages of justice over every other alternative open to him, and thereby be moved to follow the rules of justice and to approve of their being followed by everyone. But if the man I envisage is a real possibility, then Hume must explain why the alternative that kind of man seeks is not better for him and those he cares about than his acting justly every time it is required of him.

One factor that should certainly influence the deliberations of such a man is the probability of his violations' being discovered. If he is known to be unreliable in repaying debts and the like, others will not trust him and he will eventually be worse off than he would have been. There is no doubt that such considerations weigh heavily with many people in their deliberations about what to do, as does the threat of legal punishment, unemployment and social ostracism. As things are, it is often difficult to get away with blatant injustices for very long, or very often, and when they are discovered we tend to suffer. Our man will therefore take all those factors into account. But still it is not obvious how and why he would then see it to be in his self-interest to act justly every time. Given the power of the courts, of one's employer, or of a stain on one's reputation, he has good reason to try to get everyone to *believe* that he acts justly. People and the world being what they are, the easiest way for him to do that is usually simply to act justly, and then others will get true beliefs about him. But if in some cases he sees he can make it look as if he is acting justly while still profiting from injustice, then according to Hume's theory of human motivation that is the course of action that will recommend itself to him. Nothing in Hume's theory of the origins of justice so far rules that out.

In fact, as we have seen, Hume himself acknowledges the point. If concern for one's reputation were the motive to just action, then whenever injustice would not in fact injure one's reputation, one would have no reason to be just. And if one strongly believed that no loss of reputation would follow the injustice, one would not in fact be moved to be just at all. But Hume's account of the origin of justice is supposed to explain why we approve of, and how we can be moved towards, justice even when we know we will suffer from it. No doubt our knowledge of general facts about human abilities and human psychology will often be enough to recommend that course of action to us, but once such factors are brought in as essential to the motivation there is no way to explain how we can be motivated in a particular case if we know those factors are outweighed by others.

Hume grants that harm does sometimes result from individual just acts—a beneficent man is impoverished while a miser's riches swell. But, Hume claims, this 'momentary ill is amply compensated' for by all those advantages that justice brings us. Given the way things are, such harmful acts are inevitable—'it is impossible to separate the good from the ill'—so the institution of justice carries with it certain necessary evils. This suggests that the harm following from some individual just acts is like the pain of surgery. Although it is inevitable, and it is not something we would seek on its own, we can still be motivated to undergo surgery because we believe that the ultimate benefits compensate for the pain. All things considered, painful surgery is best.

On this interpretation it will not be true that there are individual acts of justice which lead to more harm than good, even though we approve of them. But that is what seemed to create Hume's original problem. On the present suggestion that justice carries with it certain necessary evils like the pain of surgery, the particular just acts which admittedly have harmful consequences will only *seem* to lead to more overall harm than good to those who consider them from a narrow and restricted point of view. Taking everything into account, we are said to be able to see that their harm is amply compensated for, and so on balance they remain the best thing to do in the circumstances. According to this interpretation, when Hume says that 'a single act of justice is frequently contrary to *public interest*', or that 'the public is a real sufferer' from some individual just acts, he must not be understood to be saying that the public interest suffers more than it profits from those acts. It suffers, but the suffering is more than compensated for by the benefits of having 'the whole plan or scheme' of justice. To ignore the general benefits is to assess the individual acts only 'consider'd in themselves'. Considered as contributions to the preservation of justice, which benefits us all, they do not lead to more harm than good. So it is only when the 'artifice' of justice is brought into our assessments of the acts that we are led to approve of them. Justice is an artificial virtue.

But this is really no better than the view already found to be inadequate. What compensates for the evil resulting from individual acts of justice is presumably the greater security in preserving our goods which society provides. To reject justice, Hume argues, is to reject all the advantages of society. But the only way this could help explain an individual person's approval of, or motivation for, being just on a particular occasion is if, as Hume puts it, 'even every individual person must find himself a gainer, on ballancing the account'. And what reason is there to suppose that that is so? The only reason Hume gives is that 'without justice, society must immediately dissolve'. Even if that is true it does not help.

As we have seen, given that an 'avid' person wants the benefits of society, and he agrees that without justice there would be no society, he will be motivated to be just on a particular occasion only if he believes that if he is not just on that occasion society will tend to be undermined. And that would often be obviously not true. There have been countless unjust acts over the centuries, but justice and society go sturdily on. Nor is it true that society would tend to collapse if an individual person were unjust on every occasion on which he thought he could get away with it. No doubt there have been people like that.

Hume tries to reach the conclusion that every individual person will be better off by being just on each particular occasion than by being unjust some of the time. Only if that is so will each of us, 'on ballancing the account', 'find himself a gainer'. But the gap in his argument comes right after the contention, which can be granted, that the institution of justice is essential to every man's well-being. That shows only that if a particular man did not act justly on this occasion, *and no one else ever acted justly*, then that would be the end of justice, and society would collapse, to everyone's detriment. But even if that is true, it is irrelevant to the motivation of a particular person on a particular occasion if he has good reason to believe that other people are not going to violate the principles of justice all the time, or often enough to bring society down.

Hume sometimes suggests that no one can reasonably have that kind of conviction, and that each act of injustice does tend to undermine society, if only very indirectly.

The consequences of every breach of equity seem to lie very

remote, and are not able to counterbalance any immediate
advantage, that may be reap'd from it. They are, however,
never the less real for being remote; and as all men are,
in some degree, subject to the same weakness, it necessarily
happens, that the violations of equity must become very
frequent in society, and the commerce of men, by that means,
be render'd very dangerous and uncertain. You have the
same propension, that I have, in favour of what is contiguous
above what is remote. You are, therefore, naturally
carried to commit acts of injustice as well as me. Your
example both pushes me forward in this way by imitation,
and also affords me a new reason for any breach of equity,
by shewing me, that I should be the cully of my integrity,
if I alone shou'd impose on myself a severe restraint
amidst the licentiousness of others. (p. 535)

But this is only an argument against overt and publicly declared
injustice. Violations of the rules of justice will occur more frequently,
along the lines of this scenario, only if they are known. People must
believe they have an example before them in order to try to follow it.
Simply being the 'cully' of one's integrity is never enough to motivate
one to injustice; one must have reason to think one is actually in that
position, and that requires good reason to believe that others are really
profiting from injustice. What this shows is that the man who resolves
to be just only when he will not suffer from it obviously has an interest
in promoting respect for justice among the other members of society. It
is a way of guaranteeing for himself the advantages of social living,
without having to pay as high a price as he might.

Once again, this man no doubt strikes us as evil, ruthless, perhaps
inhuman. Certainly he is not 'playing the game'. But that is not the
point. We regard justice as a virtue; we believe people should not act
the way he is proposing to act. But that belief or attitude of ours is
precisely what Hume has to explain. He wants to show why we regard
justice as a virtue, and why we are motivated to be just even when some
harm results. And he tries to do so by appealing, at least in the first
instance, to virtually self-interested motivation alone. Man's natural
avidity is supposed to be enough in itself to bring him into society and
to enable him to see the advantages of being just. So although we
condemn and do not seek to emulate the man I am imagining, because
he is unjust, that can hardly be used as a device to rule him out of
consideration.

The weakness of Hume's position comes out in another way. No
doubt society or mankind in general is better off with some procedures
for preventing or punishing wrongs committed against it, and in so far

as each individual person is a member of society and thus enjoys its benefits, he has reason to support those procedures. But it is scarcely credible to argue from that to the conclusion that each individual person will find that he profits from each act of justice, however harmful its consequences. We need only think of the beneficent man who is impoverished by returning what he owes to a bigot or a miser, not to mention the victim of capital punishment, to see that not *everyone* is better off. This is not to say, for example, that a person could not morally approve of his own hanging. That certainly seems possible, but if it is, it is because the man would see that particular just act as virtuous or right, and not because he would see it as furthering his own self-interest.

Hume concedes that the beneficent man about to repay the debt has 'reason to wish, that with regard to that single act, the laws of justice were for a moment suspended in the universe' (p. 497), but he claims the man is much better off, even in his impoverished state, than he would be if there were no laws of justice at all. But whatever gives the man reason to wish (hopelessly) that the laws of justice be momentarily suspended also gives him reason to violate those binding and inflexible laws if he thinks he can get away with it. In short, there are more than two possibilities for him to envisage. He is not forced to choose, as Hume seems to suggest, between a world in which everyone including himself is always just, and a world in which he and everyone else is always unjust. He can try to bring about a world in which almost everyone except himself is always, or almost always, just while he acts justly only when he will not be worse off because of it. If Hume relies only on the undeniable fact that that is not easy to do, then he cannot successfully explain how someone is motivated to be just on *every* occasion. If there are any occasions on which a man reasonably thinks he can get away with injustice and profit from it then there will be nothing to recommend justice to him at all.

The point is not that Hume's theory is inadequate because it makes it possible for men to be unjust. No theory could make that impossible. The point is rather that we regard justice as a virtue, and so even when we act against it there must be something that recommends it to us, even if we allow it to be outweighed by other factors. Hume thinks he can explain what recommends it to our avidity or self-interest alone, and that is what I think he fails to do.

Hume's theory seems to leave out of account what might be called the *obligation* to be just. Justice is thought to be binding in the sense that I ought to obey the laws of justice even though, in a particular case, I will be worse off. Hume tries to account for that obligation, and how it can motivate us, in terms of virtually self-interested motivation alone. He thinks men's reasons for joining society and adopting principles of justice are purely self-interested, or concerned only with themselves and those closest to them. One way many have tried to explain the obligation is to argue that in joining society or adopting the principles of justice, men put themselves under an obligation to obey those principles. On this view, to be a member of society is to be party to an agreement or contract, and thus to be obliged to obey its rules, and in particular to be obliged to do so even when the particular act in question leads to more harm than good for you. Not to do so is to go back on your original promise, commitment or contract. It is to break your word, and thus to violate the condition responsible for your being a member of society and being able to enjoy its benefits.[6]

Hume emphatically rejects any such account. The convention or agreement on which society is based, he says, 'is not of the nature of a promise' (p. 490). He appeals to a convention or agreement on which society and interpersonal obligations are based to explain how people come to have the rights and obligations they have. It is supposed to explain their source; without the original convention there would be no rights or obligations at all. But if the original convention is thought of as a promise then it could not be the source of all obligations, since a promise is something we are obliged to keep, and no source of that particular obligation would have been provided. If a promise were not something we are obliged to keep, it could not help explain the obligation to be just. Since promises themselves, like justice, arise from human conventions, promise-keeping, like justice, is an artificial virtue. So the original convention or agreement must be understood some other way.

According to Hume the convention that gives rise to society:

. . . is only a general sense of common interest; which sense all the members of the society express to one another, and which induces them to regulate their conduct by certain rules. I observe, that it will be for my interest to leave another in the possession of his goods, *provided* he will act in the same manner with regard to me. He is sensible of a like interest in the regulation of his conduct. When this common sense of interest is mutually express'd, and is known to both, it produces a suitable resolution and behaviour. And this may properly enough be call'd a convention or agreement betwixt us, tho' without the interposition of a promise; since the actions of each of us have a reference to those of the other, and are perform'd upon the supposition, that something is to be perform'd on the other part. Two men, who pull the oars of a boat, do it

by an agreement or convention, tho' they have never given
promises to each other. (p. 490)

In joining society, then, I resolve to act in a certain way towards other
people on condition that other people also act in a certain way towards
me. According to Hume, I see that it will be in my interest to act that
way *if* others act similarly, and I think others will draw the same
conclusion and therefore adopt the same resolution with respect to
themselves. My resolution is conditional—I resolve to act in certain
ways if others do—and I have reason to believe that the condition will
be fulfilled and that others will act in those ways. Consequently I act in
those ways. Each of us then can be said to refrain from taking the goods
of others by convention or agreement, although no promise was
actually made. That is how the institution of justice or property arises.[7]

Hume offers the same kind of explanation of the origin of promises,
and of the obligation to keep them, as he does of the origins of justice. I
can come to see that it is in my interest to keep my promises just as it is
in my interest to make promises in the first place.

> Your corn is ripe today; mine will be so to-morrow. 'Tis
> profitable for us both, that I shou'd labour with you to-day,
> and that you shou'd aid me to-morrow. I have no kindness
> for you, and know you have as little for me. I will not,
> therefore, take any pains upon your account; and shou'd
> I labour with you upon my own account, in expectation of
> a return, I know I shou'd be disappointed, and that I should
> in vain depend upon your gratitude. Here then I leave you
> to labour alone: You treat me in the same manner. The
> seasons change; and both of us lose our harvests for want
> of mutual confidence and security. (pp. 520–1)

It might look as if our natural avidity and partiality, and our
knowledge that everyone else is like us in that respect, would inevitably
lead us into a desperate situation like the one Hume describes, but he
thinks we can 'give a new direction' to those impulses, and thus be
better off than we would be if we followed them blindly. Even though
the prospect does not otherwise attract me, I can see that it is in my
interest to do a service for someone when he needs it, as long as I can
expect that he will do the same for me. And if both of us recognize
that, and act accordingly, we both benefit. Thus each of us presumably
sees that promise-keeping promotes his own interests.

Hume's account of promise-keeping really adds nothing to his
explanation of the motivation to be just. In fact, he regards promise-
keeping as a part of justice. Consequently, what he says would seem to
be open to the same difficulty noticed earlier. Does Hume really

explain how a man could come to see, on each particular occasion, that it is in his interest to keep his promise on that occasion? If the man is naturally as selfish or self-interested as Hume claims, surely he will be motivated primarily to get others to *believe* that he will perform, or has performed, his part of the bargain. Another person's actions towards me can be based only on his beliefs about what I will do, or have done, so what I must do in order to get him to perform those actions for me is to get him to believe that I will do, or have done, what he expects. That will usually be most easily done by actually returning the service—after all, how could I convince someone that I am helping him harvest his corn when I am not?—but that is not always true. For example, in income-tax evasion by the rich or by large corporations, the more resources one has to implement evasive tactics the more successful one is, and consequently one develops even more resources to develop even more efficient methods of deception the next time. When we think of such cases, perhaps the ruthless, self-interested man who does what justice requires only when he thinks he will profit from it does not seem so unreal.

The only thing Hume explicitly mentions as a factor to motivate a person to keep his promises is the hardship he would eventually encounter if he refused. Others would no longer trust him and would not enter into agreements with him, so he could not get the help he needed, and he would be worse off than he would be if he kept his promises and sometimes did not profit from it. No doubt many people keep their promises simply because they believe they ought to, or that it is a good thing if promises are kept. But Hume is trying to explain precisely how they can come to have such beliefs. There are many social influences—parents, schools, governments, etc.—operating on a person to get him to keep his promises and to be just, but Hume is looking for a more primary or natural motive than those. He thinks the forces of society can influence people only if they mould or divert a previously existing motive or impulse. And, as we have seen, Hume seems to acknowledge that simply a concern for one's reputation could not account for one's sense of obligation. So it is difficult to see how he can explain how one can be virtually self-interestedly motivated to be just or keep promises, as opposed simply to doing whatever is required to get people to believe that one is.

Clearly, he thinks the key is to be found in his notion of an 'artificial virtue'. Self-interest is connected with the performance of 'artificially' virtuous acts only indirectly. In fact, that is primarily what their 'artificiality' consists in.

> The only difference betwixt the natural virtues and justice
> lies in this, that the good, which results from the former,

213

arises from every single act, and is the object of some
natural passion: Whereas a single act of justice, consider'd
in itself, may often be contrary to the public good; and
'tis only the concurrence of mankind, in a general scheme
or system of action, which is advantageous. (p. 579)

Although men have no natural motive to perform particular acts of
justice or promise-keeping when they will suffer from them, they do
have an interest in there being such general institutions. Without
them, men would be much worse off. But Hume nowhere explains
how a man's interest in the existence of an institution is transmitted to
the performance of each particular act that accords with the principles
or constraints of that institution. If a man universally follows a practice
because he believes it will collapse if he does not act in accord with it,
then his action is simply based on a false belief. There is no particular
act or no particular man on whom the whole institution of justice so
crucially depends. And if one follows the practice only because one
fears the consequences of being found doing otherwise, then one will
not be motivated to comply with the practice on *every* occasion on
which compliance is required, unless one is particularly inept, or meek,
or lacks self-confidence, or one lives in an especially vigilant society.

It is more likely that we follow the principles of justice or promise-
keeping at least partly out of a concern for fairness—a reluctance to
take unfair advantage of those whose compliance benefits us.[8] But
Hume is not in a good position to explain how we could be so
motivated. He would regard fairness as an artificial virtue, like justice
itself. Avid and virtually self-interested men would have no natural
motivation towards it, although perhaps they can see that a society
with a practice of fair treatment is better than one without it. Certainly
they can see the advantages of being treated fairly by others. But once
again the 'oblique and indirect' connection between the value of the
institution and the value of a particular act falling under it has not been
drawn.

Hume perhaps reveals his own personal good nature when he says that
he would be motivated to leave others in possession of their goods,
provided they did the same for him. But if he were in fact motivated
only by the virtually self-interested impulses he ascribes to man in his
'natural' condition, he would long ago have observed that his interests
are best served by making sure only that others do not *believe* he has
deprived them of their goods. The fact that David Hume, and most of
the rest of us, will inevitably reach the former conclusion and will be
motivated to act justly and honestly, is something that Hume's theory
of action and morality fails to explain.

214

There is perhaps a partial concession of the point at the end of the *Enquiry*, where Hume admits that:

> though it is allowed, without a regard to property,
> no society could subsist; yet according to the imperfect
> way in which human affairs are conducted, a sensible knave,
> in particular incidents, may think that an act of iniquity
> or infidelity will make a considerable addition to his fortune,
> without causing any considerable breach in the social union and
> confederacy. That *honesty is the best policy*, may be a good
> general rule, but is liable to many exceptions; and he, it
> may perhaps be thought, conducts himself with most wisdom,
> who observes the general rule, and takes advantage of all the
> exceptions. (*E*, pp. 282–3)

Such a man is difficult to convince 'if his heart rebel not against such pernicious maxims' (*E*, p. 283), and Hume despairs of convincing him. But it is not really a matter of getting an evil opponent to change his mind, or his ways. Hume thinks that, since justice is an artificial virtue, we come to approve of it and to be motivated towards it only by the intervention of 'judgment and understanding'. He thinks we can reason to the conclusion that something that on occasion might seem to be contrary to our own interest or to the public interest really serves those interests after all, and so we will naturally approve of it, because of the operation of sympathy. That view requires that the person who follows the rules when it profits him and violates them the rest of the time does not 'conduct himself with most wisdom'. But it must be shown that the path of justice all the time is a 'wiser' path, one that 'the judgment and understanding' would choose—or, more accurately, that that is the path 'the judgment and understanding' would guide or channel our natural motives into. That is what I am arguing Hume never shows. The difficulty is certainly not new. It is at least as old as Plato's *Republic*.

There are traces of a Platonic type of solution in Hume's suggestion that those without 'antipathy to treachery and roguery' might well achieve all they seek in the way of 'profit or pecuniary advantage' (*E*, p. 283), but they will miss other things equally worth having in life.

> Inward peace of mind, consciousness of integrity, a satisfactory
> review of our own conduct; these are circumstances, very
> requisite to happiness, and will be cherished and cultivated by
> every honest man, who feels the importance of them. . . . How
> little is requisite to supply the *necessities* of nature? And in a
> view to *pleasure*, what comparison between the unbought
> satisfaction of conversation, society, study, even health and

215

the common beauties of nature, but above all the peaceful
reflection on one's own conduct; what comparison, I say,
between these and the feverish, empty amusements of
luxury and expense? (*E*, pp. 283–4)

This is a fine passage rhetorically, and perhaps it has a place in the
Enquiry, but for Hume actually to establish that the just man is better
off he must show how a man could and would be motivated by his
original interests to develop a sense of justice, honesty or fairness which
would then lead him to act justly although he does not gain from it.
Putting it another way, he must show how someone's original approval
of what satisfies his own interests and those of his closest associates can
be rationally directed or guided into an approval of actions that clearly
go against those interests, or how his original sympathetic approval of
whatever contributes to the well-being of mankind in general can be
extended to acts which make no such contribution at all.

There seems little doubt that this actually happens, but there is
some question whether it is compatible with Hume's theory of
motivation. A man could come to believe that his life would be richer
in the things he wants if he were the sort of person who wanted to act
justly and honestly, and to keep his promises. He could see that a man
unshakably attached to the values of justice and honesty might find
more pleasure and enjoyment in life than the shifty opportunist who
also seeks pleasure and enjoyment.[9] And such a man might then take
steps to cultivate that attachment, to develop a firm sense of, or
disposition towards, justice and fair dealing. He need not believe that
acting justly on each occasion will itself give him more pleasure and
enjoyment than it will give the opportunist, but simply that being the
sort of person who wants, or has a settled intention, to act justly on each
occasion will itself be a source of pleasure. His original concerns for his
own well-being might be seen to be best served by his having an
unshakable attachment to the requirements of justice—by his being,
and being known to be, a just man. And that in turn could lead him to
act justly on a particular occasion even though he knew his original
concerns would not thereby be served on that occasion. There is
certainly nothing inconsistent or even unusual about such a person.
Some noble individuals can even approve of, and acquiesce in, their
own death in the name of justice. It remains to be seen whether a
theory like Hume's can explain how such approval and such behaviour
is possible.

The difficulty arises primarily because of the special kind of theory
Hume advances, or because of the special philosophical character of his
investigation. In one respect, it is not difficult to understand, in very
general outline, how and why each of us comes to approve of justice

216

and to be motivated towards it. We are born and brought up into a society that values justice, and so understanding our eventual approval is a matter of understanding our moral development from infants to fully socialized adults. I do not mean to suggest that the details of that development and the precise nature of the causal factors involved are already known to us—I mean only that the psychological question of why we approve of justice and are motivated towards it is as susceptible of investigation by observation and experiment as any other question about human socialization. Hume would not disagree, but that is not the question he asks.[10] He does not concern himself in any detail with the mechanisms by which particular people come to share the attitudes of their society; he is interested in what he calls the 'origin' of justice. And by that he means that he seeks its source in human nature—what it is about us and the world we live in that is responsible for there being such a thing as justice at all, and for anyone's approving of it as we do.

For most of the basically human attributes he is interested in Hume finds a fairly straightforward explanation in primitive dispositions of the mind. Getting beliefs about the unobserved is a result of our natural propensity to expect a B, given an experience of an A and a conjunction of As and Bs in our past experience. Approving of benevolence or generosity results from our natural sympathetic propensity to feel certain sentiments of approval on the contemplation of acts of those kinds. These are dispositions each of us has, their unwitting operation accounts for the observable phenomenon in question, and they are primitive at least in the sense that Hume does not attempt to explain them further. But when he sees that this simple model will not work in the case of justice Hume supposes that 'the judgment and understanding' must be brought in to supplement our natural dispositions towards approval and disapproval. The 'artificial' contrivance of a 'whole plan or scheme' of justice is discovered by reason to provide the best means of achieving what we primitively approve of and are motivated towards. And, given his conception of reason and his rather simple conception of man's virtually self-interested 'natural' condition, I think this appeal to reason does not succeed.

I suspect that our 'natural' or primitive condition, which is to form the basis of an explanation along Humean lines of the 'origin' of justice, must be understood to be much richer and more complex than he allows. It may well be that an elaborate scheme of justice does not serve merely to channel or direct our acquisitive 'avidity' in more mutually beneficial directions, but that a more or less disinterested concern for justice and fairness is a natural outgrowth of outward-looking or socially-oriented emotional needs that human beings inevitably develop.[11] Except for some talk of familial concern, there is scarcely a mention of social or communal feelings or needs in Hume's individualistic, property-oriented picture of man's fundamental nature. But rather than representing justice as an artificial device necessary to help us acquire and keep the things we want, we might well illuminate more of its 'origin' by examining the connections between our sense of, and motivation towards, justice and other natural feelings, attitudes and needs that we regard as characteristically human. But can it be shown that an unshakable attachment to justice is really connected with, or an expression of, natural human feelings and needs? And if so, could justice any longer be regarded as an 'artificial' virtue? It is certainly not obvious that the answer to either of these questions is 'Yes'.

X

Problems and Prospects of Humean Naturalism

And all our Knowledge is, OURSELVES TO KNOW.

Hume's philosophy has been more highly valued during this century than ever before. That is not necessarily because the real interest and importance of his views have come to be correctly understood and appreciated, but perhaps partly because recent philosophers have claimed to find in Hume the clearest origins of important contemporary ideas. In any case, his virtual canonization by the generally positivistic philosophy of the twentieth century was certainly not the result of his having repudiated or reduced to absurdity the assumptions of his empiricist forbears. That conception of his achievement was congenial to Hume's idealist critics in the nineteenth century, but other aspects of his thought have attracted more recent and more sympathetic interpreters.

I have tried to show that his original contributions to philosophy are not to be found in his espousal of the theory of ideas or in his having reduced that theory to sceptical absurdity, so in at least that respect my understanding of Hume is in accord with the dominant reading of him in recent philosophy. But I believe the prevailing contemporary interpretation of Hume still involves a fundamental distortion in its attempt to assimilate him too closely to the positivism or 'analytic empiricism' of this century.

Hume's present reputation is based partly on his efforts in the service of empiricism—his illustration and defence of the view that all our ideas and beliefs have their origin in sense-experience. But that alone does not explain his special appeal. Locke and Berkeley, not to mention Bacon or Hobbes and, later, Mill or James or Mach, were empiricists too, sometimes to a more radical degree. But Hume is thought to occupy a unique place among the precursors of twentieth-century empiricism. Merely being of empiricist persuasion is not enough.

He was also seen as the pre-eminently anti-metaphysical philosopher of the tradition, partly on the basis of attitudes thought to be expressed in the famous rallying-cry at the end of his first *Enquiry*.

> It seems to me, that the only objects of the abstract science or of demonstration are quantity and number, and that all attempts to extend this more perfect species of knowledge beyond these bounds are mere sophistry and illusion. . . . All other enquiries of men regard only matter of fact and existence; and these are evidently incapable of demonstration. . . .
> When we run over libraries, persuaded of these principles, what havoc must we make? If we take in our hand any volume; of divinity or school metaphysics, for instance; let us ask, *Does it contain any abstract reasoning concerning quantity and number?* No. *Does it contain any experimental reasoning concerning matter of fact and existence?* No. Commit it then to the flames: for it can contain nothing but sophistry and illusion. (*E*, pp. 163–5)

Some positivists, in their zeal, even took this as an expression of their thesis that only the propositions of mathematics and empirical science are *meaningful*, and hence that metaphysics is not.[1] It is an extreme exaggeration to say that that was Hume's concern, although no doubt he was not disposed towards what he would call 'abtruse' metaphysics. But in that respect he scarcely differed from most important philosophers of the eighteenth century.

It was not just his empiricist, anti-metaphysical bent that made Hume specially important for twentieth-century philosophers. He was seen to differ from others of similar inclinations in his alleged grasp of the real *source* of the poverty and confusions of metaphysics. He was regarded as the best early exponent of a view of human knowledge that would once and for all put metaphysics in its place beyond the sphere of cognitive concern. The key was his distinction between 'abstract reasoning concerning quantity and number' (or 'relations of ideas') and 'experimental reasoning concerning matter of fact and existence', and his claim that these are the only kinds of reasoning, and therefore the only routes to knowledge, that there are. This was thought to leave no room for genuine metaphysics—either it reduces to science, broadly construed, or it is nothing that can yield knowledge.

Recent philosophers made two distinct claims in the name of this theory of knowledge, and attributed both of them to Hume, thus enlisting him as a founder of the philosophy dominant in this century.[2] Just here, I think, is the beginning of the distortion that would represent Hume as repudiating what he saw as the very 'experimental', naturalistic basis of his own philosophical results.

The first claim is that of the indispensability of sense-experience for any knowledge of the world. This empiricist denial of *a priori* insight into reality is of course one that Hume would endorse. That was precisely the point behind his 'attempt to introduce the experimental method of reasoning into moral subjects'. Given his distinction between two kinds of knowledge, it amounts to the view that 'matters of fact and existence' are discoverable only by experience or by inference from experience. The importance Hume attached to this idea can hardly be over-emphasized, and there is no doubt that it was a large part of what attracted twentieth-century empiricists.

But the positivists, drawing the map of all human knowledge, were concerned with the status of their own results, with the nature of the map-drawing itself, and that is where the second of the two claims comes in (e.g. Carnap (2), pp. 36ff). How was philosophy to be fitted into what they saw as essentially the Humean picture? The answer was found in the other half of Hume's exhaustive distinction, the knowledge of 'relations of ideas'. In so far as there are results in philosophy at all, they were to be seen as merely 'analytic' propositions made true solely by the relations among the ideas or concepts we use in understanding and gaining knowledge about the world.[3] On this picture, all knowledge the philosopher reaches as a philosopher will be purely *a priori*, known independently of the way things in the world happen to be. Anything else he claims to know will either be part of mathematics or some empirical science, and hence not philosophical, or else it will be meaningless nonsense. Since Hume formulated the fundamental distinction, he was thought to share—or at least to be committed to—this conception of philosophy. That is what I think goes against the whole spirit of his most original and most important contributions.

The view he was thought to share and, although at times perhaps unwittingly, to follow, was thought to imply that the only proper task of philosophy is logical or conceptual analysis. Mathematics and empirical science constituted the domain of 'real' knowledge, and since philosophy itself belonged to neither it would be a worthwhile study only if it could be fitted into, or alongside, the scientific enterprise in some way. It was to acquire any cognitive legitimacy it could attain only from the unquestioned legitimacy of its master, science. Thus philosophy came to be seen as a study of what was called the 'logic of science'—an analysis of the structure of scientific concepts and procedures. And that study itself was thought to be *a priori*. This is a picture of philosophy as a certain kind of handmaiden or 'underlabourer' to science, one whose value is to be assessed only by the contributions it manages to make to the understanding or growth of 'real', i.e. scientific, knowledge. Positivism is a form of scientism,[4] and twentieth-century positivism accorded philosophy the status of a service enterprise.

What in this picture goes against the spirit of Hume's philosophical work is not the attitude towards science and the primacy of experience, but the conception of the nature and status of that philosophical work itself. A 'critical' and fundamentally rationalistic[5] conception of the philosophical enterprise is foreign to Hume. He would see it as too restricted, and also as too servile to the science (or to a dominant picture of the science) of its day. Hume, after all, was a pre-Kantian philosopher. He was interested in human nature, and his interest took the form of seeking extremely general truths about how and why human beings think, feel and act in the ways they do. He did not seek an 'analysis' or a 'rational reconstruction' of the concepts and procedures employed by his contemporaries in thinking scientifically about the world and about themselves; he wanted to answer the more fundamental philosophical questions of how people even come to have a conception of a world, or of themselves, and to think about it scientifically (or morally, or politically, or religiously or aesthetically) at all.

These questions were to be answered in the only way possible—by observation and inference from what is observed. Hume saw them as empirical questions about natural objects within the sphere of human experience, so they could be answered only by an admittedly general, but none the less naturalistic, investigation. He thought we could understand what human beings do, and why and how, only by studying them as part of nature, by trying to determine the origins of various thoughts, feelings, reactions and other human 'products' within the familiar world. The abstract study of such things as 'meanings', 'concepts' and 'principles' was to be engaged in only in so far as they could be grounded in what people actually think, feel and do in human life.

Of all the ingredients of lasting significance in Hume's philosophy I think this naturalistic attitude is of greatest importance and interest. He saw it as his most original contribution, and it gives rise to the most far-reaching and challenging issues raised by his philosophy. Its most direct legacy is not recent positivism or analytic empiricism, which tends to deny or obscure its presence, but rather that scientific naturalism that suffused so much of the thought about man, animals and nature in the nineteenth century and shows signs once again of encouraging and influencing philosophical reflection about human beings. Hume's philosophical aims would best be carried out today not by a 'logical construction of the world' or by an 'analysis of the concepts' of meaning, causation, goodness, and so on, but by pursuing in a truly empirical, naturalistic spirit the very questions he raised about human thought, feeling and behaviour.

But if we insist on locating Hume's importance in his naturalistic science of man, it might easily seem that that importance fades, and that he becomes much less interesting than has been supposed. If his contributions are to be judged as part of the empirical science of man, if he is properly seen as what would now be called a 'social scientist', then his 'results' will appear ludicrously inadequate, and there will be no reason to take him seriously. He was perhaps important historically, in conceiving and sketching an outline of an empirical study of human nature, but, the objection would continue, that does not endow his views with any lasting interest or significance for theorists today. On present standards, he does not really pursue his questions experimentally, he makes no systematic effort to discover or control his data, his 'explanations' are simple-minded and appeal to 'principles' or 'dispositions' the characterizations of which amount to little more than redescriptions of the data to be explained. It can easily be felt that the growth in complexity, sophistication and rigour of the social sciences has left Hume forever behind.

Although this is perhaps a natural result of considering Hume as a contemporary social or human scientist, to so judge him is to misjudge him, and also to fall victim to that very scientism that is foreign to his thought and to the thought of his century. What is important is not how well Hume measures up to the contemporary standards of social scientists, or what precise and 'scientifically' established results he has once and for all deposited in the archives of human knowledge. The question is what can be gained philosophically by following up his naturalistic attitude towards the study of man. What contributions does he make to our understanding of human nature, and how do they derive from his conception of the proper study of man? The answers to these questions are obviously not independent of what one takes a 'contribution to our understanding of human nature' to be.

It would be a mistake to infer from the alleged poverty or naïveté of Hume's specific 'results' that a naturalistic understanding of man was not what he was primarily interested in, or was not what he rightly saw as his most original contribution. It is true that the 'explanations' he offers are often false in their details, simplistic in conception, and scarcely *explain* the phenomenon in question. The method often consists in little more than an attempt to find some 'principles' of the mind that are slightly more general, or cover at least some other kinds of events, than the particular phenomenon being explained. But that shows at most that Hume had what now appears to be a rather limited conception of how his aim could be achieved, and not that he did not have that aim.

If his importance does lie generally in his naturalistic science of man, it does not follow that that importance is to be found in any of the specific answers he actually gives to the questions he raises, or in the specific procedures he adopts in arriving at them. What are of greatest interest are the problems raised, or the issues exposed, by even so much as the possibility of the sort of investigation or mode of understanding he proposes. It is the very idea of a completely comprehensive empirical investigation and explanation of why human beings are the way they are, and why they think, feel and behave as they do, that attracts philosophical attention. What sort of position would we be in if the spirit of Hume's naturalistic programme could be extended into a more sophisticated and more comprehensive account of human phenomena? When we are confident we understand the philosophical significance of such a prospect we will be in a better position to assess the importance and depth of Hume's vision.

II

One thing that works against a consistent and comprehensive naturalism in Hume's own thought is his unshakable attachment to the theory of ideas. That theory impedes the development of his programme in several directions in which he might otherwise have pursued it. Recent philosophers have tended to varying degrees to follow Hume himself, and not the spirit of his programme, in this regard.

For one thing, the theory of ideas tends to direct attention away from, and even to deny, the intricacy and complexity of the very phenomena that are the 'objects' or *explananda* of any naturalistic study of human beings. Hume's philosophical preconceptions lead him drastically to oversimplify, and hence to distort, those aspects of human life that interest him most. I suggested at several points that in his science of man he concentrates more on the 'explanation' than on what is to be explained. At those points the theory of ideas is at work.

Explanation for Hume is fundamentally developmental or genetic. We understand human thoughts, beliefs, feelings, actions and reactions when we understand their origins by seeing how the nature of human experience and the primitive properties of the mind combine to produce them. I have tried to show that his main concern is always with the origin of perceptions in the mind, and not primarily with their content or definition. His programme therefore does not commit him to providing 'analyses' or 'definitions', in the strict sense of expressions of the meaning in alternative but precisely equivalent terms, of the thoughts, beliefs and reactions themselves. He need not be able to specify without circularity exactly what the ideas 'cause' or 'good' or 'self' stand for, or exactly what 'distinct objects continue to exist unperceived' means, but there is a closely related question about which he ought to, but does not, say a good deal. One who seeks to explain how and why human beings come to think and feel in the ways they do must have some conception of what he wants to explain—some way of identifying, describing and understanding what it is for human beings to think and feel in those ways. He must at least be able to say what it is to 'have' the idea of causality, or of goodness or of the self, or what it is to 'think of' and 'believe in' a world of distinct, enduring objects. Those are some of the phenomena the science of man is to account for.

Of course, there is no difficulty in characterizing those phenomena in terms of the theory of ideas. On that view, to have the idea of causality, or goodness or the self, is for there to be a certain item in the mind, and to believe in continued and distinct existence is for a certain other item to be there 'in a certain manner'. And to lack those ideas and beliefs is for certain items to be absent. Explaining the origins of such thoughts and beliefs is therefore for Hume a matter of discovering by experience the 'principles' in conformity with which mental entities or items make their entrances into minds that originally lack them.

But how are these alleged mental occurrences—these 'comings' and 'goings', 'presences' and 'absences', 'entrances' and 'exits'— themselves to be understood? How are they connected with ordinary observable occurrences among human beings—those facts gleaned 'from a cautious observation of human life'—that Hume set out to explain? Not only must the principles and operations of the mind appealed to in Humean explanations be drawn from what can be discerned within the natural, observable world, but the very 'data' themselves that those explanations are supposed to explain must be similarly 'naturalized'. Under the pressure of the theory of ideas, Hume does not extend his investigations in that direction.

The theory of ideas restricts him because it represents thinking or having an idea as fundamentally a matter of contemplating or viewing an 'object'—a mental atom that can come and go in the mind completely independently of the comings and goings of every other atom with which it is not connected. One idea is connected with another only by 'containing' it, so for any two thoughts, beliefs, or in general, perceptions in Hume's sense, it is always possible for someone to 'have' the one without the other as long as the first perception does not itself 'contain' the second. It is just this atomistic picture of distinct and separable perceptions, according to which having a certain thought or belief is a relatively discrete event or state isolated from the having of most other thoughts or beliefs, that leaves Hume without the resources for describing realistically what is actually involved in what he refers to as 'having' an idea or a belief. Consequently he is left with a false and simplistic picture of our possession of the pervasive and fundamental notions he is interested in.

That certainly detracts from the interest and the wider significance of Hume's own pursuit of his naturalistic programme as he conceives it, but the philosophical importance of a more accurate and, perforce, more complicated application of that programme can scarcely be denied. Understanding more fully, in terms of more familiar, recognizable phenomena, precisely what 'having' the idea of necessity, or goodness or the self, amounts to, or what it is to 'believe' in the continued and distinct existence of objects, might be just what is needed, and in fact the most that can be done, towards understanding what has traditionally been found philosophically puzzling and in need of 'analysis' in the cases of causality, goodness, personal identity and the external world. There is good reason to suppose that the task is not an easy one, but at least a few steps away from the restrictive theory of ideas would be steps in the right direction.

The point comes out perhaps most clearly in the case of causality. Hume believes that it is a contingent fact that human beings ever get the idea of necessary connection. That is precisely the fact he wants to explain. He also takes it as a contingent fact, which could have been otherwise, that people who observe constant conjunctions between kinds of phenomena and then come to expect one of the second kind, given one of the first, then come to have the idea of necessary connection. The 'generalizing' behaviour itself, the tendency we have to make inferences or transitions from what has already been observed to what has not, is completely explained by him in terms of the principle that observed constant conjunctions establish a 'union in the imagination' between perceptions of the two kinds of things found to be conjoined, and the principle that an impression transmits some of its force and vivacity to an idea with which it is associated in the imagination, thus producing belief. That whole story comes early, and is obviously an extremely important part of Hume's account, but he goes on later to search directly for the source of what he calls the idea of necessary connection. So he means more by 'having the idea of necessary connection' than simply engaging in the 'generalizing' behaviour of making inferences from the observed to the unobserved. He is committed to at least the possibility of people's getting beliefs about the unobserved on the basis of observed constant conjunctions without their having the idea of necessary connection. To see what is involved in our own 'possession' of that fundamental idea, then, it is tempting to speculate about what any such people would have to be like, and how in their feelings, thoughts and actions, they would differ from us.

It is implausible to suggest that they would differ in being less *certain* than we are about, say, billiard balls, falling bodies or death. If their minds worked according to the two principles of the imagination mentioned earlier, there is no reason to suppose that less force and vivacity, and therefore less certainty, would be transmitted from impression to idea in their case than in ours. So it seems at first glance as if, given the same past experience, they would have all the same beliefs as we do about the actual world, past, present and future, and they would hold those beliefs with the same degrees of conviction as we do.

But by hypothesis they lack the idea of necessary connection, and so they would presumably differ from us in never saying or believing that certain things *must* happen, or that two sorts of things come together *of necessity*. What does that difference really consist in? If what has been suggested along Humean lines so far is genuinely possible, it would seem that the notion of necessity does not serve to describe or refer to some objective feature of the world that we, but not they, have discovered. All their beliefs about the actual course of their experience would be the same as ours. And although our minds do differ from theirs in 'possessing' the idea of necessary connection, surely we are not actually describing or referring to that difference, or to anything else in our minds, when we use the word 'must' or attach the idea of necessity to something we believe. What then is the difference? According to the theory of ideas, we, but not they, are simply the beneficiaries of an additional mental item that forces itself into our minds on certain occasions, and we then go through the otherwise empty ritual of adding that unanalysable idea of necessary connection to some of our beliefs.

But this is a far from satisfactory account of what is really involved in our 'having the idea' of necessary connection. We need some way of understanding the function, or point, of our notion of necessity. What does it do, or what does it enable us to do that those who lack it cannot do? What else of significance is our 'possession' of it connected with? Because of his atomistic picture of thinking or having an idea as a matter of contemplating or 'viewing' an object, Hume is not in a strong position to answer this question realistically.

The notion of necessity or the use of the word 'must' seems intimately tied to inference, or to the relation between one state of affairs and something that can be derived from it, and this could suggest a real difference between us and the hypothetical beings we are trying to imagine. It might be thought that in having the idea of necessity we can move from one belief to another, and defend those transitions on the basis of past experience, in a way they cannot, since we can appeal to connections between phenomena that they have no way of appealing to.

Although there is something in this suggestion, it is not immediately obvious what it is. If, when asked why we believe that the billiard ball will move, we appeal to nothing more than past regularities and the virtually present impact, we would seem not to differ from those others at all, since there seems to be nothing to prevent them from appealing to the same facts. If our 'must' is used merely to signal or mark the fact that an inference is being drawn from past constant conjunctions and present data, and if those others make the same inferences as we do, and present and comment upon those inferences and their bases when required, then the difference between us shrinks and threatens to vanish. We believe everything they believe, and if they and we both appeal only to past conjunctions and present experience to support those beliefs, the only difference between us would seem to be that we mysteriously use the word 'must' or the idea of necessity in concluding our inferences, and they do not. They would seem to do the very same things without it.

But do they do the very same things we do? Even if it is granted that those others could be said to share with us all our categorical beliefs about the actual course of events in the world, they might still be thought to differ from us in their conditional beliefs, or in their general beliefs, or in both, and so the inferences they make, and the reasons they have for their expectations, would not be the same as ours after all. This raises complicated issues about the nature of our conditional and general beliefs and how they are best to be understood.[6]

So far it has emerged that the beings we are trying to imagine might be said to have conditional and general beliefs of a sort, and hence to be able to infer from the observed to the unobserved and to specify and comment in a certain way upon those inferences. They can observe the constant conjunction between, say, being unsupported and falling, and so perhaps can give to the statement that for all xs, if x is unsupported then x falls, the sense that being unsupported and falling are in fact universally correlated. That goes beyond their actual experience, of course, but if the correlation had been found to hold in all observed cases, then because of the principles of the imagination they would simply generalize from the observed to the unobserved. In so far as we also believe in that universal correlation, they and we will share the same belief. And they can perhaps also be said to believe that *if* a particular body is, was or will be unsupported, then at the time in question it is, was or will be falling. Such beliefs would seem to enable them to give at least some answer to questions about why they believe the categorical statements they do, or how they infer one from another.

When they believe that a particular billiard ball will move, for example, and are asked for their reasons for that belief,[7] they could point out that it is now in a certain situation on the table and is about to be struck, and if anything is a billiard ball in such a situation and is struck then it moves. They could see their belief as supported in that way on the basis of past experience.

What is most important, however, is not whether we can make complete sense of the possibility of such people, but rather what our own situation is really like. The only point of the contrast is to illuminate the special role of our own notion of necessity, and perhaps that can be suggested even if we cannot fully comprehend the alleged possibility of not having it.

Part of that role can be discerned in our sense that people with only the conditional beliefs described above would be appealing to much less than we appeal to when we invoke the conditionals or generalizations behind our own categorical beliefs. We believe that the body will fall *because* it is unsupported, or we believe that its falling when unsupported is an instance of a *law of nature*, and not simply an instance of a generalization that is true as long as phenomena of the first kind never in fact fail to be followed by phenomena of the second kind.

This comes out in another way in our reliance on subjunctive, or what are often misleadingly called 'counterfactual', conditionals. Our dependence on laws or law-like connections between phenomena is expressed in our belief that if this particular body *were* to be unsupported then it *would* fall, even though we might know that it is not, and never was or will be unsupported. Here we countenance a certain possibility, and in doing so come to believe that certain consequences would ensue if it were realized. But that is to go beyond beliefs about the course of all actual events, past, present and future. It is something that those who were imagined to lack the idea of necessity presumably could not do. They are restricted to the actual in a way we are not. But it should not be surprising to find that having the idea of necessity and being able to countenance various unrealized possibilities go hand in hand. To believe that something *must* happen is to reject any possibility of its not happening.

Having the idea of necessary connection is therefore a much richer and more complicated matter than simply having a certain mental particular present to the mind, but Hume cannot give a satisfactory account of that richness. To find an intimate connection between having the idea of necessary connection and being able to countenance and trace the implications of various unrealized possibilities must seem, on Humean grounds, simply to add to, but not really to illuminate, the puzzle. According to the theory of ideas, to discover that having the idea of necessity involves our having an equally mysterious notion of possibility is simply to discover that we are the passive beneficiaries of not just one, but perhaps a complex set of interconnected mental items, and that the ritual we go through of 'adding' certain unanalysable ideas to the things we believe is more complicated than we had originally supposed, but is still otherwise as empty and mysterious. But this simply draws a veil over what needs to be understood before Hume's programme can succeed, viz. how it is possible for us to think about more than the actual course of events in the world, or what is involved in our accepting statements whose modality is stronger than 'existence' or what is actually the case. The theory of ideas cannot adequately express what difference our having the whole set of interconnected ideas of necessity, possibility, and so on, actually makes.

That theory obstructs understanding of the role of those notions by giving us an illusion of a perfectly hard, clear and distinct conception of 'what is actually the case'. For when we regard 'what is actually the case' as residing in, at most, the occurrence of particular, discrete events, and we find problematic any notions that are not straightforwardly instantiated in those particulars, or which go beyond them and imply in addition something that strikes us as mysterious, then I think we are still feeling the seductive force of Hume's impressions.

In trying to imagine what it would be like for people to get on in the world without the idea of necessary connection we are in effect trying to imagine what it would be like if there were nothing more to 'what is actually the case' than what can be gleaned from Humean impressions alone. And then it is no wonder that anything we believe in addition to those austere data appears 'epiphenomenal', empty or without a counterpart in the 'real' world.

But the notion of causality or necessary connection is more central and more deeply embedded in our very conception of 'what is actually the case', or 'what happens', than this picture would allow. This is revealed in one way by the pervasiveness of causal verbs in our language. The hypothetical beings we are trying to imagine would presumably lack them, at least with anything like the sense those verbs bear for us. That is not to say that one is in a position to specify in an illuminating and non-circular way just what those senses are. But when one thing is said to 'push' another, or to 'pull' it, or to 'break' it, more is being said than that one event or state of affairs immediately follows another, and more too than that plus the generalization that whenever something of the first sort happens something of the second sort does. There is an assertion of a causal connection between two events or states of affairs. So those who lack what Hume calls 'the idea of necessary connection' would lack all such verbs. Nothing they said could be translated into English in those ways, since that would amount to attributing to them the idea of necessary connection after all.

Such reflections make it increasingly difficult to get a grip on what the life and thought would be like of those who completely lack the idea of necessary connection. And we also perhaps begin to appreciate more fully what having that idea means to us. Can we even conceive of what it would be like to think and speak of the world without any causal verbs, or verbs of efficacy or action, or not to take talk of one thing's pushing, pulling or breaking another, or of a person's lifting, grasping or knocking on something, as reports of 'what is actually the case' or 'what happens'? The question whether we can conceive of that or not is less important than the realization that in any case it would be a world very different from our own. But is Hume even in a position to understand how we could have such a world?

The situation of those hypothetical beings is actually worse than has been imagined so far. They have been represented as being acquainted only with discrete events and having no more than the generalizing ability to sort them into kinds and notice correlations among them. But even that exceeds the severely restricted limits of Humean impressions. Many events take time and are therefore beyond the purview of a single impression. One billiard ball's striking another might be said to be, for all practical purposes, instantaneous, but the same cannot be said of the event of the second ball's moving. That takes time, and so that event is not something of which we could ever have an impression. Strictly speaking, the most that could be discovered by someone restricted to impressions alone would be momentary states of affairs and their succession, and that might be thought too little to give one even so much as a notion of an event, or of something's happening, especially when it is remembered how those 'states of affairs' would have to be described.

Kant, for instance, opposed this Humean theory by demonstrating that having the idea of necessary connection and being capable of even so much as the thought of an objective happening are more intimately connected than Hume could have supposed (Kant (1), B233–56). He did not accept the challenge of showing that necessity is a discernible feature in our experience. Nor did he simply show by 'analysis' that one discrete mental item ('the idea of an objective happening') 'contains' a certain other one ('the idea of necessary connection'). Rather he explored the depths of the role that the idea of necessary connection can be seen to play in our thought about the world, and thereby came closer than Hume could have come to an understanding of what our 'having the idea of necessary connection' consists in. But his approach was explicitly based on a rejection of one of the

231

fundamental preconceptions of the philosophical theory of ideas.

The theory of ideas obstructs proper understanding of the role, or function, or point, of various ideas in our thought about the world because in representing 'having' an idea as a matter of a certain object's simply being 'in' the mind, it leaves out, or places in a secondary position, the notion of judgment, the putting forth of something that is true or false. For Hume, ideas exist in the mind and have their identity completely independently of any contribution they might make to judgments or statements that have a truth-value. He sees judging as just a special case of an object's being present to the mind. Characteristically, he is more explicit about this feature of the theory of ideas than its earlier advocates had been,[8] but he does not see the difficulties it creates. He does not see that without an account of how ideas combine to make a judgment or a complete thought he can never explain the different roles or functions various fundamental ideas perform in the multifarious judgments we make, or in what might be called the 'propositional' thoughts we have. Consequently, he does not arrive at even the beginnings of a realistic description of what 'having' the idea of causality actually consists in. And that is an indispensable first step in his naturalistic science of man.

Despite his un-Humean reliance on completely *a priori* procedures, Kant could be said to follow the spirit of Hume's programme more closely in this crucial respect. He concentrates on what is involved in, or required for, people's 'having' or employing certain ideas or concepts, rather than on straightforward 'analyses' or definitions of the ideas themselves. But he is in a better position than Hume to show what difference 'having' the idea in question makes to a person—what a person 'with' the idea can do, or think or feel, that a person 'without' it cannot—since he takes 'having' a certain idea to be a matter of having a certain ability, capacity or competence. This more functionalist treatment of ideas or concepts is a result of his conception of the primacy of judgment—the view that the 'possession' of a certain concept consists precisely in the ability to make judgments of certain kinds, and that the employment of that concept is to be found nowhere but in the making of actual judgments. For Kant, concepts are 'predicates of possible judgments' (Kant (1), A69 = B94), and 'the only use which the understanding can make of . . . concepts is to judge by means of them' (Kant (1), A68 = B93).

Hume's distance from this insight is partly obscured in his account of morality, since that part of his theory is in one respect more in accord with the underlying spirit of his naturalistic programme than is his account of the idea of necessary connection. His investigation of the notion of goodness, or of the virtues and vices, does not take the form of a search for the origins of a certain idea in the mind; in fact, he does not speak of an 'idea' of goodness, or of virtue, at all. He wants to explain what might be called the very phenomenon of morality itself—people's regarding some things as virtuous and others as vicious, their approving of certain things and disapproving of others, and their acting, or being moved to act, one way rather than another. And that is something that presents itself fairly directly to any observer of human life. It is, in short, people's moral 'pronouncements' that Hume is interested in, and they reveal themselves in something other than 'comings' and 'goings', 'entrances' and 'exits', on some hidden ghostly stage. Feelings, emotions, 'pronouncements' and propensities to act are not things we must identify and describe only in terms of the theory of ideas. They are exhibited 'in the common course of the world, by men's behaviour in company, in affairs, and in their pleasures' (p. xxiii). Hume is much closer to the data here than in his treatment of what he sees as the more purely intellectual cases of necessary connection, continued and distinct existence, and the self.

If it is possible, in a strictly Humean frame of mind, to get into the position of finding our 'possession' and employment of the idea of necessary connection mysterious, or of finding that it remains an empty ritual somehow tacked onto, but adding nothing substantial to, our beliefs about what is actually the case, nothing comparable seems possible in the case of morality, even on Hume's own terms. That is not because good and evil, virtue and vice, are themselves something present in what we directly observe to be the case, but rather because regarding or responding to the world in moral terms does not seem empty. It serves to express human feelings and desires, and thus to connect the observed world to human propensity and action, so trying to imagine people for whom the notions of good and evil played no role would involve trying to imagine 'people' with no affections, desires or propensities at all—'people' who are completely inactive because they are never moved to act. We cannot get very far in that imaginative direction. That helps us appreciate the importance and pervasiveness of Hume's *explananda* in a way that the official theory of ideas alone can never do, since the psychological phenomena of morality that are to be explained are directly linked to other things that people do, and think and feel.

But although approving or disapproving of things, or 'pronouncing' an action or character to be virtuous, or vicious, is thus more accessible to common observation and intelligible in more naturalistic terms, that is not because Hume sees the 'pronouncements' in question as genuinely 'propositional' thoughts. Having a moral 'opinion', or regarding something as virtuous, or vicious, is not for him a matter of having a 'thought' at all. If it were, he thinks it would follow that 'we distinguish betwixt vice and virtue and pronounce an action blameable or praise-worthy' by means of our *ideas* and not our impressions, and that is what he explicitly wants to deny (p. 456). His view is that 'morality . . . is more properly felt than judg'd of' (p. 470), so he sees our making moral 'pronouncements' as a matter of having impressions or feelings rather than thoughts or beliefs. And despite his tendency to describe his task as that of explaining why we 'pronounce any action or character *to be vicious*' (p. 469, my italics), or how observing or contemplating an action can lead us to 'feel *that it is virtuous*' (p. 471, my italics), he cannot really represent those 'pronouncements' or feelings as 'propositional'.[9] Officially, they are nothing more than feelings or sentiments 'of approbation', or 'of satisfaction', and those are just pleasant feelings of certain kinds. In Chapter VIII I tried to reveal some of the difficulties Hume faces in identifying or describing those feelings accurately and in a way that illuminates their special moral character. They are partly the difficulties of explaining how it is possible for us to 'pronounce' or feel *that* a certain action or character is virtuous, and that is a special case of explaining how one can have a thought or perception that such-and-such is the case, or indeed a thought or perception with any 'content' at all.

The treatment of the idea of the continued and distinct existence of objects labours under those same difficulties. When Hume tries to determine 'what causes induce us to believe in the existence of body', he takes believing in the continued and distinct existence of body to be a 'state' all of us are in, and he tries to explain how we get into that 'state'—how we acquire a belief we originally lack. But, as in the case of necessary connection, the official theory of ideas makes it difficult to see the belief in question as anything other than empty and idle— something merely tacked onto, and not engaged with, our active beliefs about the course of our experience.

The 'constancy' and 'coherence' we notice in our experience are said to operate on certain basic properties or 'principles' of the imagination to produce in us the idea of, and the belief in, continued and distinct existence. So Hume would allow as a possibility, though not of course a causal possibility, someone's acknowledging the 'constancy' and 'coherence' of much of his experience without believing in the continued and distinct existence of body. His question is how those features of our experience actually produce that belief. So he is committed to there being some describable difference between one who notices or acknowledges only the 'constancy' and 'coherence' exhibited in his experience and one who, in addition to that, also believes in the continued and distinct existence of body. What account could Hume give of that difference?

A non-believer in continued and distinct existence would seem to be capable of all the same memories of his past experiences as a believer, and given that his mind 'generalizes' in the same way on the basis of observed constant conjunctions, he could have all the same expectations about his future experience as well. So the two need not differ in any beliefs about the course of their actual experiences, past, present or future. And if the non-believer could have the idea of causality, or necessary connection, as well, and hence could be said to have a conception of possibility, and to be capable of believing that, under certain conditions, a certain kind of event *must* occur, then he would be capable of going beyond the course of his actual experience to beliefs about what experiences *would be* forthcoming if certain other experiences *were to* occur. Such a person might then share with the believer in continued and distinct existence all the same beliefs about both actual and possible experiences, past, present and future. He would not be aware of, or expect, or remember, anything different in experience from what the non-believer believes, nor would he believe anything different about what *would* be experienced if certain other experiences were to occur. If to have the belief in the continued and distinct existence of bodies is only for a certain complex idea to be 'before the mind' with a high degree of force and vivacity, it can easily look as if that is a belief we could well do without. 'Having' it does not seem to make a difference to any of our thoughts, feelings and actions, or even to our hopes, desires and fears. It is just an additional mental item that makes its vivacious appearance in the mind on certain occasions.

For Hume the world of enduring bodies is a 'fiction', something we 'feign', but never find in our experience, however rich. The 'fiction' or 'supposition' is one the mind makes in order to free itself from conflict. But the act of 'feigning' the continued existence of objects can only be understood as a purely cognitive or intellectual operation of thought that somehow 'produces' the very ideas that would seem to be needed for that act of 'feigning' itself to occur. I suggested in Chapter V that the impossibility of explaining, within the theory of ideas, how this 'feigning' or 'supposing' is possible, is responsible for the incoherence of Hume's putative explanation of the origin of the belief in continued and distinct existence.

Even the task of describing in more realistic detail the phenomena Hume had in mind in speaking of people's 'belief in the continued and distinct existence of body' is not a simple one. It is probably possible, although by no means easy, to describe some of the important ways in which a person who believes, for example, that there are seeds in grapes or stars in the sky differs from one who lacks those beliefs. But Hume is interested in what he sees as 'the belief in bodies' (in general), and not beliefs in this or that specific kind of body. 'Having' that 'belief' would involve our fulfilling the conditions that make it even so much as possible for us to acquire specific beliefs about seeds or stars or any other definite kind of thing. It is our having a conception of an enduring world, and our thereby being in a position to come to believe it populated with various specific sorts of things, that is at stake. And our fulfilling those conditions is much more a matter of our having the capacity to make and understand judgments of a certain kind than simply a case of our 'possessing' one more, albeit more general, belief. How it is possible for us to have any objective beliefs at all is what needs to be explained. The theory of ideas leads Hume to miss the depth and complexity of what he wants to explain, and to represent our having and endorsing a conception of an enduring world as a straightforward matter of the 'presence before the mind' of a certain mental particular.

Similar difficulties beset the account of the idea of the self. Hume is once again unable to account for the importance and centrality of the very idea he sees needs investigation. Why should that mental item that is the idea of the self be more interesting or important than any one of a thousand others? What is especially significant about whether or not that particular light-bulb is glowing in the mind? We need some understanding of the role or function of that idea, and that requires a more complicated and sophisticated picture of what 'having' it consists in.

For Hume it is perfectly possible for a conscious subject to have thoughts, feelings and desires without having any idea of the self. That idea arises only after certain features of the person's experience have combined with various properties of his mind to produce it. But in explaining how we move from simply taking in the passing show to being able to think of ourselves and others as subjects of consciousness, Hume has to explain how it is possible for a conscious subject to think about and refer to his thoughts, feelings and desires as *his*, and even how it is possible for him to realize that there are such things as thoughts, feelings and desires (or indeed, a passing show) at all. Only someone with a conception of self could think about psychological states belonging to him or to anyone else. That is a major part of the role that the 'possession' of the idea of the self plays in our thoughts and feelings; it is what a person who 'has' that idea can do that those who lack it cannot.

Kant argued that the possibility of our having the thought that a certain psychological state belongs to us is itself a condition of that state's belonging to us (Kant (1), B131–2). Having the capacity to make judgments of a certain kind was seen as a requirement for being a subject of consciousness. And the judgments in question are ascriptions of thoughts, feelings, desires, and so on, to ourselves. For Kant the capacity to make such judgments was also intimately connected with our ability to make and understand judgments about the enduring existence of objects independent of our perceiving them, and that in turn was seen to involve our having a conception of laws of nature according to which events in the objective world follow one another of necessity.

So when Kant focused on what is involved in our 'having the ideas' of necessary connection, continued and distinct existence, and the self, he found them to be much more closely connected than Hume supposed, or than the official theory of ideas would allow. But Kant's inquiries into the conditions of our having various thoughts, feelings and desires were informed by the non-atomistic notion of the primacy of judgment, and so he could describe, in a way Hume could not, the roles or functions those various 'representations' perform. Such investigations would bring us closer to completing the indispensable first step in Hume's naturalistic science of man. They would provide more varied and more complicated, because more realistic, descriptions of the phenomena Hume wants to explain.

Although a serious interest in what is involved in our 'possession' of certain concepts, rather than in the analysis or definition of those concepts themselves, is in the spirit of Hume's naturalistic programme, Kant also deviated from that spirit in his insistence on purely *a priori* procedures. That is primarily because he saw his philosophical results as necessary, and hence as attainable only *a priori*. Recent analytic philosophers have tended to side with Kant in seeing philosophy as proceeding completely independently of all experience in the search for necessary truths. And they have also tended to abandon Hume's atomism in favour of a conception of the sentence or the proposition, and not the term or idea, as the basic unit of meaning and hence of analysis.[10]

A typical analysis or definition of causality or personal identity would now focus, not on the word 'cause' or the word 'self' or 'person' alone, but on whole sentences in which those terms occur essentially. An analysis of the meaning of singular causal statements, for example, is normally intended to yield a set of conditions necessary and sufficient for the truth of 'A caused B', and there need not be any term in the definition that is itself equivalent in meaning to the English word 'cause'. And analyses of personal identity concentrate on the conditions necessary and sufficient for the truth of identity-statements about persons, e.g. 'This is the same woman who was here last week.' In each case the necessary equivalences are held to be true in virtue of meaning alone, hence analytic, and therefore discoverable only *a priori*.

With respect to these aims recent analytic philosophers are further from the real spirit of Hume's naturalistic programme than was Kant. Like Kant, they see the philosophical task as completely *a priori*, but unlike him, they also see it as one of analysis of meanings or concepts alone. It is centred on the 'content' of our thoughts, beliefs and reactions, rather than on the conditions of our having them. Questions about how it is possible for us to think or understand the thoughts we have, or what their being intelligible to us consists in, or what is involved in our having the 'ideas' we do, are either themselves construed as questions about the meaning of certain psychological expressions (and largely ignored), or else they are explicitly avoided in the name of 'anti-psychologism'. The 'subjective', and therefore merely contingent, is rejected in favour of the purely 'objective'—those relations of 'containment' or inclusion holding necessarily among our concepts, thoughts and beliefs. On this conception, philosophy can contribute to our understanding of what is involved in having and employing the concepts we do only by analysis. It can show that the content of a certain thought or belief implies, and therefore contains, certain others, and can thereby add to our understanding of what is involved in what we understand and think. Its task is only to provide a schematic logical geography—a map of the complicated inter-relations among our concepts.

But Hume's main interest is in our understanding and thinking the things we do. His concern with human nature is not so much a concern with the intricacies of *what* we understand or think, as with the conditions of our understanding and thinking it. He can hardly be said to have given a satisfactory account of those conditions in any particular case he considers, but that should not blind us to the fact that his project as he envisages it is not one simply of the *a priori* analysis of meanings. It is not that such analysis would be incompatible with Hume's programme,[11] but it would not produce the kind of illumination he seeks. It would stop short of full acknowledgment that:

> all the sciences have a relation, greater or less, to human
> nature; and that however wide any of them may seem to
> run from it, they still return back by one passage or
> another. Even *Mathematics, Natural Philosophy, and Natural
> Religion*, are in some measure dependent on the science of
> MAN; since they lie under the cognizance of men, and are
> judged of by their powers and faculties. (p. xix)

That is why for Hume talk of such abstract things as 'meanings', 'concepts' and 'principles' must finally be grounded in what people actually think, feel and do in human life.[12]

Kant sought the essential or necessary ingredients of human thinking and perceiving, and so he thought only *a priori* methods could succeed. But a Humean concern with the conditions of our thinking in certain ways need not be construed exclusively in that way. The competences, capacities and abilities involved in our conceiving of ourselves as subjects of consciousness in a world of enduring, causally interacting objects, are themselves natural phenomena that can be investigated like any others, and perhaps even their 'origins' in some sense can be discovered. But the most important and most difficult step is first to describe them, to understand what 'having' the ideas in question consists in and what makes it possible. That descriptive task would not require truths of a mysterious, unempirical psychology somehow deduced *a priori* from the knowledge and skills we so clearly exhibit, but it would require a fully 'naturalized' investigation of the actual human situation in real life—what people come to be able to do, think and feel, that constitutes their having a conception of an objective world of causally interacting bodies in which they themselves have a role.[13] Simplistic theories of the mind, such as the theory of ideas, would mislead us into thinking we understand that already. More sophisticated analytic philosophers concentrate on the 'contents' of our thought, and hence ignore it. But there remains something there to be understood. Thinking and feeling human beings are Hume's subject-matter, and not simply the 'contents' of those thoughts and feelings themselves, but the theory of ideas prevents him from appreciating the full complexity of that subject-matter and leads him to concentrate prematurely on the later, more explanatory, parts of his naturalistic science of man.

The theory of ideas also restricts the scope of Hume's naturalism in a very different way by leading him to ignore an area of investigation at least as puzzling and difficult as any of those he considers, and equally important for an understanding of human thought.

We have seen that his treatment of causality is itself causal. He explains how we 'project' necessity onto the connections between things (where it does not objectively 'reside') because of what happens in our minds after we have had experiences of constantly conjoined phenomena. This explanation is meant to render more intelligible our thinking of things as causally connected without appealing to any mysterious relation of causality objectively holding between things in our experience. No such connection is there to be observed, and so the source of our thinking causally must be found in our minds, and not in the phenomena we observe.

An essential part of the explanation consists in showing that the connection between cause and effect is not to be understood as requiring the 'absolute' impossibility (pp. 87, 89), 'in a metaphysical sense' (Hume (2), p. 14), of the cause occurring without the effect. When one thing causes another there is held to be no 'contradiction' involved in asserting that the first happened and the second did not. That is the heart of Hume's proof that we have no 'demonstrative' or 'intuitive' certainty of the truth of the general causal maxim or of any particular causal statement (pp. 79, 87). Any assurance we have in either case must come from experience, since only that whose negation is contradictory or 'absolutely' impossible can be known with 'demonstrative' or 'intuitive' certainty, and no causal statement is 'necessary' in that sense. 'Absolute' necessity or possibility resides in, and is guaranteed by, the 'relations of ideas' alone.

Hume's treatment of the whole subject of 'reasoning from ideas alone' is rudimentary and perfunctory. [14] He accepts almost uncritically talk of 'the same' and 'distinct' ideas, and of 'the relations of ideas', as if they inhabited a determinate objective domain immediately open to our minds for inspection. The theory of ideas encourages this picture of a set of autonomous, interconnected 'things' among which certain relations can be discovered to hold merely in virtue of our 'possessing' the ideas in question. Hume's confident assertions about which ideas are 'the same', and which 'distinct', with their consequences about what is, and what is not, 'absolutely' impossible, are an expression of this picture. In fact, in his reliance on a putatively unproblematic notion of the relations amongst ideas, and of the 'absolute' necessities which hold as a result of them, Hume speaks of ideas and their interconnections in just the way someone who quite naturally and uncritically accepts the idea of *causal* necessity would speak about the world of observable events and the causal connections between them. In our ordinary and scientific dealings with the world we think the causal necessities we 'discover' are there to be discovered.

Hume does not wish to put an end to our thinking of causality as an objective feature of the world, but as a scientist of man he wants to examine it, to discover its source, and to explain how and why we are led to think that way. Because of its centrality in human life, he wants to stand back from our causal thinking and examine it in the way we might examine any other natural phenomenon. That is where the theory of 'projection' comes in. Is something analogous to his naturalistic examination of the idea of causal necessity possible with respect to our thought of 'absolute' (or what is usually called 'logical') necessity? [15] Having such an idea of necessity, we must, according to Hume, get it somehow. Is it possible to explain its origin along the general lines of the theory of 'projection' that Hume uses elsewhere?

The only passage in all his writings that suggests that such a thought occurred to him is the tantalizing remark:

> Thus as the necessity, which makes two times two equal
> to four, or three angles of a triangle equal to two right
> ones, lies only in the act of the understanding, by which we
> consider and compare these ideas; in like manner the necessity
> or power, which unites causes and effects, lies in the
> determination of the mind to pass from the one to the
> other. (p. 166)

I have argued that what Hume means by 'the necessity or power, which unites causes and effects, lies in the determination of the mind to pass from the one to the other', does not commit him to the psychologistic view that 'A caused B' implies, or includes in its meaning, anything about the mind.[16] Nor need it mean that the idea of necessity itself adds nothing, and that 'A caused B' serves to assert only the presence of those objective conditions that actually produce in our minds the superfluous idea of a necessary connection between A and B.[17] He means that we get the idea of causal necessity and 'project' it where it does not objectively 'reside' only because something happens in our minds on certain occasions. If that is right, then the analogous suggestion that the necessity with which two times two equals four 'lies only in' an 'act of the understanding' need not have the fatal implication that statements like 'necessarily, two times two equals four' are all statements at least partly about the mind. Nor would we have to assume from the outset that they are merely equivalent to their non-modalized counterparts ('two times two equals four'), and that the idea of necessity is therefore otiose.[18] In drawing the analogy with the idea of causal necessity Hume would be saying that the idea of 'absolute' or 'logical' necessity is also a 'fiction' we inevitably 'project' onto what we think about only because something happens in our minds on certain occasions. The explanation of the origin of the idea would concentrate on the mental occurrences giving rise to it and would thereby render more intelligible our thinking of things as holding 'absolutely' necessarily without appealing to any unexplained 'necessity' objectively true of the things we regard as holding necessarily.[19]

The explanation of the origin of the idea of causal necessity first identifies the experimental occasions on which that idea arises, and then explains how those experiences actually produce the idea. And Hume suggests analogously that our idea of the necessity with which two times two equals four arises from some act of the understanding that occurs on those occasions when 'we consider and compare' the idea of the product of two and two and the idea of four. No such idea of necessity arises when we 'consider and compare' the idea of a body's being unsupported and the idea of its falling, since we do not regard it as 'absolutely' necessary that all unsupported bodies fall. Some considerings and comparings give rise to an idea of 'absolute' necessity and some do not.

It is tempting to distinguish between the two sorts of occasions by saying that the idea of 'absolute' necessity arises only when we consider and compare ideas that are not 'distinct', or are such that one of them 'contains' the other, and that that is why we attach the idea of 'absolute' necessity to 'two times two equals four' and not to 'all unsupported bodies fall'. But even if that is right as far as it goes, it cannot contribute to an explanation of the origin of the idea of 'absolute' necessity. The explanation must describe the occasions on which that idea arises in such a way that our noticing them, or their having their effect, does not require that we already have the idea of 'absolute' necessity. And I argued in effect in Chapter III that the notion of 'the same' or 'distinct' ideas makes sense to us only if the notion of 'absolute' necessity also makes sense to us. To say that the idea of the product of two and two is not 'distinct' from the idea of four is to say more than that two times two equals four, since not every truth is guaranteed by the 'relations of ideas' alone. Two ideas are 'distinct' only if it is *possible* for the first to apply to something without the second applying to it, and they are 'the same' only if the one *must* apply if the other does. So anyone who understood the notion of 'the same' or 'distinct' ideas would already have to have the idea of 'absolute' necessity, and so his recognition of 'sameness' of idea could not be the source of his idea of necessity.

Hume explicitly tries to avoid such explanatory circularity in his treatment of causality. He recognizes the inadequacy of saying, for example, that we get the idea of causal connection whenever we observe something that *produces*, or is *produced* by, something else. Because 'the terms of *efficacy, agency, power, force, energy, necessity, connexion,* and *productive quality*, are all nearly synonimous' (p. 157),[20] they cannot be used for explanatory purposes to describe those experiences that operate on our minds to produce one or the other of those ideas in us in the first place. It could not be because they strike us *as* instances of, say, 'production' that such experiences give rise to the idea of causality.

There is considerable initial plausibility in Hume's claim that our recognizing, or being affected by, nothing more than constant conjunctions of observable phenomena does not require that we already possess the very idea of causal necessity that those conjunctions are said to produce.[21] But nothing strictly parallel seems available in the case of 'logical' necessity. It is not merely because contemplating the product of two and two has always in the past been followed by the thought of four that we are led to regard 'two times two equals four' as 'absolutely' necessary. That is something Hume must insist on, since the idea of *causal* necessity is produced by just such conjunctions, and for him it is demonstrable that causal necessity and 'absolute' necessity are not the same.[22]

One difference between the two kinds of cases, according to Hume, is that the constant conjunctions that produce the idea of causal necessity come only from past experience, whereas the idea of 'absolute' necessity arises when we 'consider and compare' the ideas themselves, without having to rely on a backlog of constantly conjoined phenomena. We can reflect on, and arrive at necessary truths about, a unicorn, or a right-angled triangle, even though we have never encountered them in experience at all. But again that could not serve as part of the explanation of the 'origin' of the idea of 'absolute' necessity unless there were some way in which reflecting on 'the ideas themselves' differed from reflecting on, say, unsupported bodies and finding that they fall. And the difference would have to be one that could eventually produce the idea of 'absolute' necessity in someone who originally lacked that idea. So 'reflecting on the ideas themselves' would have to involve more (or less) than asking whether or not it is *possible* for one idea to apply to something without a certain other one applying to it. If that were all there was to it, any explanation of the 'origin' of the idea of necessity that appealed only to such 'reflecting' would be circular and hence could not get started.

The need to break out of the circle and find in common to all those occasions on which the idea of 'absolute' necessity arises some feature that does not require for its recognition, or its efficacy, that we already have that very idea, is undoubtedly what leads Hume to the question of what we can, and cannot, conceive. He thinks that if we try to conceive of an unsupported body's not falling we do in fact succeed, but if we try to conceive of the product of two and two's not being four we fail. If this extremely oversimplified account adequately described the facts, and held quite generally, it could well contribute to an explanation of the source of the idea of 'logical' necessity along Humean lines.[23] The 'act of the understanding' out of which the idea of necessity arises might be that of *inevitably* thinking of Y when thinking of X, or being *unable* even to think of X without thinking of Y, and that inevitability or inability need not itself be thought of as anything but causal. One does not obviously need the idea of 'absolute' impossibility in order to find out that one *cannot* lift a certain stone. That is a relatively straightforward deliverance of experience, undoubtedly involving as well certain causal views.

Of course, if the facts about what we can and cannot conceive were as

243

Hume perhaps imagines them to be, they would still themselves be open to further explanation. There must be reasons why we can, or cannot, do the things we do, or fail to do, and it would be fully in the spirit of an empirical science of man to try to discover those reasons—to explain what might be called our conceptual or intellectual abilities and inabilities.[24] One thing that would not be in the spirit of that programme, however, would be to appeal at this advanced stage to the still-unexplained notion of objective 'relations' independently holding among 'ideas'. To try to explain our inability to conceive of the product of two and two's not being four by appealing to the 'fact' that the idea of the product of two and two is 'the same' idea as that of four would be a fruitless backward step. It could not explain how we come to have that idea in the first place. Explanations of our inabilities must appeal to empirically discoverable, natural facts about *us*, something true about human beings and the world we live in that accounts for our thinking of some things as 'absolutely' necessary. That is essential to any science of man, and especially to one whose aim is to explain our fundamental ideas by locating their source in the 'fictions' or 'projections' of the human mind.

But the facts are not as simple as Hume would appear to suppose. Our having the idea of 'absolute' necessity is not simply the result of our trying, and failing, to perform a particular mental act. In fact, as in the cases considered earlier, the very phenomenon of our 'having the idea' of 'absolute' necessity is much more complicated and far-reaching than the atomistic structure of the theory of ideas would allow. It seems undeniable that we do regard some things as necessary in a sense stronger than that of causal necessity; we can get nowhere in trying to understand what it would be like for them to be false. Those are some of the most minimal 'data' to be accounted for, and no doubt in some sense they can be explained. But even if the deceptively rigid theory of ideas were abandoned, and along with it the search for the genesis of a person's idea of necessity from experiences that do not presuppose it, there would still be need for a descriptive, naturalistic investigation of our thought about 'logical' necessity.

We need to know why the falsity of some of the things we believe strikes us as, and therefore is, unthinkable in a fairly direct way, and what kinds, and depths, of unintelligibility are involved. We do not understand the relations between our use of the word 'must' and various 'epistemic' considerations—the present state of our knowledge about the particular matter in question, and the centrality or relative 'unrevisability' of the truths invoked in discussing it.[25] Nor do philosophers even have an adequate representation of what in a fairly straightforward sense could be called the 'grammar' of the words 'must', 'necessary', 'possible', and so on. There is much about our 'possession' of the idea of necessity that is not understood. But these and other aspects of its use are natural facts that would reveal the point or function of the notion of necessity in our thought; they are not recondite facts about some mysterious super-sensible entities with a life of their own. That is not to say that we have no difficulty in discovering the facts we need, or in arranging perspicuously and grasping correctly those we already know. But that is a reason for pursuing more carefully questions about the human mind and its capacities, not for abandoning them.

Recent analytic philosophers would concentrate on 'analysing' or 'defining' necessity, and so would tend to deviate from the spirit of Hume's programme. They would focus, not on what 'having the idea' of 'logical' necessity consists in, or on what makes it possible for us to regard some things as necessary and others as contingent, but simply on what 'necessary', or 'contingent' *means*.[26] But the prospects of genuine illumination in that direction seem dim; terms like 'possible' or 'must' in which any such 'definition' would presumably be expressed 'are all nearly synonimous' with the term to be defined. If we find necessity and our thought of it puzzling we are not likely to get the kind of understanding we want by tracing its fairly obvious connections with other notions we find equally puzzling for the same reasons. At least that is not the kind of understanding Hume seeks in his science of man. He recognizes the dead-end represented by the appeal to 'power', 'efficacy' or 'productive quality' in the clarification of the idea of causal necessity, and the same pessimism would undoubtedly have carried over to an analogous account of 'absolute' necessity if he had pushed his investigations more resolutely in that direction.

III

There remains the question of the specifically philosophical interest or importance of Hume's achievement. The end result of the naturalistic science of man that he recommends would be an empirically based description and explanation of human actions, thoughts and feelings—in short, a general theory of human nature. It is nothing more than a dream to think of such a project's being completed, but even if talk of its 'completion' makes no real sense we are still faced with the question whether unlimited access to all the knowledge such a science could provide would give us more of the kind of understanding of ourselves that we seek. I think Hume feels this worry deeply, and in his suggestions towards its 'solution' he not unwittingly expresses a deep affinity with the ancient sceptics.

It is an essential part of Hume's explanations of our most fundamental ideas, beliefs and reactions, that they are in one way or another 'fictions', or 'illusions', produced primarily by various happenings in our minds and lacking instances or counterparts in the objective world of experience onto which we 'project' them. If the ideas of causality, continued and distinct existence, the self, and goodness, for example, were not thought of as 'fictions' or 'projections', but were said to be abstracted directly from instances of them encountered in experience, then the explanations of their origins in the mind would perhaps be simple and straightforward, but they could not help to make our thinking in those ways a little less puzzling or mysterious. Those modes of thought would be brute facts beyond which our explanatory powers could not reach.

For example, to say simply that we get the idea of causality by perceiving instances of it in our experience would leave completely unexplained what causality is, and what it is to perceive it. It would not make our causal thinking any more intelligible to us than it was before we began the unproblematic and largely unmotivated search for its origin. Hume's genetic investigations derive their interest and complexity precisely from his contention that the ideas he examines in that way are 'fictions' or 'illusions'. He is concerned with our 'possession' of certain ideas and with our 'acquisition' of them from perceptual experience, and if he were to suppose that the ideas he examines are acquired directly from instances of them in experience, then because of his views about the severe constraints on what is, strictly speaking, perceived, the only problem left to him would be to provide reductive analyses of those ideas, to show that their contents can be fully analysed into nothing more than combinations of the simple features that can be directly encountered in experience. I have argued that the kinds of definitions or reductions required for any such explanation are not to be found in Hume. 'Phenomenalism', the 'regularity theory of causality', the 'bundle theory of personal identity', moral 'subjectivism', 'psychologism' in morals, or in causality, or in mathematics—all these, understood as semantic theses about the meanings of various terms or the contents of our ideas, I think are not among his most considered views. His explanatory aims, plus the theory of ideas, push him towards his theory of 'projection', according to which there is nothing in our experience answering to those fundamental ideas we use in making sense of it. That is at once both the most distinctive and the most paradoxical feature of Hume's theory of human nature.

The paradox is not simply that his theory of man attributes a number of false or unjustified beliefs to people. Although that is true, it is not paradoxical. It is not a requirement on an adequate explanation of a person's belief that it represent that belief as true or justified; if it were, there would be no accounting for error or unreasonableness. Nor is there anything paradoxical in the general idea that there are many things that people are wrong about, or that they have always been wrong about. It is not simply because of his attribution of error, but rather because of the completely general nature of the theory that attributes such error to human beings, that the Humean scientist of man is put in an unstable, perhaps paradoxical, position.[27]

The theory is meant to apply to all human beings, and to show how and why, given their experiences, they will inevitably get the various fundamental ideas, beliefs and reactions that they do. But since the theory is to be true of all human beings, it is to be true in particular of David Hume, the human being who asserts it and believes it. Therefore, since it is essential to Humean explanations that they represent our fundamental beliefs as 'fictions' or 'illusions', when Hume comes to think of himself and his beliefs from the detached point of view of his own theory of man, he must see those beliefs themselves as false, as nothing more than 'projections' of various mental happenings onto an objective world which, strictly speaking, contains nothing that makes them true. Hume's theoretical investigations reveal to him that 'necessity is something, that exists in the mind, not in objects' (p. 165), that ' 'tis a false opinion that any of our objects, or perceptions, are identically the same after an interruption' (p. 209), that 'there is properly no *simplicity* in [the mind] at one time, nor *identity* in different' (p. 253), and that 'vice and virtue . . . are not qualities in objects, but perceptions in the mind' (p. 469). He must then see his own, and not just other people's, most fundamental beliefs as nothing more than elaborately produced 'fictions' or 'illusions'.[28]

Even that in itself might not be totally depressing. If knowledge were power, then the full realization that one's beliefs are ill-based or downright mistaken could be seen as a liberation. One could finally throw over the old ways and believe and live according to one's new and more penetrating perceptions of the world. But that optimistic response is not open to Hume. His theory of man explains those fundamental beliefs as the inevitable or unavoidable outcome of the interaction of human nature and human experience. To suppose that they could simply be jettisoned in the light of theoretical discoveries, however reasonably arrived at, would be to abandon the very core of the Humean theory of the relative roles of 'reason' and 'passion' or 'the imagination' in human life. On that theory, there is for man no practical problem, and no possibly efficacious deliberation, with respect to the 'acceptance' or 'rejection' of his most fundamental beliefs and reactions. 'Nature has not left this to his choice, and has doubtless esteem'd it an affair of too great importance to be trusted to our uncertain reasonings and speculations' (p. 187). The primacy of nature, or the imagination or passion, over reason is the whole point behind Hume's naturalistic, non-Cartesian theory.

So a Humean must find himself in conflict. As a theorist he discovers that the fundamental beliefs of human beings are false and have no counterparts in reality. But his theory also implies that those beliefs cannot be given up—human beings cannot succeed in bringing their lives more into accord with the truths his theory has discovered. So in particular even he cannot accommodate himself to his new discoveries in that way. If he could he would refute his own theory, since such a successful accommodation would be living proof that it is *not* inevitable or unavoidable for people with certain kinds of experiences to believe in objective counterparts of their ideas of causality, continued and distinct existence, the self, and goodness. According to the theory, that *is* unavoidable, and so anyone who accepts the theory will have to accept that fact about himself.

But then what sort of 'discovery' is it that Hume's science of man claims to provide? The 'results' it arrives at to the effect that there really are no causal connections, no continuously existing objects, nor selves nor minds in the world, are literally incredible—beyond belief. No human being can believe them, at least for more than a few moments in the stillness of his study, and even then a sudden knock on the door could be enough to destroy his 'conviction' for weeks. That is scarcely our ideal of scientific achievement. We aspire to something more than brief periods of what at the time we must regard as certainty and illumination while knowing and confidently predicting that it will not last when we return to our natural practical and cognitive interactions with the world. Why then pursue the Humean science of man? Why seek those fleeting moments that only momentarily can be taken to reveal the truth about man and his relation to his world?

Such doubts might tempt us to resolve the conflict by abandoning the general Humean theory of man and remaining solidly immersed in those practical and intellectual endeavours that take fully for granted the existence of causal connections, continuous objects and human persons. If those natural beliefs and reactions are unavoidable there is presumably much to be gained by renouncing the ultimately absurd attempt to get outside of them and see them as 'fictions' and 'illusions'. The attempt is absurd because 'nature is obstinate, and will not quit the field, however strongly attack'd by reason' (p. 215), so no such 'discoveries' could last or could alter our understanding of our world while we are engaged with it. But for the Humean, renunciation of the attempt to appreciate the 'fictional' or 'illusory' character of our most fundamental beliefs, in favour of engagement in 'action, and employment, and the occupations of common life', is tantamount to renunciation of the quest for understanding of human beings and their relations to their world, and that is not easily given up.

> At the time, therefore, that I am tir'd with amusement
> and company, and have indulg'd a *reverie* in my chamber,
> or in a solitary walk by a river-side, I feel my mind all
> collected within itself, and am naturally *inclin'd* to carry
> my view into all those subjects, about which I have met
> with so many disputes in the course of my reading and
> conversation. I cannot forbear having a curiosity to be
> acquainted with the principles of moral good and evil, the
> nature and foundation of government, and the cause of
> those several passions and inclinations, which actuate and
> govern me. I am uneasy to think I approve of one object,
> and disapprove of another; call one thing beautiful, and
> another deform'd; decide concerning truth and falshood, reason
> and folly, without knowing upon what principles I proceed. . . .
> These sentiments spring up naturally in my present disposition;
> and shou'd I endeavour to banish them, by attaching
> myself to any other business or diversion, I *feel* I shou'd
> be a loser in point of pleasure; and this is the origin of
> my philosophy. (pp. 270–1)

The curious student of human nature will inevitably find himself in this conflict. There are rationally lucid moments when he can no longer unquestioningly follow nature and see himself unproblematically placed in a world objectively populated with causal connections, continuing objects and human minds—and yet, being human, for most of the time he cannot see those putative denizens of his world as the 'fictions' he sometimes knows them to be. This conflict, in one form or another, should be familiar to anyone who philosophizes, since to philosophize is perhaps inevitably to try to see the world and oneself in it 'from outside' or *sub specie aeternitatis*, and there is a constant tension between two roles or positions the human philosopher finds he can never quite adequately occupy simultaneously. Yet neither one is fully satisfactory on its own.

Refusing to theorize with complete generality would leave us with no understanding of the kind we seek about ourselves. And simply accepting the positive general theory (if we could) would leave us with unstable 'results' of marginal relevance to our actual situation. Perhaps the real philosophical value of the Humean study of human nature lies in neither position on its own, but in the illumination gained from the constant and inevitable passing to and fro between them. Only then is the true significance of the poverty of reason and the dominance of nature in human life brought to the surface. We reason conclusively to the 'discovery' that our most fundamental beliefs and reactions are without rational foundation, but if that were enough to bring home to us the full significance of the poverty of reason then reason would not be fully impoverished after all. It alone would have brought us to the final discovery of the 'illusory' character of our ways of thinking about the world. But we fully acknowledge and appreciate that 'discovery' only when, having reasoned our way to it, we immediately and inevitably return to those same fundamental beliefs and reactions when we live our lives.

Notes

For full bibliographical details please see the bibliography.

I The Study of Human Nature

1 Hume (1). All page numbers appearing alone in parentheses in the text refer to this book.

2 Hume (3). All page numbers preceded by an 'E' in parentheses in the text refer to this book.

3 See, for example, the first sentence of the first *Enquiry*, which begins: 'Moral philosophy, or the science of human nature. . .' (*E*, p. 5). It is clear that the 'or' serves to introduce what the *OED* calls a 'mere synonym'.

4 Jeremy Bentham apparently was unimpressed by Hume's implicit claim to greatness, and he made use of the same parallel to support the same claim on his own behalf. He wrote: 'What Bacon was to the physical world, Helvetius was to the moral. The moral world has therefore had its Bacon; but its Newton is yet to come.' Quoted in Halévy (1), p. 19.

5 See his 'Dedication' at the beginning of Reid (1) and the autobiographical remarks in Reid (2), p. 172.

6 See the letter Hume wrote to a physician in March or April 1734, when he was almost twenty-three, describing his life since he left the university (Hume (7), vol. 1, pp. 12–18).

7 The importance of Hutcheson for the origin and development of Hume's view has been stressed in the masterly work of Norman Kemp Smith. See Kemp Smith (2), esp. chapters 1–3, 7, 14.

8 For example, compare Hume (p. 458) with Hutcheson (1), p. 120, or Hume (*E*, p. 293) with Hutcheson (1), p. 123.

9 Kemp Smith was the first to suggest that Hume's work on morals was composed first, and that the point of view taken there was then generalized to other parts of human psychology. So Books I and II of the *Treatise*, which were published before Book III, were actually written later. See Kemp Smith (2), esp. pp. 12–20. I suggest some further evidence for this conjecture in Chapter VIII, pp. 186–7.

10 See, for example, Descartes (1), vol. 1, p. 116. In referring to Descartes' views here and in what follows I do not mean to suggest that Hume in his philosophizing had Descartes explicitly in mind. It is only the general type of view which is forcefully expressed in Descartes that is in question.

11 Hume's position on, for example, our beliefs about the future is often represented as the view that those beliefs are not reasonable, or are unjustified, *because* they arise simply from 'custom' or 'habit'. This unsupportable interpretation fails to distinguish the negative and the positive phases of Hume's investigation. Although Hume nowhere explicitly argues that an inference from 'this belief is caused in such-and-such a way' to 'this belief is not reasonable' is not a good one, from the fact that he never makes such an inference perhaps we can conclude that he would endorse that assessment of it. For some recent demonstrations of the invalidity of similar inferences see, for example, Davidson (1) and Pears (7).

II   The Theory of Ideas

1 See, for example, pp. 3, 5, 6, where Hume either asserts, or says something that implies, that ideas of colours, or of particular shades of a colour, are simple ideas.

2 Hume actually asserts a one-one correlation between simple ideas and simple impressions, but all he actually relies on in his subsequent argument about the origin of simple ideas is the presence of an impression for each idea. If the correlation also held in the other direction it would follow that every simple impression is followed by a simple idea, and hence that the mind never perceives a simple quality that it does not retain at least for a little while 'in thought'. I can see no good reason for Hume to insist on this controversial point. He wants to explain the origin of all the ideas that actually arise in human minds. The fact that some impressions do not give rise to any ideas would not undermine that explanation.

3 See Berkeley (1), esp. the *First Dialogue*.

4 A full discussion of this view and the philosophical interests and inclinations that seem to lead inevitably to it would take up much more than a big book on its own. Although it is certainly a fundamental belief for Hume, and one that has far-reaching consequences for the whole of his philosophy, most of my discussion will provisionally concede its intelligibility and truth, or else will try to determine the extent to which his treatment of particular issues can survive without it. Any other course would lead to a book on perception and the peculiarities of philosophizing about it, and not one especially about Hume.

5 This of course makes the outrageously unacceptable assumption, which Hume relies on throughout, that our impressions can somehow 'remain' in the mind after they have been 'had', so that we can then notice their similarities with their 'corresponding' ideas. He seems to be engaging here and elsewhere in the fiction that all (or a sizeable number) of our

past perceptions can be 'present' to us, or at least that they remain available for inspection. But on the theory of ideas, strictly speaking, we can make no sense of this alleged possibility.

6 A natural reply on Hume's behalf is to say that the detective has a more forceful and lively perception on the second occasion only because he *notices* something different, or because he *believes*, for example, that the victim was right-handed, that right-handed people usually put pokers back on the right-hand side of fireplaces, and so on. But even if that is so, it remains true that the second occasion was in fact one of thinking and not perceiving, and that the perception then present to the mind was more forceful and lively than the earlier one. A perception that is more forceful and lively than its counterpart only because of the presence of some additional causal factor is, after all, more forceful and lively than that counterpart.

7 The point of the example is only to support the first of these two alternatives. It is not put forward to 'refute' Hume's way of making the distinction, but only to show that talk of 'force and liveliness' cannot be taken very literally. Hume concedes as much, at least when he tries to use the same terms to explain the nature of belief. See, for example, p. 629.

8 I return briefly to Hume's difficulties in explaining different 'attitudes' involving the same perception in Chapter IV, pp. 74-6.

9 Hume cannot accept the plausible suggestion that the man fills in the missing shade by noticing certain features common to all previously perceived members of the spectrum and also noticing a certain respect or degree in which they all differ. That implies that the perceptions of the particular shades are complex, since they would have distinguishable features, whereas it is the very fact that the particular perceptions are supposed to be simple that gives rise to the problem. Someone's getting a *complex* idea without having had a corresponding impression poses no threat to Hume's principle about the origin of ideas.

10 This is a further instance of the difficulties Hume gets into in trying to distinguish different mental 'acts' or 'attitudes' solely on the basis of differences among their 'objects'. See above, pp. 74-6 and pp. 225-39.

11 Hume thinks the 'great' Berkeley has made 'one of the greatest and most valuable discoveries that has been made of late years in the republic of letters', and he tries only to 'confirm it by some arguments, which I hope will put it beyond all doubt and controversy' (p. 17).

III Causality and the Inference from the Observed to the Unobserved: The Negative Phase

1 Even in the so-called 'definitions' of 'cause' at the end of Section VII, 'Of the Idea of Necessary Connexion' (*E*, pp. 76-7) no mention is made of contiguity.

2 This argument (p. 76) is extremely puzzling, and Hume does not seem entirely happy with it himself. It uses a certain 'establish'd maxim' to

derive from the assumption that there is one cause that is simultaneous with its effect the consequence that all causes are simultaneous with their effects. That in turn is held to imply 'no less than the destruction of that succession of causes, which we observe in the world; and indeed, the utter annihilation of time'. So no cause can be simultaneous with its effect, but must exist or occur prior to it. The difficulty is that the 'maxim' used to derive this strong conclusion is: 'an object, which exists for any time in its full perfection without producing another, is not its sole cause; but is assisted by some other principle, which pushes it from its state of inactivity, and makes it exert that energy, of which it was secretly possest'. And that implies directly that no cause can exist 'in its full perfection' at any time before its effect exists, which contradicts the desired conclusion.

3 The difficulties raised in the previous two pages will be familiar to all students of recent philosophy from the writings of Quine. See especially the classic Quine (1). The fact that Quine's objections to positivism carry over so easily to Hume's theory of ideas perhaps shows how little progress had been made on the nature of 'demonstrative' knowledge since Hume. It would be just as misplaced to say that the present objection to Hume's argument rests only on arbitrarily or unreasonably strict requirements for an adequate explanation of 'same idea' as it was to say of Quine in 'Two Dogmas' that he simply imposed arbitrarily or unreasonably strict standards of adequacy on any explanation of synonymy.

4 Hume speaks only of 'objects' as causes and effects, or sometimes of an object's 'beginning to exist' as an effect. In what follows I will usually speak of events as the terms of the causal relation. In doing so I depart from the letter of Hume's doctrine, but it remains to be seen whether any important view of his is denied or damaged by the change.

5 Hume says his detour in the search for the source of the idea of necessary connection will consist in trying to answer the two questions: (i) why we believe that everything that begins to exist must have a cause, and (ii) how and why we come to believe, of some particular cause, that it will have such-and-such particular effects (p. 78). But having shown that the appeal to 'reasoning from ideas alone' will not answer (i), and therefore that experience must be appealed to, he does not go on to try directly to answer the question of how experience brings about that general belief. Rather, he finds 'it will be more convenient to sink this question in the following, *Why we conclude, that such particular causes must necessarily have such particular effects, and why we form an inference from one to another?* . . . 'Twill, perhaps, be found in the end, that the same answer will serve for both questions' (p. 82). The long explanation of our belief in particular causes and effects can then be used to account for the general belief as well.

6 He concentrates on cases in which the correlation is perfect—*every* A has been followed by a B. But of course most of our experiential reasoning is not like that; it proceeds on less than perfect correlations. Hume agrees, and in the sections 'Of the probability of chances' and 'Of the probability

of causes' he discusses the origins of our beliefs when they are based on 'the chances' or when our experience is 'mixed'. But if he shows that our inferences to the unobserved are not reasonable or justified when based on exceptionless correlations, then he will have shown that they are not reasonable or justified in the 'mixed' cases either. For the sake of brevity I, like Hume, will concentrate on cases in which the correlation is perfect.

7 I use 'PE' to stand for a statement of this form about *past experience*, 'PI' for a description of a *present impression*, and 'FE' for a statement about a *future experience* or, since the predicted event need not be experienced, for a *future event*. I thereby put the problem in terms of the past and the future, for the usual dramatic effect, although that does not express Hume's concern in its full generality. What is in question is any inference at all from the observed to the unobserved, so even beliefs about unobserved events in the past or the present will arise in this way.

8 It would be absurd to suggest that in inferring from the past to the future one is committed to something as clearly false, or even incoherent, as 'the future is exactly like the past in every respect', 'every sort of thing that has happened once will happen again', or 'every generalization that has been observed to hold so far will continue to hold in the future'. For the purposes of considering its role in Hume's argument, we need have only a relatively weak and restricted version of the principle in mind. It must say something about the relation between the observed and the unobserved, but it need not be any stronger than, e.g. 'with respect to being followed by Bs, unobserved As will continue to resemble observed As (at least for a short time into the future)'.

9 In suggesting that an inference's being 'founded' on a certain supposition must be understood 'epistemically' and not in purely logical terms, I appear to differ with, among others, D. C. Stove, who has given the most recent and most elaborately defended interpretation of Hume's sceptical argument. For Stove:

> Sometimes when we say of an argument from p to q, that it presupposes [or is 'founded on the supposition' that] r, our meaning is as follows: that, as it stands, the argument from p to q is not valid, and that, in order to turn it into a valid argument it would be necessary to add to its premises the proposition r. I believe that this is the sense in which 'presuppose' [or 'is founded on the supposition' that] occurs in . . . Hume's argument. (Stove (2), p. 43; see also Stove (1), p. 203)

But this, taken strictly, is too weak to capture Hume's meaning. There are indefinitely many different ways of adding premises to make a previously invalid argument deductively valid, if that were our only goal. The simplest would be simply to add the conclusion itself to the premises or, in my schematic example, to add the conditional 'If PI then FE'. To reply that such *ad hoc* suggestions are irrelevant since they are not the sorts of premises on the basis of which one could *know* or have *reason to believe* the conclusion would show that one takes Hume to be really making an 'epistemic', and not a purely logical, point after all. This of course does not affect the soundness of Stove's overall interpretation of Hume's argument, but it at least leaves open the question of what assumptions about reasoning or inference lie behind the first step of that argument. Stove admits that his is simply the best suggestion he can think of, but it settles the matter in favour of his general interpretation right from the beginning. I sketch and discuss the merits of an alternative suggestion on pp. 60-7.

10 Its obviousness is perhaps what leads most commentators, including Stove, to say that what Hume *means* by saying that the inference is founded on a certain supposition is that a certain supposition is needed to make the argument deductively valid. But the obvious invalidity might be part of Hume's *reason* for saying what he does without its being simply what he *means*, or what what he says means. If so, we can grant that inferences from the observed to the unobserved are obviously invalid as they stand and still go on to ask how, if at all, that supports Hume's claim that they are all founded on the supposition that the uniformity principle is true. It might even turn out that their obvious deductive invalidity is not what Hume primarily has in mind.

11 This view, in one form or another, is so widespread that it is difficult to document it adequately. It comes easily to mind on first acquaintance with Hume's argument, and it finds more sophisticated expression in, for example, Edwards (1), Strawson (1), ch. 9, and Stove (1) and (2). Partly for want of a better name, and partly because of its popularity, I call this the 'standard interpretation'.

12 Most critics of Hume have been content to show that his apparently general scepticism does not follow from his argument, or that it follows only on a certain implausible and unjustified assumption about 'good' reasoning, and that therefore we need not accept it. Stove (in Stove (2)) has gone on from Stove (1) to 'prove' that Hume's scepticism is actually false. The 'proof' of that apparently very strong result (I take it that it would amount to a direct 'solution' to 'the problem of induction') depends essentially on understanding Hume's sceptical conclusion that 'even after the observation of the . . . constant conjunction of objects, we have no reason to draw any inference concerning any object beyond those of which we have had experience' as simply equivalent in meaning to the negation of a certain 'statement of logical probability' which is derivable from the probability calculus with the help of two other extremely weak 'statements of logical probability'. The 'proof' of the falsity of Hume's view consists of that derivation.

13 See, for example, Russell (1), ch. VI; Kemp Smith (2), pp. 374-5; von Wright (1), ch. VII; Salmon (1), pp. 5-11; Ayer (7), ch. I; and many others.

14 Of course, I will have such grounds on the basis of the evidence described only if Hume's scepticism is not true. But here I am not discussing his argument for that sceptical conclusion, but rather looking for principles

implicit in the ways we ordinarily 'justify' our inferences that might then be used in reaching the sceptical conclusion.

15 Statements restricted to what I have observed before the new information do not imply that the next person to come out of the door will be male, nor do those statements plus the new information imply that that person will not be male. But in each case I take it that those are the reasons I have for my belief.

16 In developing this line of thought I am much indebted to Judith Jarvis Thomson (see Thomson (1)). I have no reason to suppose that she would endorse my application of her suggestion to Hume's, or to anyone else's, sceptical argument.

17 It is really too strong to require without qualification that the man straightforwardly *believe* that experience of a past constant conjunction between As and Bs and a present A gives him good reason to believe that a B will occur, since, for one thing, ordinary belief might be said to require some *understanding* of what is believed. The most that I have tried to make plausible in the previous paragraph, and the most I mean to put forward here, is that 'he must somehow take his past and present experience with respect to As and Bs as good reason to believe that a B will occur'. As long as such 'takings' are the sorts of things that could be reasonable or unreasonable I think the suggested line of thought can be given the kind of plausibility I want. Having made this qualification, I will continue for the sake of brevity to speak of the man's having (higher-order) beliefs about the reasons for his (lower-order) beliefs.

18 It is well known that this quest for unimpeachable foundations for rational belief is expressed perhaps most forcefully in Descartes, but again in pointing this out I do not mean to suggest that Hume has Descartes in particular in mind.

19 This point is made explicitly in Thomson (1), pp. 294-5.

20 This is still to be understood as subject to the qualifications introduced in note 17 above.

21 This way of taking the sceptical sting out of Hume's argument has been suggested in one form or another by many authors, most notably Edwards (1) and Strawson (1), ch. 9.

22 Here I rely on examples of merely 'accidental' or 'non-law-like' generalizations of the sort brought to prominence by Nelson Goodman (see Goodman (1), chs 1, 3).

23 The term is borrowed from Kneale (2), p. 229. In saying that the idea makes perfect sense I am agreeing with Kneale.

IV Belief and the Idea of Necessary Connection: The Positive Phase

1 This way of putting the problem is closest to Hume's when he speaks of 'those ideas, to which we assent' (p. 97), or 'an idea assented to' (p. 629), or when he says 'we conceive many things, which we do not believe' (p. 94). Strictly speaking, we do not believe or assent to the very same thing of which we have an idea. We have an idea of, e.g. the book's being

on the table, but when that idea figures in a belief it is a belief *that* the book is on the table. I suggest on pp. 74–6 that Hume's theory of belief or assent does not account for this fact.

2 Parts of this argument appear in the body of the *Treatise* (pp. 66–7, 94) and it is presented in summary form in Hume (2), pp. 17–18. It is dropped from the first *Enquiry*.

3 The phenomena here described seem to be just further cases of a belief arising from an impression, and not merely analogous instances of the principle of the transmission of force and vivacity.

4 For an interesting recent illustration of the importance of the inter-relationship between belief, desire and other mental states see Davidson's outline of the 'holism of the mental' in Davidson (3) and (4).

5 For a brief explanation of this term and an outline of various theories of intentionality see Chisholm (1).

6 He puts it most explicitly, but still (for reasons I suggest below) not fully satisfactorily, in a letter in 1751:

> We feel, after the constant Conjunction, an easy Transition
> from one Idea to the other, or a Connexion in the Imagination.
> And as it is usual for us to transfer our own Feelings to the Objects
> on which they are dependent, we attach the internal Sentiment
> to the external Objects. If no single Instance of Cause & Effect
> appear to have any Connexion, but only repeated similar ones,
> you will find yourself oblig'd to have Recourse to this Theory.
> (Hume (7), vol. 1, pp. 155–6)

7 In the *Treatise* (p. 157) Hume first seems to allow that the idea of necessity or power might be either simple or 'compound', but to Locke's view that we acquire the idea by reasoning from the 'new productions' we find in experience to the conclusion that there must be a power that produces them, he objects that 'reason alone can never give rise to any original idea' (p. 157). In the first *Enquiry* there is a strong suggestion (*E*, p. 62) that he regards the idea as simple, and when he repeats his objection to Locke's account of the origin of the idea he expresses it more fully as, 'no reasoning can ever give us a new, original, simple idea; as this philosopher himself confesses. This, therefore, can never be the origin of that idea (*E*, p. 64n).

8 The section 'Of the idea of necessary connexion' in the *Treatise* begins with the question '*What is our idea of necessity when we say that two objects are connected together*' (p. 155). The corresponding section of the first *Enquiry* discusses 'power', 'force', 'energy' and 'necessary connexion' and tries 'to fix, if possible, the precise meaning of these terms' (*E*, p. 62).

9 Unfortunately, this is precisely what Hume does sometimes say. See, for example, pp. 167, 469.

10 Alastair Hannay has suggested that this be described as the operation of 'spreading must'.

11 Hume need not be committed to the unacceptable view that, say, 'agency'

and 'connexion', or 'force' and 'necessity', are synonyms in English. In saying they are 'nearly synonimous' he can be taken to be saying only that a full explanation of the meaning of any of those words would make essential use of one and the same problematic idea, viz. that of causal connection, causal efficacy or necessary connection.

12 I elaborate a little on these difficulties, and on Hume's inability to account for them, in Chapter X, pp. 226–32.

13 See, for example, pp. 2n, 84, 275–6.

14 A not altogether fruitful exchange on the relations between these two 'definitions' is to be found in Robinson (1) and (2) and Richards (1).

15 I return to speculations about this alleged possibility, and try to give it more sense, in Chapter X, pp. 226–32.

16 The fact that this objection to Hume is not as widespread among commentators as some other weaker objections can perhaps be attributed to the fact that most commentators have not taken Hume to be primarily interested in giving a causal explanation of the origin of the idea of causality.

17 The importance of these considerations for the question of the nature of our inferences from the observed to the unobserved can scarcely be over-emphasized. They have permanently transformed the subject. An elegant exposition and generalization of Goodman's view and its implications can be found in Scheffler (1).

V The Continued and Distinct Existence of Bodies

1 And certainly nothing as subtle or elaborate as that to be found in twentieth-century critics of traditional philosophy such as J. L. Austin and, especially, Wittgenstein.

2 Hume thinks these two beliefs are so 'intimately connected together' that 'the decision of the one question decides the other' (p. 188). But although the continued existence of objects unperceived does imply that their existence is independent of and distinct from their being perceived, it is not so obvious that what Hume says is correct about the implication in the other direction. He says 'if their existence be independent of the perception and distinct from it, they must continue to exist, even tho' they be not perceiv'd (p. 183). But it seems that the things we perceive might, quite coincidentally, last only as long as the intervals during which we perceive them (see Price (1), p. 18). Perhaps Hume could invoke his theory of causality to argue that any such 'coincidence', if we knew of it, would lead us to believe in a causal connection and hence to deny 'distinctness'.

3 Hume's view of what the vulgar believe, or what position they take themselves to be in, is not easy to understand. I raise and discuss some of its difficulties on pp. 105–9.

4 In admitting that 'coherence' alone is 'too weak to support so vast an edifice, as is that of the continu'd existence of all external bodies' (pp. 198–9) Hume is perhaps half acknowledging that on his account the

'hypothesis' of the continued existence of bodies, once we have it, is used to *explain* the 'coherence' we find in our experience, but that 'coherence' alone would never give rise to that 'hypothesis' in the first place, without some additional 'principles'. If we simply 'infer the continu'd existence of the objects of sense from their coherence, and the frequency of their union, . . . in order to bestow on the objects a greater regularity than what is observed in our mere perceptions' (p. 197), it would seem that the notion of the continued existence of objects must already make sense to us.

5 Something like this tension is briefly noted in Kemp Smith (2), pp. 548–9.

6 I return to Hume's conception of the opposition between philosophical scepticism and ordinary life in Chapter X, pp. 245–50.

VI   The Idea of Personal Identity

1 Here he appears to be looking for properties of the perceptions themselves that could lead the mind to 'slide easily' along them and to form the idea of their constituting one continuous thing, and since it makes no literal sense to speak of the contiguity of two perceptions, perhaps he rules out contiguity as irrelevant for that reason. Resemblance and causation are then thought of as relations holding among the very perceptions themselves, and thereby having an effect on the mind. But 'natural relations' and the corresponding principles of the association of ideas were originally described as relations holding between the 'objects' of our ideas, or the things our ideas are ideas of, which have the effect of leading the mind from the thought of one of those things to the thought of another. For example, 'the relation of cause and effect betwixt their objects' is what Hume says 'makes one idea . . . recall another' (p. 11). See also the illustrative examples in the first *Enquiry* (*E*, p. 24). It would therefore be the contiguity of the things thought about that leads the mind from an idea of one of them to an idea of another, and some of the perceptions we contemplate when regarding a bundle we take to be one person could be expected to be perceptions of contiguous things. So contiguity might have an effect after all.

  Hume's declaring contiguity irrelevant here might be taken as some indication that throughout the discussion he is thinking primarily of the case in which I contemplate, or 'see clearly into the breast of' (p. 260) *another* person. If what I am then contemplating, or having perceptions of, are his perceptions, and if those perceptions themselves cannot be contiguous, then it cannot be any contiguity holding between the things I contemplate (or the 'objects' of my perceptions) that leads my mind to think of him as one person. So contiguity would be irrelevant. I suggest on pp. 129–30 that Hume does seem to have this third-person picture in mind, and that it tends to obscure some of the difficulties in his account.

2 Obviously Hume intends his explanation of the origin of the idea of identity and of our tendency to regard certain series of perceptions as 'a

continu'd view of the same object' to carry over from the section 'Of Scepticism With Regard to the Senses'. Since I dealt in Chapter V with some of the problems raised by that account, in this chapter on personal identity I, like Hume, concentrate on what is special about *personal* identity.

3 By 'such' regularities I mean regularities of the kind Hume has in mind when he explains the origins of our causal beliefs. I do not mean that our experience exhibits no regularities at all. The point of the fundamental criticism of Hume's explanation of our causal beliefs (outlined pp. 93–5 above) is to show that for any stretch of experience ABCDEFGH . . . , however varied, there will always be *some* classes to which, say, G and H belong, which are such that every member of the first class has been followed by a member of the second. But Hume needs correlations that will actually produce a belief in a causal connection between the two.

4 Nor, of course, is the 'object' of the first perception, or what the perception is a perception of, a cause of the second perception, or of the 'object' of that second perception. The tree does not cause the impression of the building, nor does it cause the building. So on whichever account of 'natural relation' Hume might be adopting (see note 1 above) it is not true that each member of a series of my impressions of sensation bears the natural relation of causality to its successor. In fact, very few of them are so related.

5 See the discussion in Chapter III, pp. 47–50 above.

6 Passmore (1), pp. 81–2, briefly notes the peculiarities of shifting Hume's theory of the 'fictional' character of the idea of the self from the third-person to the first-person case. The asymmetry between the two cases with respect to memory is discussed in Shoemaker (1), pp. 152–9.

7 For some recent discussions in which the problem of individuation plays a prominent role see, for example, Penelhum (1), Williams (1) and (3), Quinton (1), Pears (1), Shoemaker (1) and (2).

8 One reason Hume's treatment of personal identity is so remote from our actual ways of thinking about and identifying embodied persons is that he leaves out bodies and speaks only of those 'internal and perishing' perceptions that he thinks constitute a person or mind. But even among those perceptions themselves there are no relations or connections which constitute sufficient conditions of identity of a self over time. Identity itself (as we saw above, pp. 102–3) is a 'fiction of the imagination'.

9 The same ambiguity is present on the previous page of the *Treatise* in Hume's recognition of the inadequacy of his view 'when I proceed to explain the principle of connexion, which binds [our perceptions] together, and makes us attribute to them a real simplicity and identity', since 'they form a whole only by being connected together' and 'no connexions among distinct existences are ever discoverable by human understanding' (p. 635).

10 Here and in what follows I am indebted to an unpublished paper on Hume's theory of personal identity by Paul Grice and John Haugeland,

and to discussions with them about their suggestion. I am not completely certain precisely where my interpretation of Hume's misgivings begins to diverge from theirs. I try to show (pp. 136–9) that Hume can avoid the charge of circularity as here advanced.

11 Some such point is perhaps what Passmore has in mind when he writes:

> For if all that happens is that a series of very similar
> (or causally linked) perceptions succeed one another, there is no
> possible way in which this series of itself could generate
> the fiction of personal identity. Nor, the fiction once generated,
> could this series ever reveal its fictional character. Both the
> original fiction and the discovery that it is a fiction are
> possible only if there is something which is at first misled
> by, and then, after reconsideration, can discover that it was
> misled by, a series of similar perceptions. (Passmore (1),
> pp. 82–3)

12 David Pears has located Hume's difficulties in the Appendix in his inability to account for certain 'peculiarities of the ownership of mental objects' that 'have to be accommodated in any viable theory of personal identity' (Pears (6), p. 216).

Certainly ownership is somehow at the centre of Hume's problem, but the peculiarity of ownership Pears concentrates on is the fact that one of my sense-impressions could not have been one of yours instead, and it could not have existed on its own. He thinks Hume in the Appendix is lamenting his inability to explain that fact because of the high degree of 'independence' he accords to impressions, on the analogy with physical atoms. But the degree of 'independence' Hume accords to impressions is actually so high that he is led to deny the alleged fact that a particular perception of mine could not have belonged to anyone else, or could not have existed on its own (pp. 207–8, 233).

13 The abandonment would consist, as it does in Kant, in making judgments, and not ideas, primary in human thought. For some general reflections on the significance of this shift see pp. 231–9.

VII Action, Reason and Passion

1 It is not clear how basic Hume thinks these differences are, or what he thinks accounts for them. He compares them here with the differences among 'different trees, which regularly produce fruit, whose relish is different from each other' (p. 401). But he insists on the social origin of important differences among people when he writes:

> The skin, pores, muscles, and nerves of a day-labourer are
> different from those of a man of quality: So are his sentiments,
> actions, and manners. The different stations of life influence
> the whole fabric, external and internal; and these different
> stations arise necessarily, because uniformly, from the necessary

and uniform principles of human nature. Men cannot live without
society, and cannot be associated without government. Government
makes a distinction of property, and establishes the different
ranks of men. This produces industry, traffic, manufactures,
law-suits, war, leagues, alliances, voyages, travels, cities, fleets,
ports, and all those other actions and objects, which cause such a
diversity, and at the same time maintain such an uniformity
in human life. (p. 402)

2 For an early and influential expression of the idea that Hume did all that
ever ought to have been needed in this subject, see Schlick (1), p. 143. For
a more recent expression of the same idea see Davidson (5), p. 139.

3 It has been widely believed, for example, that we tend to confuse laws of
nature, which are discovered by science, with prescriptions or requirements, which we might feel we are somehow compelled to follow. This
diagnosis has been offered by, for example, Schlick (1), pp. 146–8,
University of California Associates (1), pp. 602–4, and Ayer (2), p. 283.

4 This argument is reproduced almost *verbatim*, with only small alterations
and improvements, from the *Treatise* (pp. 408–9).

5 It could be, for example, that actions 'belong' to a particular agent only if
the wants, beliefs, etc., of that person contribute in a certain way to
explanations of those actions, but the explanations in question are not
causal or do not fit Hume's model of causal explanation. The controversy
about the production and explanation of human actions is one of the most
complicated issues in recent philosophy.

6 For an elaboration of the idea that Hume's causal theory of action is what
leads him astray, and that his errors on that question undermine his
support for the strong thesis that the ascription of responsibility requires
'the doctrine of necessity', see Foot (1).

7 Hume's causal theory of action might also be seen as a result of the severe
constraints imposed by his conception of the self. That conception leaves
no room for a self or agent as the initiator of a causal sequence, and the
idea of agency, or initiating, is of central importance in our ascriptions of
responsibility. I owe this observation to Hans Sluga.

8 For a more detailed elaboration of the argument I sketch here see Wiggins
(1), esp. pp. 43–4.

9 Similar considerations are advanced in Hutcheson (1), pp. 120–1.

10 This is perhaps further evidence for Kemp Smith's conjecture that
Hume's views on action and morals were composed first, before
generalizing the point to all cognitive activity in Book I of the *Treatise*.
The 'reasoning' that Hume here contrasts with 'feeling' or 'passion'
includes ordinary causal reasoning, the conclusions of which he here
regards as 'calm and indolent judgments of the understanding' (p. 457),
whereas in Book I he holds the more radical view that even those
conclusions do not belong to 'reason' or to 'the understanding', but to
'the imagination'. However, the two different contrasts remain present
in the *Enquiries* as well. The first *Enquiry* parallels Book I of the *Treatise* in

contrasting 'reason' or 'the understanding' with 'sentiment or feeling', while the second *Enquiry* continues to contrast only the 'cool assent of the understanding', which 'begets no desire or aversion' (*E*, p. 172) with 'an active feeling or sentiment' (*E*, p. 290), which 'takes possession of the heart' (*E*, p. 172).

11 I have altered the passage as it appears in the text in accord with Hume's directions on p. 636.

12 There are great difficulties in any very simple dispositional theory of wants or desires, but there is no need for such a theory to be objectionably reductionistic or behaviouristic. It is quite likely, for example, that the notion of desire cannot be understood separately from that of belief, and vice versa. See, for example, Davidson (3) and (4).

13 Very similar considerations, along with explicit reference to Aristotle, can be found in Hutcheson (1), p. 123.

14 For the most interesting recent account of this type see Nagel (1). Nagel grants that for every action there is a want, but he denies that at least one of the wants involved must always be underived or basic. The presence of what he calls 'motivated wants' is not enough, he claims, to establish Hume's conclusion. That is not to say that Nagel himself succeeds in explaining how rational considerations alone actually move people to act.

VIII   Reason, Passion and Morality

1 Hume only rarely (e.g. p. 456) uses the term 'judgment' to speak of our moral 'decisions', verdicts or 'pronouncements', partly because it is one of his main aims to argue that 'morality . . . is more properly felt than judg'd of' (p. 470). He more often uses the term 'pronouncement', which denotes more than a mere feeling. It suggests at least the putting forward of a claim with respect to the moral nature of an action or character. No traditional term is exactly right, for reasons I try to suggest below.

2 One of the great difficulties in understanding Hume's argument is that of understanding clearly the 'rationalist' views he is opposing. This is a part of the history of moral philosophy that needs much more, and more sophisticated, investigation. The best outline of some of the central issues is Prior (1). For an elementary general sketch see Hudson (1).

3 I have tried to suggest some reasons for believing this above, pp. 90–1.

4 I argue in Chapter VII that Hume never really establishes this conclusion, and in saying here that he relies on the additional or independent consideration that reason is impotent in the production of action I do not mean to suggest that he has somehow managed to establish it. But he does believe it. He believes that arriving at a moral 'pronouncement' is sometimes enough in itself to lead us to act, and if we arrived at such 'pronouncements' by reasoning alone then this theory of the role of reason in action would be refuted. But his ground for saying that they are not arrived at by reason is that reason alone can never produce action, and that moral 'pronouncements' alone can.

5 See above, pp. 83ff.

6 For an uncompromising statement of this view see Ayer (1), ch. VI.

7 Its central position in recent discussion of the relation between 'factual' and 'moral', or 'descriptive' and 'evaluative', judgments has given it an importance and point out of all proportion to its actual role in the text of the *Treatise*. R. M. Hare sees it as an 'observation on the impossibility of deducing an 'ought'-proposition from a series of 'is'-propositions' (Hare (1), p. 29), and he even comes to regard it as an expression of something he calls 'Hume's Law ('No "ought" from an "is" ')' (Hare (2), p. 108). If Hume had discovered such an important 'Law' to serve as the foundation of his (and apparently most subsequent) moral philosophy, it is curious that he did not give it a more prominent place in the *Treatise*, and that he omitted it entirely from his second *Enquiry*.

   For an important dissent from what had come to be the standard reading of this passage see MacIntyre (1).

8 For an interesting explanation of Hume's aims in this passage, and an explicit comparison with the case of causality, see Beck (1).

9 This part of Hume's moral philosophy has led some to find in him (and in Hutcheson and others) an expression of an 'ideal observer' theory of the meaning of moral judgments, according to which 'X is good' is equivalent in meaning to a statement about how a disinterested observer would react to X. See, for example, Firth (1). I argue below that no such theory could be acceptable to Hume, since it would commit him to the view that moral judgments, so understood, can be arrived at by reasoning alone. I would hold, in fact, that Hume commits himself to no 'meta-ethical' semantical thesis about the meanings of moral judgments at all.

IX   *Morality and Society*

1 This classification appears explicitly in only a few pages in the *Treatise* (pp. 587–91), but it is much more prominent in the second *Enquiry*, where each one of four kinds of virtues has a section of its own (Sections V–VIII).

2 Hume regards the classification as complete and points out that no other qualities will be regarded as 'part of personal merit':

> where men judge of things by their natural, unprejudiced
> reason, without the delusive glosses of superstition and false
> religion. Celibacy, fasting, penance, mortification, self-denial,
> humility, silence, solitude, and the whole train of monkish
> virtues; for what reason are they everywhere rejected by men of
> sense, but because they serve to no manner of purpose; . . . We
> observe, on the contrary, that they . . . stupify the understanding
> and harden the heart, obscure the fancy and sour the temper.
> We justly, therefore, transfer them to the opposite column,
> and place them in the catalogue of vices; nor has any
> superstition force sufficient among men of the world, to pervert

entirely these natural sentiments. A gloomy, hair-brained enthusiast, after his death, may have a place in the calendar; but will scarcely ever be admitted, when alive, into intimacy and society, except by those who are as delirious and dismal as himself. (*E*, p. 270)

3 Even after giving 'the vulgar definition of justice', according to which justice is '*a constant and perpetual will of giving every one his due*' (p. 526), he goes on to discuss nothing but property and one's right to it as that which is secured by the institution of justice.

4 As time passes on this planet it becomes more and more difficult to find a clear example of something essential for life that is so plentiful that there need be no laws or restrictions governing its use and distribution. That brings Hume's point home to us in an especially direct way.

5 Our natural passions are therefore the original source of the laws of justice:

Whatever restraint [those laws] may impose on the passions of men, they are the real offspring of those passions, and are only a more artful and more refin'd way of satisfying them. Nothing is more vigilant and inventive than our passions; and nothing is more obvious, than the convention for the observance of these rules. Nature has, therefore, trusted this affair entirely to the conduct of men, and has not plac'd in the mind any peculiar original principles, to determine us to a set of actions, into which the other principles of our frame and constitution were sufficient to lead us. (p. 526)

In his 'therefore' Hume suggests that it is precisely *because* the need for justice is so obvious to people with passions like ours in a world like ours that nature decided not to provide us with any natural or primitive propensities towards justice. There was no need to build them in since it was inevitable that they would arise anyway. In this respect nature shows a benign tolerance towards the integrity of its creatures, and one wonders how far this knowing *laissez-faire* attitude could be extended. Compare, for example, the belief in enduring bodies, which nature has not left to our choice, 'and has doubtless esteem'd it an affair of too great importance to be trusted to our uncertain reasonings and speculations' (p. 187).

6 For classic statements of the social contract theory see Hobbes (2), Locke (2), Rousseau (1).

7 A very similar theory of convention, indebted to Hume but described in more contemporary, game-theoretic terms, can be found in Lewis (1).

8 The most thorough elaboration and defence of the view that fairness is an essential ingredient in justice and in our motivation towards it is found in Rawls (1). It is essential reading in connection with the problems raised by Hume's theory of justice and the 'artificial' virtues.

9 For an outline of a view along these lines see, for example, Foot (2).

10 In saying that Hume does not ask questions of individual psychology or of

the socialization of particular groups I of course do not mean to imply that he is not asking empirical questions about contingent matters of fact.

11 For some interesting connections between moral attitudes (in particular, a sense of justice) and 'natural' attitudes, see Rawls (1), ch. 8, esp. pp. 485–96.

X   Problems and Prospects of Humean Naturalism

1 This connection between Hume and logical positivism is explicitly drawn by, for example, Carnap (2), pp. 35–6, and Ayer (1), p. 54.

2 The assimilation of Hume to logical positivism or 'analytic' empiricism is perhaps most explicit in some of the earlier writings of A. J. Ayer, but it has come to be widely shared in Anglo-American philosophy. In what follows I try to express the essential ingredients of that dominant picture.

3 The actual development of the logical positivists' conception of philosophy was much more complicated than this oversimplification suggests. Schlick, for example, in the first issue of *Erkenntnis*, officially endorsed the view derived from Wittgenstein that 'philosophy does not consist of statements at all' (Schlick (2), p. 58). Carnap was still partly supporting that idea the following year in his view that what remains for philosophy 'is not statements, nor a theory, nor a system, but only a *method*: the method of logical analysis' (Carnap (1), p. 77). But he also thought that that method yields results, the nature of which requires careful examination. The view that philosophy provides 'definitions', perhaps of various sorts, is explicit in Ayer (1), chs II, III.

4 It is perhaps with respect to its scientism that twentieth-century logical positivism (and therefore much of the rest of twentieth-century philosophy) is most firmly tied to the original positivism of Comte and his followers. Nothing comparable is easily discernible in the eighteenth century.

5 For the idea that logical positivism, deriving from Frege, embodies many of the essential features of traditional rationalism, see Sluga (1).

6 The people I am trying to describe would appear to fulfil all the conditions of a 'regularity' theory of causality, which is often attributed to Hume. They infer from one particular to others on the basis of general truths of the form '$(x)(Fx \supset Gx)$', understood completely extensionally. If 'regularity' or 'laws', so understood, gave an adequate account of our notion of causality, then those people would not differ from us at all. But they do, and on my interpretation Hume thinks they do as well.

7 In saying that they can respond to a question about their reasons for their belief I mean only that at most they could perhaps learn to respond to the question 'Why do you believe that the billiard ball will move?' by giving the facts of their past and present experience I have mentioned. Since by hypothesis they lack the idea of causality I do not think they could really be said to be *explaining why* they believe what they do. That would require them to give sense to 'because', or some such notion, and by hypothesis they only understand generalizations in a purely extensional

way. Nor do I think they could ever explain *why* the ball moves, even though what they believe (but not what they have experienced) implies that it will. For that too they need a notion of 'because'.

8 See the long footnote to p. 96 of the *Treatise* in which Hume is at some pains to point out 'a very remarkable error' that has come to be 'universally received by all logicians', viz. that of distinguishing 'the acts of the understanding' into *'conception, judgment* and *reasoning'*. To correct the error:

> What we may in general affirm concerning these three acts of
> the understanding is, that taking them in a proper light,
> they all resolve themselves into the first, and are nothing
> but particular ways of conceiving our objects. (p. 97)

9 This is in effect the substance of Thomas Reid's criticism of Hume's moral philosophy to be found in Section VII ('That Moral Approbation Implies a Real Judgment') of Reid (3).

10 This move from the idea or term to the judgment or sentence as primary is one of the most decisive influences on twentieth-century philosophy of Frege and Russell, despite Russell's ambivalence or partial back-sliding on the matter for primarily epistemological reasons.

11 In fact, one popular defence of philosophical analysis is that we need an adequate representation of *what* we understand, of its 'content', before we can begin to explain what it is to understand, think, or mean something.

12 Wittgenstein issued a reminder of a similar point in the philosophy of mathematics: '. . . mathematics is after all an anthropological phenomenon' (Wittgenstein (2) V, 26).

13 The philosophical importance of this task, but not a common conception of how to pursue it, has been appreciated by philosophers as apparently diverse as Wittgenstein and Quine. The purely 'descriptive', but certainly not scientific, task of philosophy is emphasized throughout Wittgenstein (1). Much of Quine's later work, summed up in, for example, Quine (3), stresses his conception of the scientific, but still naturalistic, character of the enterprise.

14 In 'Of Scepticism With Regard to Reason' in the *Treatise* he does not go into the question of what reasoning 'from ideas alone' consists in, and how it works. His aim there is to show that so-called 'demonstrative reasoning' is no more immune to sceptical challenge than is non-demonstrative reasoning. But in neither case, of course, are we to draw the conclusion that we should not indulge in such reasoning. 'Drawing' that 'conclusion' would be perfectly idle in either case. I have tried to indicate that the point of the sceptical arguments is a different one.

15 The parallel between demonstrative and non-demonstrative reasoning is explicitly drawn in Pears (2), but it is drawn in terms of a simple theory of association and not the theory of 'projection' that I suggest. Pears is there concerned with the inferences or transitions we make, and not with the ideas themselves of causal and logical necessity.

268

16 See above, pp. 83–6.

17 This is argued above, pp. 90–1.

18 Nor would a Humean view of 'logical' necessity, according to which it is a contingent, explainable fact that we attribute that status to (or 'project' it onto) some of the things we believe, imply that we should strictly speaking withhold that notion from all the things we believe and regard them all as contingent after all. The theory that we simply 'project' a certain idea is perfectly compatible with our believing that that idea is objectively true of the things onto which we 'project' it, and so we could regard some truths as objectively necessary after all. This would perhaps provide Hume with the beginnings of an answer to Kant's charge that if Hume had considered mathematics his good sense would have saved him from the 'destructive' view that what we take to be necessity is really nothing more than 'the illusory semblance of necessity', merely 'borrowed . . . from experience, . . . under the influence of custom' (Kant (1), B20). I suggest that on the theory of 'projection' Hume is not committed to this admittedly 'destructive' view of necessity in either the causal or the 'logical' case.

19 The strategy of rendering 'necessary' truth or the 'logical "must"' more intelligible by pursuing such a descriptive, naturalistic programme can be discerned in Wittgenstein's later writings. Just as in the case of Hume, I do not think that it commits him to psychologism, or to the view that 'necessary' adds nothing, or to the view that everything is contingent. Needless to say, the strategy is envisaged as being pursued in very different ways by the two philosophers.

20 See above, pp. 258–9, note 11.

21 If Kant is right (see above, pp. 231–2), what here seems initially plausible is actually false, and so Hume's strategy for explaining the origin of the idea of necessity cannot really get off the ground. The objection of Goodman (see above, pp. 93–5) raises in quite another way the question whether Hume could be right in saying that we rely on nothing more than constant conjunctions in arriving at our views of causal necessity.

22 The 'act of the understanding' which gives rise to the idea of 'logical' necessity must therefore be something more than that of finding the idea of a B in the mind whenever one has the idea of an A. To distinguish the two kinds of necessity Hume must believe that ideas of them result from two different kinds of mental occurrence. The present problem is just what the 'occurrence' could be in the case of 'logical' necessity.

23 I argued above (pp. 48–50) that this oversimplified account does not work, and that there is no simple step from conceivability to possibility. That alone does not show that there is no relation at all between our being able, or unable, to conceive of certain things and our regarding certain things as possible, or as necessary.

24 On the non-psychologistic view I am suggesting, to try to explain how and why certain contingent facts make us unable to conceive of certain things, or make us regard some of the things we believe as necessarily true, would not commit one to the view that necessary truths are not really

necessary after all, or that they merely assert that those contingent facts obtain. Fear of psychologism, or of some other form of unpalatable reductionism, is therefore not reason enough in itself to eschew what I am calling naturalism.

25 Quine is one recent philosopher who has emphasized the different degrees of 'centrality', or likelihood of revision in the face of recalcitrant experience, among all the things we believe, but he has not seen any such epistemic matters as contributing to an explanation of the notion of necessity. That is probably because he rightly assumes that his opponents, the defenders of necessity, would reject any such epistemic *definition* or *analysis* of the notion. But that is not what the theory of 'projection' would provide. As far as I can see, there is no incompatibility between Quine's theory of knowledge and an account of necessity along the lines of the Humean theory I have sketched. That is not to say that I think Quine, or the traditional defenders of necessity, would welcome it.

26 This was the focus of earlier analytic philosophers, in so far as they distinguished 'necessary' from '*a priori*' and 'analytic'. With the recent popularity of the appeal to 'possible worlds' to explain modal notions like 'necessary', the project of giving an adequate analysis or definition of 'necessary' would seem to have been abandoned. That is not to say that all its advocates regard themselves as having abandoned it.

27 And it might well be nothing more than the complete generality of Hume's theory that makes it philosophical, or gives it its philosophical importance and interest.

28 This is perhaps what leads the philosopher who reaches this position to try to give up, or at least to deny, the vulgar beliefs. See, for example, the interesting discussion in Hampshire (1), esp. pp. 12–14, in which it is claimed that we cannot retain our beliefs, but at most only 'inclinations to believe', once we know that the truth of those beliefs plays no role in the causal explanation of their origin. That is precisely the nature of Hume's complaint about, for example, his belief in the continued and distinct existence of objects (p. 217).

Bibliography

This bibliography is not intended to be exhaustive. It lists only works explicitly referred to, plus some others, not explicitly referred to, that I have found especially interesting or helpful. Even the coverage of this second class is not exhaustive. In most cases, recent and readily available editions are cited.

ÁRDAL, P. S.
(1) *Passion and Value in Hume's Treatise*, Edinburgh University Press, 1966.
AYER, A. J.
(1) *Language, Truth and Logic*, Dover Publications, New York, n.d.
(2) 'Freedom and Necessity', in Ayer (3).
(3) *Philosophical Essays*, Macmillan, London, 1959.
(4) *Logical Positivism* (ed. A. J. Ayer), Free Press, Chicago, 1959.
(5) 'Man as a Subject for Science', in Ayer (6).
(6) *Metaphysics and Common Sense,* Macmillan, London, 1969.
(7) *Probability and Evidence*, Macmillan, London, 1973.
BECK, LEWIS WHITE
(1) ' "Was-Must Be" and "Is-Ought" in Hume', *Philosophical Studies,* vol. 26, 1974.
BERKELEY, G.
(1) *Three Dialogues Between Hylas and Philonous*, Liberal Arts Press, New York, 1954.
BLACK, M. (ed.)
(1) *Philosophy in America*, Allen & Unwin, London, 1965.
BROWN, S. C. (ed.)
(1) *Philosophy of Psychology*, Macmillan, London, 1974.
CARNAP, R.
(1) 'The Elimination of Metaphysics Through Logical Analysis of Language', in Ayer (4).
(2) *Philosophy and Logical Syntax*, Kegan Paul, Trench & Trubner, London, 1935.
CHAPPELL, V. C. (ed.)
(1) *Hume,* Doubleday, New York, 1966.
CHISHOLM, R.
(1) 'Intentionality', in Edwards (2), vol. 4.
CHURCH, RALPH W.
(1) *Hume's Theory of the Understanding,* Allen & Unwin, London, 1968.

DAVIDSON, D.
(1) 'Actions, Reasons, and Causes', *Journal of Philosophy*, vol. lx, 1963.
(2) 'Causal Relations', *Journal of Philosophy*, vol. lxiv, 1967.
(3) 'Mental Events', in Foster and Swanson (1).
(4) 'Psychology as Philosophy', in Brown (1).
(5) 'Freedom to Act', in Honderich (1).
DESCARTES, RENÉ
(1) *Philosophical Works of Descartes*, 2 vols (ed. E. S. Haldane and G. R. T. Ross), Dover Publications, New York, 1955.
EDGLEY, ROY
(1) *Reason in Theory and Practice,* Hutchinson, London, 1969.
EDWARDS, PAUL
(1) 'Bertrand Russell's Doubts About Induction', in A. Flew (1).
(2) *Encyclopaedia of Philosophy*, 8 vols (ed. P. Edwards), Macmillan and Free Press, New York, 1967.
FEIGL, H. and SELLARS, W. (eds)
(1) *Readings in Philosophical Analysis,* Appleton-Century-Crofts, New York, 1949.
FIRTH, R.
(1) 'Ethical Absolutism and the Ideal Observer', *Philosophy and Phenomenological Research*, 1952.
FLEW, A.
(1) *Logic and Language, First Series* (ed. A. Flew), Blackwell, Oxford, 1951.
(2) *Logic and Language, Second Series* (ed. A. Flew), Blackwell, Oxford, 1953.
(3) *Hume's Philosophy of Belief*, Routledge & Kegan Paul, London, 1961.
FOOT, PHILIPPA
(1) 'Free Will as Involving Determinism', *Philosophical Review,* vol. lxvi, 1957.
(2) 'Moral Beliefs', *Proceedings of the Aristotelian Society*, vol. 59, 1958–9.
(3) 'Hume on Moral Judgement', in Pears (3).
FOSTER, LAWRENCE and SWANSON, J. W. (eds)
(1) *Experience and Theory*, University of Massachusetts Press, Amherst, Massachusetts, 1970.
FOSTER, MARGUERITE H. and MARTIN, MICHAEL L. (eds)
(1) *Probability, Confirmation, and Simplicity*, Odyssey Press, NY, 1966.
GOODMAN, NELSON
(1) *Fact, Fiction, and Forecast*, Harvard University Press, Cambridge, Massachusetts, 1955.
GUSTAFSON, DONALD F. (ed.)
(1) *Essays in Philosophical Psychology*, Doubleday, New York, 1964.
HALÉVY, ELIE
(1) *The Growth of Philosophic Radicalism*, Beacon Press, Boston, 1960.
HALL, ROLAND
(1) *A Hume Bibliography from 1930*, University of York, 1971.

HAMPSHIRE, STUART
(1) *Freedom of Mind and Other Essays*, Princeton University Press, Princeton, N.J., 1971.
HARE, R. M.
(1) *The Language of Morals*, Oxford University Press, 1952.
(2) *Freedom and Reason*, Oxford University Press, 1963.
HARMAN, GILBERT
(1) 'Practical Reasoning', *Review of Metaphysics*, 1976.
HENDEL, CHARLES W.
(1) *Studies in the Philosophy of David Hume*, Bobbs-Merrill, Indianapolis, 1963.
HOBBES, THOMAS
(1) *The English Works of Thomas Hobbes*, 11 vols (ed. Sir William Molesworth), John Bohn, London, 1839.
(2) *Leviathan*, in Hobbes (1), vol. 3.
HONDERICH, TED (ed.)
(1) *Essays on Freedom of Action*, Routledge & Kegan Paul, London, 1973.
HUDSON, W. D.
(1) *Ethical Intuitionism*, Macmillan, London, 1970.
HUME, DAVID
(1) *A Treatise of Human Nature* (ed. L. A. Selby-Bigge), Oxford University Press, 1958.
(2) *Abstract of a Treatise of Human Nature* (ed. J. M. Keynes and P. Sraffa), Cambridge University Press, 1938.
(3) *Enquiries Concerning the Human Understanding and Concerning the Principles of Morals* (ed. L. A. Selby-Bigge), Oxford University Press, 1962.
(4) *The Natural History of Religion* (ed. H. E. Root), Stanford University Press, Stanford, California, 1967.
(5) *A Dissertation on the Passions,* in Hume (9), vol. 2.
(6) *Dialogues Concerning Natural Religion* (ed. Norman Kemp Smith), Bobbs-Merrill, Indianapolis, n.d.
(7) *The Letters of David Hume*, 2 vols (ed. J. Y. T. Grieg), Oxford University Press, 1969.
(8) *New Letters of David Hume* (ed. R. Klibansky and E. C. Mossner), Oxford University Press, 1969.
(9) *Essays, Moral, Political and Literary*, 2 vols (ed. T. H. Green and T. H. Grose), Longmans, Green, London, 1875.
(10) *Writings on Economics* (ed. Eugene Rotwein), University of Wisconsin Press, Madison, Wisconsin, 1970.
HUTCHESON, FRANCIS
(1) *Illustrations on the Moral Sense* (ed. Bernard Peach), Harvard University Press, Cambridge, Massachusetts, 1971.
KANT, IMMANUEL
(1) *Kant's Critique of Pure Reason* (tr. Norman Kemp Smith), Macmillan, London, 1953.

KNEALE, W. C.
(1) *Probability and Induction*, Oxford University Press, 1949.
(2) 'Natural Laws and Contrary to Fact Conditionals', in Macdonald (1).
KYDD, RACHEL M.
(1) *Reason and Conduct in Hume's Treatise*, Oxford University Press, 1946.
LEWIS, DAVID K.
(1) *Convention: A Philosophical Study*, Harvard University Press, Cambridge, Massachusetts, 1969.
LOCKE, J.
(1) *Essay Concerning Human Understanding*, 2 vols (collated and annotated by A. C. Fraser), Dover Publications, New York, 1959.
(2) *The Second Treatise of Government*, Liberal Arts Press, New York, 1952.
MACDONALD, MARGARET (ed.)
(1) *Philosophy and Analysis*, Philosophical Library, New York, 1954.
MACINTYRE, A. C.
(1) 'Hume on "Is" and "Ought"', in Chappell (1).
MACNABB, D. G. C.
(1) *David Hume: His Theory of Knowledge and Morality*, Blackwell, Oxford, 1966.
MOSSNER, ERNEST CAMPBELL
(1) *The Life of David Hume*, Oxford University Press, 1970.
NAGEL, THOMAS
(1) *The Possibility of Altruism*, Oxford University Press, 1970.
NELSON, J. O.
(1) 'The Conclusion of Book One, Part Four of Hume's *Treatise*', *Philosophy and Phenomenological Research*, vol. xx, 1964.
NOXON, JAMES
(1) *Hume's Philosophical Development*, Oxford University Press, 1973.
PASSMORE, J. A.
(1) *Hume's Intentions*, Cambridge University Press, 1952.
PEARS, DAVID
(1) 'Hume on Personal Identity', in Pears (3).
(2) 'Hume's Empiricism and Modern Empiricism', in Pears (3).
(3) *David Hume: a Symposium* (ed. David Pears), Macmillan, London, 1963.
(4) *Bertrand Russell and the British Tradition in Philosophy*, Fontana, London, 1967.
(5) *Ludwig Wittgenstein*, Viking Press, New York, 1970.
(6) 'Hume's Account of Personal Identity', in Pears (8).
(7) 'Sketch for a Causal Theory of Wanting and Doing', in Pears (8).
(8) *Questions in the Philosophy of Mind*, Duckworth, London, 1975.
PENELHUM, TERENCE
(1) 'Hume on Personal Identity', in Chappell (1).
PERRY, JOHN (ed.)
(1) *Personal Identity*, University of California Press, Berkeley and Los Angeles, 1975.

PIKE, NELSON
(1)   'Hume's Bundle Theory of the Self: a Limited Defence', *American Philosophical Quarterly*, vol. xx, 1967.
POPKIN, RICHARD H.
(1)   'David Hume: His Pyrrhonism and his Critique of Pyrrhonism', in Chappell (1).
PRICE, H. H.
(1)   *Hume's Theory of the External World*, Oxford University Press, 1963.
PRIOR, ARTHUR N.
(1)   *Logic and the Basis of Ethics*, Oxford University Press, 1961.
QUINE, W. V.
(1)   'Two Dogmas of Empiricism', in Quine (2).
(2)   *From a Logical Point of View*, Harvard University Press, Cambridge, Massachusetts, 1953.
(3)   'Epistemology Naturalized', in Quine (4).
(4)   *Ontological Relativity and Other Essays*, Columbia University Press, New York, 1969.
QUINTON, ANTHONY
(1)   'The Soul', in Perry (1).
RAWLS, JOHN
(1)   *A Theory of Justice*, Harvard University Press, Cambridge, Massachusetts, 1972.
REID, THOMAS
(1)   *The Philosophy of Reid, as contained in the 'Inquiry Into the Human Mind on the Principles of Common Sense'* (ed. E. H. Sneath), Henry Holt, New York, 1892.
(2)   *Essays on the Intellectual Powers of Man*, MIT Press, Cambridge, Massachusetts, 1969.
(3)   *Essays on the Active Powers of the Human Mind*, MIT Press, Cambridge, Massachusetts, 1969.
RICHARDS, THOMAS J.
(1)   'Hume's Two Definitions of "Cause" ', in Chappell (1).
ROBINSON, J. A.
(1)   'Hume's Two Definitions of "Cause" ', in Chappell (1).
(2)   'Hume's Two Definitions of "Cause" Reconsidered', in Chappell (1).
ROUSSEAU, J.-J.
(1)   *The Social Contract*, Hafner, New York, 1955.
RUSSELL, BERTRAND
(1)   *The Problems of Philosophy*, Oxford University Press, 1954.
SALMON, WESLEY C.
(1)   *The Foundations of Scientific Inference*, University of Pittsburgh Press, Pittsburgh, 1967.
SCHEFFLER, ISRAEL
(1)   'Inductive Inference: a New Approach', in Foster and Martin (1).
SCHIRN, MATTHIAS (ed.)
(1)   *Studien zu Frege—Studies on Frege*, 3 vols, Fromann-Holzboog, Stuttgart-Bad Canstatt, 1976.

SCHLICK, MORITZ
(1)   *Problems of Ethics* (tr. David Rynin), Dover Publications, New York, 1962.
(2)   'The Turning Point in Philosophy', in Ayer (4).
SHOEMAKER, SYDNEY
(1)   *Self-Knowledge and Self-Identity*, Cornell University Press, Ithaca, 1963.
(2)   'Personal Identity and Memory', in Perry (1).
SLUGA, HANS
(1)   'Frege as a Rationalist', in Schirn (1).
SMITH, NORMAN KEMP
(1)   'The Naturalism of Hume', I and II, *Mind*, vol. xiv, 1905.
(2)   *The Philosophy of David Hume*, Macmillan, London, 1949.
STOVE, D. C.
(1)   'Hume, Probability, and Induction', in Chappell (1).
(2)   *Probability and Hume's Inductive Scepticism*, Oxford University Press, 1973.
STRAWSON, P. F.
(1)   *Introduction to Logical Theory*, Methuen, London, 1952.
(2)   *Studies in the Philosophy of Thought and Action* (ed. P. F. Strawson), Oxford University Press, 1968.
(3)   'Imagination and Perception', in Foster and Swanson (1).
THOMSON, JUDITH JARVIS
(1)   'Reason and Reasoning', in Black (1).
UNIVERSITY OF CALIFORNIA ASSOCIATES
(1)   'The Freedom of the Will', in Feigl and Sellars (1).
VON WRIGHT, GEORG HENRIK
(1)   *The Logical Problem of Induction*, Macmillan, New York, 1957.
WIGGINS, DAVID
(1)   'Towards a Reasonable Libertarianism', in Honderich (1).
WILL, F. L.
(1)   'Will the Future be Like the Past?', in Flew (2).
WILLEY, BASIL
(1)   *The Eighteenth-Century Background*, Beacon Press, Boston, 1968.
WILLIAMS, BERNARD
(1)   'Personal Identity and Individuation', in Gustafson (1).
(2)   'Imagination and the Self', in Strawson (2).
(3)   'The Self and the Future', in Perry (1).
WITTGENSTEIN, LUDWIG
(1)   *Philosophical Investigations* (tr. G. E. M. Anscombe), Blackwell, Oxford, 1953.
(2)   *Remarks on the Foundations of Mathematics* (ed. G. H. von Wright and G. E. M. Anscombe and tr. G. E. M. Anscombe), Macmillan, New York, 1956.
WOLFF, ROBERT PAUL
(1)   'Hume's Theory of Mental Activity', in Chappell (1).

Index

277